Postcolonial Criticism

Postcolonial Criticism

History, Theory and the Work of Fiction

Nicholas Harrison

polity

First published in 2003 by Polity Press in association with Blackwell Publishers Ltd, a Blackwell Publishing Company.

Editorial office:
Polity Press
65 Bridge Street
Cambridge CB2 1UR, UK

Marketing and production:
Blackwell Publishers Ltd
108 Cowley Road
Oxford OX4 1JF, UK

Published in the USA by
Blackwell Publishers Inc.
350 Main Street
Malden, MA 02148, USA

A catalogue record for this book is available from the British Library.

  Library of Congress Cataloging-in-Publication Data
Harrison, Nicholas.
Postcolonial criticism : history, theory and the work of fiction / Nicholas Harrison.
p. cm.
ISBN 0–7456–2181–3 (hard : alk. paper)—ISBN 0–7456–2182–1 (pbk. : alk. paper)

1. Developing countries—Literatures—History and criticism. 2. Literature, Modern—20th century—History and criticism. 3. Imperialism in literature.
4. Decolonization in literature. l. Title.

PN849.U43 H37 2003
809'.891724—dc21

                                                                      2002010495

Typeset in 10.5 on 12 pt Sabon
by Kolam Information Services Pvt. Ltd, Pondicherry, India
Printed in Great Britain by MPG Books, Bodmin, Cornwall

This book is printed on acid-free paper.

Contents

Acknowledgements   vi

Introduction:
Postcolonial Criticism and the Work of Fiction   1

1   **Colonialism and Colonial Discourse**   11

2   **Racism, Realism and the Question of Historical Context**   22

3   **'Race', Reading and Identification**   62

4   **Representation, Representativity and 'Minor' Literatures**   92

5   **Writing and Voice: Women, Nationalism**
    and the Literary Self   112

6   **Conclusion: Literature and the Work of Criticism**   136

7   **Afterword: Theory and Relativism (Fanon's Position)**   151

Notes   164

References and Bibliography   194

Index   216

Acknowledgements

In writing this book I have benefited greatly from support from various quarters. For the stimulation and encouragement they offered I must first thank past and present colleagues and students from St Catharine's College, Cambridge (where a Research Fellowship allowed me to begin work on this project), from Trinity Hall, Cambridge and from the Departments of French at the University of Cambridge and University College, London.

Much of the material here I tested out on research seminars, and I would like to thank those who gave me the chance to do so and those who participated, especially Simon Gaunt, Patrick ffrench, and friends and colleagues at King's College, London; Geoff Gilbert, Robert Hampson and the London Modernism seminar; Chris Johnson and his former colleagues at the University of Keele; James Williams and the School of European Languages and Cultures at the University of Kent; the Association for the Study of African and Caribbean Literature in French; the Society for French Studies; and Danielle Allen and the Workshop on the Reproduction of Race and Racial Ideologies at the University of Chicago. I am grateful to the staff of the Huntington Library, Pasadena, and the Lewis Walpole Library, Farmington, for giving me the chance to write in such agreeable surroundings, and to Anne Welschen, librarian at the Musée Royal de l'Afrique Centrale, Brussels, who dealt with my enquiries knowledgeably and efficiently and drew my attention to the image that now appears on the cover of this book (and is explained on page 15).

Chapter 3 is based on an article that appeared in *Nottingham French Studies*, and chapters 4 and 6 on articles published in *Paragraph: A Journal of Modern Critical Theory*. I am grateful to the editors of those journals for permission to reuse some of that material here, and especially to Celia Britton and Michael Syrotinski, who edited the *Paragraph* number on 'Francophone Texts and Postcolonial Theory' and made some useful suggestions (not least concerning my overuse of brackets). I would also like to thank Driss Chraïbi and Assia Djebar, who gave me permission to use extracts from their writings as epigraphs, and Andrew Brown, who put me in contact with Polity Press.

Finally, I want to say how grateful I am to all those who agreed to read my work and from whose insights I gained: Elizabeth Eger, Simon Gaunt, Robert Gordon, Azzedine Haddour, Peter Hallward, Sara Harrison, Eddie Hughes, Jean Khalfa, Benita Parry, Sally-Ann Spencer at Polity and Polity's two anonymous readers, and Mark Treharne. Lizzie had least choice in the matter, and for that reason, and many others, I dedicate the book to her.

Introduction: Postcolonial Criticism and the Work of Fiction

'it was a beautiful piece of writing. ... It gave me the notion of an exotic Immensity ruled by an august Benevolence. It made me tingle with enthusiasm. This was the unbounded power of eloquence – of words – of burning noble words.'

Conrad, *Heart of Darkness* (1899)

Fiction as a way of 'thinking', a place, a territory, a continent: this does not mean, it would seem, writing something purely fantastical, I was going to say a fantasy or a *fantasia*.

Rather it means rediscovering, thanks to an imaginary construction (be it a plot, intertwined situations, or dialogue, dangerous or banal), thanks to a *fiction*, then, inhabiting, populating or repopulating a place, a town, starting from its ghosts and at the same time, from your own obsessions...

Djebar, *Ces voix qui m'assiègent* (1999)[1]

This book is intended for readers who are interested in literature, and its relation to colonialism and its wake. It is structured around a series of case studies and explores diverse strategies and examples of reading and historicization in response to particular texts. Like most books in this area, it contains much that is non-literary, and engages with various issues in history, politics and critical theory. In choosing to centre my discussions on literary fiction I do not wish to *assume* anything much about the value or nature of literature – or of literary studies – or about the place and the ultimate significance or insignificance of works of fiction in the broad historical and ideological schemes with which postcolonial criticism connects them. Rather, I want to raise questions about those very issues.

Historicizing literary texts may seem like the bread and butter of postcolonial criticism, but I will be trying to show that this task is more intricate and multi-faceted than postcolonial critics generally allow. When confronting a work of fiction they encounter two demands that can be difficult to reconcile: on one hand they must give adequate weight to the text in its individuality and 'literarity'; on the other they must apprehend it in the socio-historical context from which it emerged and in relation to which it needs, at some level, to be understood. I shall be trying to 'work through' this difficulty, but what will become apparent is that, when one brings together different forms and levels of historicization, or different modes of attention to fiction's specificity, they may interfere with one another rather than combining into one definitive, richly historicized picture.

At the literary end of postcolonial studies there have been, broadly speaking, two main strands of work. For the first, a seminal moment came when Chinua Achebe, lecturing at the University of Massachusetts in 1975, declared that 'Joseph Conrad was a bloody racist.'[2] Achebe was not the first person to raise the issue of racism in relation to Conrad, but his paper brought it to the forefront of critical discussion, where it has subsequently remained. Achebe's iconoclastic insistence that Conrad be judged in relation to the imperial history, and especially the imperial and racial 'discourse', with which he and his writing were entangled, helped launch postcolonial studies, and has proved one of the characteristic gestures of postcolonial critics. (I will discuss the term 'discourse' in chapter 1.) Recognizing that a 'beautiful piece of writing' may be shot through with delusions and brutality, those critics have sought ways in which texts, especially canonical texts from the colonizing nations, bear the traces of or get to grips with the ideology of colonialism/imperialism, and have interpreted them as challenging or promoting orthodox views of colonialism's purposes and justifications.

Readers already familiar with postcolonial studies may be despondent to see that in this book I give a fair amount of space to *Heart of Darkness* and the argument over its alleged racism, territory that is far from unexplored. I do so partly for the benefit of those who are new to the field: one aim of my two opening chapters is to trace a path through a debate that is exemplary of that first strand of postcolonial critical practice. Beyond that, I try to clarify the theoretical and historical *basis* of any such debate, and to bring to light the tensions within it that allow it to run and run without reaching any final resolution. These tensions, I will argue, arise around different, perhaps incommensurable, notions of what literature is and does, and around competing accounts of what critical practice should be.[3]

In making that argument I will assume that it more or less goes without saying that, by today's standards, Joseph Conrad was, in fact, racist, in ways that were all but inevitable given that he lived when and where he did. As I will suggest in chapter 3, moreover, 'racial' categories still have a certain tacit currency even among those opposed to racism; will power alone is not enough to remove oneself from a history of discrimination that makes Conrad's thinking less alien than one might wish. This has at least two important implications for how Achebe's charge should, in my view, be treated, about which I will make some preliminary remarks here to give a sense of the kind of approach I am going to adopt. The first is that, to assess any particular historical instance of racism meaningfully, one needs to recontextualize it, rather than measure it by anachronistic standards, or by absolute standards by which *anyone* would be found lacking. The second is that, in this instance, the debate properly concerns Conrad's text, rather than Conrad himself.

Many critics – most recently Robert Young – have assumed or maintained that it is to Conrad's shame that *Heart of Darkness* never names the particular place, the Congo Free State (CFS), that is in some sense the story's subject as well as its setting, and clearly it is possible that this omission stemmed from timidity or indeed a certain racism.[4] If one frames the issue in the way I am proposing, however, to condemn Conrad on such grounds appears cursory both historically and literarily. From a historical perspective, as I will show in chapter 2, the text's 'failure' to name the culprit cannot be equated with a lack of specificity or pointedness. When one asks if a person or a policy is racist, one is concerned fundamentally with attitudes and effects; what my discussion of *Heart of Darkness* will show is that the decision not to name the CFS may have had positive rather than (or as well as) negative motivations and implications. For anyone thinking in literary-critical terms, meanwhile, establishing the 'attitude' or effect of a literary text such as *Heart of Darkness* appears a precarious, speculative task. Evidently it contains racist remarks, as might a history book on racism, but in each case it is crucial to consider how such remarks are presented – 'literarily', in this case. And whereas a historian, or indeed the author of a report such as Kurtz's (as described in my first epigraph), is under an obligation both to be accurate and to make his or her perspective clear, the obligations of the author of fiction – towards the reality he or she depicts, and towards his or her readers – are less clear-cut.

My chapters on *Heart of Darkness* try, then, to convey the full complexity of the dialogue, so to speak, between a fictional text and the experiences, discourses and debates it brings into play, or brought into play for its first readers in the era of high colonialism. Chapter 1 offers further introductory material in the form of reflections on the notion of colonial discourse, and a consideration of the CFS as an example of imperialism. Against that background, and with the aid of various key literary-theoretical concepts (including 'realism' and *vraisemblance*), chapter 2 pursues in detail the question of Conrad's alleged racism that I have begun to consider here. It is probably already apparent that the famous 'haziness' of Conrad's story will be matched, in a sense, by a certain hesitancy in my conclusions; both risk irritating those who fear that when we read *Heart of Darkness* we silently imbibe racist attitudes and colonial ideology and so prolong their life. By the same token, clearly, the sort of criticism that emphasizes the work's literarity or 'autonomy' may allow it to do its ideological work all the more effectively, if it exempts literature from practical and political considerations. I take such anxieties seriously, and go on to address them at some length in chapter 3, which, through a sustained consideration of issues of 'identification' in relation to Camus's *The Outsider* (*L'Etranger*, 1942), raises further questions about how readers actually read, how fiction actually works and what its impact, politically and emotionally, may be.

Those questions, I shall argue, again need to be considered historically, which implies that the responsibilities of the critic may also vary historically and contextually. That both *Heart of Darkness* and *The Outsider* are canonical texts makes them fitting objects for what I have characterized as the first strand of postcolonial criticism. The second strand, which has evolved partly in response to the accusation of continued academic Eurocentricity even within postcolonial studies, has been part of a broader trend extending literary studies beyond its traditional canons. At a certain point, this means that the very definition of literature, and of what it is appropriate to study in a literature department, is necessarily called into question: this may have many consequences, but at the very least it usually means that those devising literary syllabuses today see reasons to include writers from former European colonies, such as Achebe, who was born in Nigeria when it was still under British rule, or Assia Djebar, born in Algeria, from whose work my second epigraph is drawn.[5]

In the newer subcanonical areas, the critical stakes seem different. Critics working on 'postcolonial' writers have frequently found in their work a previously ignored perspective or unheard 'voice', and a means of breaking through the artificial confines of 'national' literatures. To some extent, chapters 4 and 5, which centre on writing by Driss Chraïbi and Assia Djebar, are meant as instances of this second strand of postcolonial criticism. (I should note that the texts on which I focus have all been published in English translation and both authors are reasonably well known, but to a degree that I felt unnecessary with *Heart of Darkness* and *The Outsider* I try to allow for readers who are unfamiliar with the material.) In this critical context, it appears crucial that the ethnic origins of Chraïbi and Djebar put them on the other side of the colonizer/colonized divide – and their writing indeed offers novel and challenging perspectives on issues around colonialism and cultural identity.

As in the earlier chapters, however, I see part of my task as being to question certain critical reflexes, to explore the relation between various forms of 'specificity', and to test the fit between some general theoretical/political models of interpretation and particular texts and contexts to which they might apply. On one level this will mean considering colonial history's relation to social divisions *other* than the split of colonizer and colonized, including divisions of class, gender and language. On this last issue I will argue that the significance of 'choice' of language has often been misrepresented and even overstated, and that it is a mistake to see the use of French by Chraïbi or Djebar – or, to take a different example, of English by various Indian writers – as somehow inherently 'compromising'. Nevertheless, it may be worth pointing out in passing that none of the principal figures in this book writes in a non-European language. It should go without saying that, for anyone wishing to form a general picture of North African or Indian literature, or indeed North Africa or India, the advantages of knowing languages other than French and English are immense.

On another level, among the histories with which I will be dealing in chapters 4 and 5, as in the earlier chapters, are histories of representation, reading and criticism. Both Chraïbi and Djebar have tried, as we shall see, to position their writing in relation to the dominant tradition of reception that they have encountered, a tradition that postcolonial studies, at least in one of its versions, may sustain.[6] Crucial here is the sort of context that is captured ambiguously by Rushdie in his controversial anthology of Indian writing or by Deleuze and Guattari in their influential essay on 'minor literature': both help crystallize the problems involved in turning to 'postcolonial' fiction, or even autobiography, for what I have referred to as 'a previously ignored perspective or unheard "voice"'. Chraïbi's first novel, *The Simple Past* (*Le Passé simple*, 1954), a literarily innovative work that was published on the cusp of Moroccan independence, was read in precisely that way by contemporary critics: and it was on that basis, as we shall see, that the author ended up receiving death threats.

In such a context, and in the face of the 'burden of representation' borne by the postcolonial writer who is perceived as a member of a 'minority' (a term analysed in chapter 4), *some* notion of literary 'autonomy' – even if that term will turn out to be unsatisfactory – clearly has something to be said for it. It may be argued, consequently, that the first responsibilities of critics responding to Chraïbi's and Djebar's work are currently towards the specifically literary facets of the text with which any sense of literary autonomy is associated. What this might mean – what the 'literary' *is*, or how it should be understood – will return as an issue throughout the book and will be at the centre of the Conclusion. Throughout the book, then, I try to demonstrate the importance to 'postcolonial' literary studies of theoretical questions that arise more commonly in other literary-critical contexts; accordingly, the theorists that I draw on and discuss include figures such as Derrida, Blanchot and Genette alongside those who habitually feature more prominently in postcolonial studies.

A certain level of abstraction may be both the precondition and the result of the sorts of comparative and theoretical approaches adopted here, especially in the Conclusion and the Afterword. The latter, focused on *theoretical* writing by Fanon (and, briefly, Freud), is intended to add a final twist to the questions of textual historicity and 'voice', and explores the notion of relativism – a crucial concept in comparative or intercultural academic work. The tendency towards abstraction of postcolonial critics could also be seen as the result of murkier pressures, however, including those exerted by publishing and academic job markets. McClintock, for one, expresses her distrust of a certain 'theoretical' vocabulary on these grounds, writing that 'Historically voided categories such as "the other", "the signifier", "the signified", "the subject", "the phallus", "the postcolonial", while having academic clout and professional marketability, run the risk of telescoping crucial geopolitical distinctions into invisibility.'[7]

Such terms are also part of what may make postcolonial theory off-putting to newcomers to the field, of course. In this book I apply theoretical tools and extrapolate general, 'transferable' lessons where I think it appropriate, and should confess now that I use some (though not all) of the terms that McClintock mentions. Any that may be unfamiliar I try to explain as I go along, either in the main text or in the notes. I do not provide summaries of the work of those eminent postcolonial critics and theorists who by now have been more or less canonized, however, and will make just a few brief remarks, in the remainder of this Introduction, about the definition of the 'postcolonial'. One reason for this decision is that other critics have already done a very good job of offering such summaries, along with some telling criticisms.[8] Another is my view that what is most interesting and often most important in postcolonial studies – at least postcolonial literary studies – remains tied up in textual and historical detail, as McClintock's remarks may imply. Indeed, if one takes these points seriously, it is no longer clear to what extent there *is* a field of the sort susceptible to systematic exposition. This, in a sense, is my starting point, and it is why I believe that working through specific case studies provides as good a way as any to enter the broad area to which the label 'postcolonial' points.

The terms colonialism, imperialism, and the postcolonial are used differently by different writers, and it may be useful for some readers if I say a little more about them here. In *Culture and Imperialism* Said works with a distinction between imperialism, by which he means 'the practice, the theory, and the attitudes of a dominating metropolitan centre ruling a distant territory', and colonialism, which 'is almost always a consequence of imperialism' and means 'the implanting of settlements on distant territory'.[9] These definitions are reasonable, but 'colonialism' is often used by other authors in ways that make it close to imperialism in Said's sense – to describe, on the one hand, a set of attitudes or an ideology and, on the other, forms of exploitation and conquest of foreign lands. The latter case includes but is not limited to the history of 'settlement', of the sort integral to the French colonization of Algeria, say.

The examples of the Roman empire and the Ottoman empire make it clear that Said's terms could be applied to many different contexts. Postcolonial studies has been concerned mainly with European colonial expansion since the Renaissance, especially in the nineteenth and twentieth centuries. In focusing on this later period many postcolonial critics have considered imperialism as a stage in the development of capitalism. Patrick Williams and Laura Chrisman, for instance, write:

> Colonialism, the conquest and direct control of other people's lands, is a particular phase in the history of imperialism, which is now best understood as the globalization of the capitalist mode of production, its penetration of previously non-capitalist regions of the world, and destruction of pre- or non-capitalist forms of social organization.[10]

By this point it is becoming clearer why the notion of 'postcolonial studies' has been so loose. The adjectives postcolonial and post-imperial were originally used to designate the post-independence period of former European colonies, but the economic emphasis of a description such as the one offered by Williams and Chrisman calls into doubt the neatness and the significance of the break between the colonial/imperial and the 'post-'. As Raymond Williams noted back in 1976 in *Keywords*,

If imperialism, as normally defined in late 19th century England, is primarily a political system in which colonies are governed from an imperial centre, for economic but also for other reasons held to be important, then the subsequent grant of independence or self-government to these colonies can be described, as indeed it widely has been, as 'the end of imperialism'. On the other hand, if imperialism is understood primarily as an economic system of external investment and the penetration and control of markets and sources of raw materials, political changes in the status of colonies or former colonies will not greatly affect description of the continuing economic system as imperialist.[11]

To talk of a culture as 'postcolonial' may then carry misleading implications concerning the cessation of imperialist influence and interference after the formal acquisition of independence by former colonies (influence that is sometimes termed 'neo-imperialist' or 'neo-colonialist', words connoting influence exercised by means other than colonial settlement). This problem is exacerbated by the fact that, in 'postcolonial' studies, what is discussed is often, necessarily, not only the period *after* a given country gained its independence, but the entire period of contact between the countries or cultures in question, from the 'precolonial' era through to the present.

Such considerations in turn raise the question of whether a 'post-colonial' perspective on colonialism and the 'colonial era' is liable to treat colonial phenomena as more self-contained and coherent than they were (or are), to attribute too great an importance to them, and indeed to continue to define former colonies in relation to the colonial powers – liable, in other words, to be drawn into and reinforce the globalizing, self-mythologizing and ethnocentric tendencies of colonialism itself. Numerous writers have criticized postcolonial studies on these grounds, adding the related charges that it tends to neglect factors such as class and gender that cut across the colonial/postcolonial division (in ways that, as I have already indicated, will be discussed in chapter 5), and to lump together cultures that are highly diverse in numerous ways, including in their relation to colonialism.[12] To take the example of the French empire, the colonial 'legacy' evidently means very different things in countries such as Algeria, Tunisia, Senegal, Vietnam and Quebec: each may be dubbed postcolonial, but each has its own history beyond colonialism as well as its own particular relationship to French culture, French government, the French language, and so on. Comparable points could be made about the British empire and the English language in relation to Ireland, India, Nigeria, the United States, and so on.

Clearly, many postcolonial critics and theorists have been sensitive to such distinctions and have duly focused on the particularities of different cultures. The issues to which they have turned their attention have included power relations and patterns of (mutual) influence between colonizer and colonized; the question of subjective and political agency; nationhood, nationalism and anti-colonial resistance; Eurocentrism, universalism and relativism; 'race' or ethnicity, gender and identity; and many more besides. Partly because the field is so eclectic and partly because it has consisted to a notable degree, and for good reasons, in cutting the ground from under its own feet in ways I have begun to describe, I can see no point in talking as if consensus about what postcolonial studies 'is' might eventually emerge, or in pursuing such consensus, or in *arguing* about distinctions between postcolonialism, postcolonial studies, postcolonial criticism and postcolonial theory (even if working distinctions along these lines are sometimes serviceable), and least of all in getting involved in the sporadic sideshow argument about the relative merits of the terms 'post-colonial' and 'postcolonial'. Postcolonial theory is not an identifiable 'type' of theory in the same (limited) sense as deconstruction, Marxism, psychoanalysis or feminism, on all of which it sometimes draws: it does not have foundational thinkers playing a role comparable to that of Marx or Freud; and whereas feminism, say, is first, both conceptually and historically, a political movement and a theory of gender relations in society, postcolonial studies as such seems to have emerged specifically within the English-speaking academic world, particularly in literature departments. Like Marxism and feminism, though, it has evolved in response to political and historical issues of vast importance and scope, such as anti-colonial militancy, and its deeper origins and many of its ends lie outside academic study.[13]

   For the purposes of this book, postcolonial studies in general may be characterized broadly and simply in terms of an attention to the history of colonialism/imperialism and its aftermath, and may in many instances be distinguished from traditional historical or political writing on the colonial or post-independence era by the particular attention that is paid to the role within that history of 'representation' or 'discourse'. To approach colonialism, and the questions it raises, in such terms – and through literature in particular, as I will here – is to lay oneself open to the accusation (from literary critics, discourse theorists and others) that one has inflated the importance of discourse and literature, and has missed what is important about colonialism. Overstating the dangerous consequences of this may be part of the same inflation, of course, but to clarify the scope of this book I should stress that, while it aims to cast light on key aspects of the relation to colonialism of literature, and especially fiction, it does not claim to

cover all aspects even of that topic, and still less to offer a full understanding of colonialism. In a sense, to put it another way, this book
mimics the evolution of the field in that it starts within the discipline of
literary studies and explores ways of moving out into other disciplines,
or of describing and theorizing the connections between literature/
literary studies and the (rest of the) world – connections that the
work of literary criticism may itself not just mediate but modify.

If, from a certain political perspective, that movement occasionally
seems meandering and the distance travelled eventually appears
modest, this is the corollary not just, I think, of my limits and the limits
of what I feel competent to talk about, but of the kind of work that this
book seeks to undertake. Although their writing often turns on the
historical embeddedness and weight of particular actions and forms of
representation, or how contexts shape texts, postcolonial critics sometimes seem wilfully oblivious to what are, in practice, the relatively
narrow bounds of the field in which they are operating and who they
are actually writing *for* – even though they may make a point of telling
their audience where they are writing 'from', so to speak, in terms of
their geographical location, institutional affiliation, and so on. That
particular ratio of self-consciousness and its lack often seems to me the
wrong way round; and, at the risk of pre-empting a point that I will
develop more fully in due course, it may be worth signalling here that I
do not consider it legitimate or meaningful *criticism* of a text to point
out that it is about one thing rather than another, or that it was written
by someone living in a former colonial nation, or of a certain gender/
class, or for that matter in a literature department. A sense of such
things may help you locate areas in which that person *may* rely on
certain unjustified presuppositions, but it does not tell you that he or
she has done so, nor does it constitute an engagement with the work as
such. I would argue, then, that although the literary affiliations of
many postcolonial critics may lead them to overestimate the importance of literary texts, they need not. Indeed, it is partly because they
have been repeatedly questioned and linked to imperial ideology by
postcolonial theorists that traditional conceptions of the value of canonical and other literature have lost much of their authority. Literary
critics may respond to this in various ways, all of which have something
to be said for them. They may abandon criticism altogether, if they
think their time would be better spent in other ways. Alternatively, they
may write theoretical, political or historical essays that simply leave
literary considerations behind – and attempt to reach an audience
outside their original professional field. Finally, they may write about
literature with due awareness of and attention to the limits of the
subject. This, in any case, is what I hope to do.

1

Colonialism and Colonial Discourse

At the time that *Heart of Darkness* was written much of the Congo region was effectively the personal property of Leopold II, king of Belgium from 1865 to 1909. Belgium had been independent only since 1830, and at the end of the nineteenth century its role in international politics was insignificant by the standards of the major imperial nations of Europe, who continued to expand and consolidate their empires overseas. Two of the main powers, the French and the Dutch, were not only the Belgians' neighbours but also their former rulers. Against this backdrop Leopold had begun early in his career to contemplate imperial expansion. He travelled widely, visiting many countries including Egypt, India and China, and was particularly impressed in the Dutch East Indies by the profitable Dutch East India Company. Searching for an arena in which to pursue his own dreams of profit and power, he settled on the Congo, a place he was never to visit but on which his impact was to prove devastating.

Leopold's attention was drawn to the region by Henry Morton Stanley's exploration of the river from 1874 to 1877. His interest was further stimulated, it seems, by a work entitled *In the Heart of Africa*, published in quick succession in English (1873), German (1874) and French (1875). Its author, Georg Schweinfurth, argued that the best way to stop slave-trading in Africa was to establish strong, independent African political entities under the protection of European powers. Leopold was also impressed by an article in *The Times* in 1876, which advertised the 'unspeakable riches' potentially offered by the area.[1] Pursuing his plans discreetly, and often mendaciously, Leopold took his first major step by convening a grandiose geographical conference in Brussels in 1876, the African Geographical Conference (Conférence Géographique Africaine), at which he assembled an impressive array of eminent explorers, missionary chiefs, military men, geographers and anti-slavery humanitarians. In his welcoming speech Leopold gave a high-minded account of his intentions in bringing them all together:

> The subject which brings us together today is one that deserves in the highest degree to engage the attention of the friends of humanity. To open to civilization the only part of our globe which it has not yet penetrated, to pierce the darkness enshrouding entire populations, that is, if I may venture to say so, a crusade worthy of this century of progress.... It seemed to me that Belgium, a centrally located and neutral country, would be a suitable place for such a meeting.... Need I say that in bringing you to Brussels I was guided by no egotism? No, gentlemen, Belgium may be a small country, but she is happy and satisfied with her fate.[2]

He went on to express the hope that the conference would manage to decide on the 'location of routes to be successively opened into the interior, of hospitable, scientific, and pacification bases to be set up as a means of abolishing the slave trade, establishing peace among the chiefs, and procuring them just and impartial arbitration.'[3] The conference led to the founding of the purportedly philanthropic International Association for Exploration and Civilization in Africa, which in 1876 gave rise to two smaller 'geographical' societies, the Belgian Geographical Society of Brussels and the Anvers Geographical Society. Later, in 1877–8, these effectively metamorphosed into the Committee for the Study of the Upper Congo (or CEHC, Comité d'Études du Haut Congo), a commercial undertaking. There followed in 1879 a further incarnation, the International Congo Association (AIC, Association Internationale du Congo), which was in fact not international at all, but primarily a political organization serving Leopold's private purposes. Leopold encouraged confusion between these various bodies, and thus confusion about the extent to which the interest in the Congo to which he gave voice was international, Belgian or personal, and whether it was philanthropic, scientific, political or economic.

Behind this smokescreen, Leopold gained a foothold in the area by employing Stanley to return to the Congo in 1879 and to establish trading posts along the upper river. On the basis of the many 'agreements' with local rulers reached in the name of the CEHC and the AIC, often obtained deceitfully and backed up by the regular use of force (the Congolese historian Isidore Ndaywel è Nziem speaks in terms of a thirty-year war of conquest from 1874 to 1904), Leopold was able to lay claim to the territory. He also worked, via lobbyists, to persuade the US government to recognize the legitimacy of that claim, which it did in 1884; and he helped ensure French support by agreeing that, if ever he relinquished his hold on the area, the French would be given first opportunity to step in. His extensive groundwork paid off at the Berlin West Africa Conference of 1884–5, at which the major European nations and the US met to decide all questions connected with their commercial exploitation of the Congo river basin. The general act of the conference guaranteed 'free trade' for all (foreign) states operating there, rejected Portugal's territorial claims, and banned slavery.[4] In effect, this opened the way for Leopold's so-called État Indépendant du Congo or 'Congo Free State' – a grotesque misnomer.

Stanley was useful to Leopold at this time not just as an agent in Africa but as a relentless and successful self-publicist in Europe. For various reasons, including the financial risks involved in colonization, Belgian public support for Leopold's scheme was initially tepid, but in Belgium as in England many people's imagination was gripped by Stanley's adventures. Stanley spread word of his exploits through a series of best-selling volumes, including *How I Found Livingstone* (1872), *Through the Dark Continent* (1878) and *The Congo and the Founding of its Free State* (1885). Nonetheless he met with hostility in some quarters, and thanks to reports of the murderous violence of his party successive waves of scandal broke over the celebrations when he returned from his search for Livingstone in 1872, again during his second African expedition in 1876, and again in 1890–91, in the wake of his journey to 'rescue' Emin Pasha.[5] A passage in William Morris's *News from Nowhere* of 1890 is one example of the criticism Stanley attracted: Morris talks of the 'use of hypocrisy and cant to evade the responsibility of vicarious ferocity' as 'force and fraud' were used to ' "open up" ' countries outside the 'World-Market'. It goes on to condemn further 'the dealings of civilization (or organized misery) with "non-civilization"; from the time when the British Government deliberately sent blankets infected with small-pox as choice gifts to inconvenient tribes of Red-skins, to the time when Africa was infested by a man named Stanley' – the same man, clearly, previously referred to as a 'bold, unprincipled, ignorant traveller'.[6] Eager to preserve the heroic air around his agent and his own projects, Leopold helped to stage-manage a celebration for Stanley on his return from the Emin Pasha expedition. In Belgium on 19 April 1890 a special train was sent to meet Stanley's party at the French border, and in London a week later Stanley was greeted at the station by cheering crowds. His latest account of his experiences, *In Darkest Africa*, came out in June 1890 and went on to sell 150,000 copies.[7]

A few short weeks after Stanley's return, and just one month after the publication of *In Darkest Africa*, Joseph Conrad left for the Congo in the pay of a Belgian company (the Société Anonyme Belge pour le Commerce du Haut-Congo). His experiences there are recorded in his 'Congo Diary', first published in 1925. It is a minimal and fragmented account, providing little that presages the imaginative resources of *Heart of Darkness*, and little to suggest that Conrad witnessed the sorts of exploitation and abuse for which the Belgian regime was to become known (and which was to become truly systematic, and reach its infamous peak, only later). Nonetheless, in his late essay 'Geography and some explorers' Conrad was to write that 'a great melancholy' descended upon him when his experience of the Congo matched neither his boyhood visions of travel nor the rhetoric of heroism surrounding Stanley, to whom he alludes in writing of 'the unholy recollection of a prosaic newspaper "stunt" and the distasteful knowledge of the vilest scramble for loot that ever disfigured the history of human conscience and geographical exploration.'[8] Before that trip, he told a friend, he had had 'not a thought in his head'.[9] What Conrad meant, it seems, was that his thinking previously had been less critical of, and more readily seduced by, the commonplace accounts, and fantasies, of imperial adventuring.

Of course, Conrad's retrospective recollections and fictional reworkings of his experiences may have been coloured by subsequent events. By the time Conrad reached the CFS, Leopold had spent most of a sizeable personal fortune on explorers, steamboats, mercenaries and armaments. He had little to show for it, however, and in 1889 had been forced to make out a will leaving the country to the Belgian government, in return for which he was granted a massive loan. This helped him realize a longstanding project, a 241-mile railway around the Matadi rapids which separated the upper part of the river from the estuary. Construction of the railway, which began in the year of Conrad's journey (indeed, the first rails arrived on the same boat as Conrad), was intended to facilitate the rapid transportation of goods from the upper Congo out to sea. It took three years to build the first 14 miles, but the project was given a new urgency by the rubber boom of the mid-1890s, when new commercial uses for the commodity in Europe (for tyres, for example) created unprecedented demand. In the pursuit of forced labour – to collect rubber and ivory, to build the railway, or for various other tasks – Belgian agents burned villages, took hostages, and mutilated and killed adults and children alike. One Swiss observer later remarked: 'If the chief does not bring the stipulated number of baskets [of rubber], soldiers are sent out, and the people are killed without mercy. As proof, parts of the body are brought to the factory. How often have I watched heads and hands being carried into the factory.'[10] The railway project alone employed up to 60,000 forced labourers at one time, and was eventually completed in 1898. Financially, things paid off for Leopold: whereas in 1891, 82 metric tons of rubber, with a value of 327,000 francs, were exported from the Belgian Congo, a decade later, with the railway running, the export figures peaked at 6023 tons, with a value of 43,966,000 francs.[11]

Fifty years after the railway was completed, a commemorative monument was raised on the Matadi road: a sculpture of three bony, exhausted porters on a pedestal bearing the irony-defying legend THE RAILWAY FREED THEM FROM PORTERAGE. As Hochschild notes, 'In a metaphor that is echoed elsewhere in Africa, local legend along the railway line has it that each tie [or sleeper] cost one African life and each telegraph pole one European life. Even in the rosy official figures, the railway death toll was 132 whites and 1800 nonwhites.'[12] These figures are a mere fraction of the total number of people who died as a direct or indirect result of Leopold's policies in the Congo; estimates vary, but the figure may have been as high as 13 million people – roughly a third of the population.[13]

* * * * *

This brief sketch of elements of the Congo's colonial history begins the work of historical contextualization that will be carried further in the next chapter, where I will say more about the period during which Conrad wrote *Heart of Darkness* and the decade or so afterwards. At this juncture, I want to make some more general points about the CFS's status as one example of European imperialism at the turn of the twentieth century.

First, it is worth noting that the violence of the Belgians, and for that matter of Stanley, was far from exceptional in this era. Addressing this issue, Hochschild writes:

what happened in the Congo could reasonably be called the most murderous part of the European Scramble for Africa. But that is so only if you look at sub-Saharan Africa as the arbitrary checkerboard formed by colonial boundaries. If you draw boundaries differently – to surround, say, all African equatorial rain forest land rich in wild rubber – then what happened in the Congo is, unfortunately, no worse than what happened in neighboring colonies: Leopold simply had far more of the rubber territory than anyone else. Within a decade of his head start, similar forced labor systems for extracting rubber were in place in

the French territories west and north of the Congo River, in Portuguese-
ruled Angola, and in the nearby Cameroons under the Germans.[14]

Secondly, it should be pointed out how easy it is, in recounting the
history of European colonialism, to adopt a narrowly Eurocentric
perspective. To say that 'the Congo' 'belonged' to Leopold, or to
Belgium, or that ownership was achieved via a series of treaties
among the European powers, or for that matter to use colonial
place-names, is already to run that risk. Even Ndaywel è Nziem,
despite drawing on a wealth of Congolese material, notes in his
introduction that there are numerous obstacles to a properly 'African'
version of his country's history, many of them stemming, of course,
from the fact that the country as such (and so the notion of the
'Congolese' as it is now used) was created under colonialism. In the
process, diverse local cultures and histories were lumped together:
Ndaywel è Nziem's book provides a map showing how the country
might be divided into fourteen regional 'cultural groupings', and he
identifies 365 different ethnic groups. Among the problems for
anyone wanting to get to grips with these varied socio-cultural elements is the variety of languages spoken, including Lingala, Kiswahili,
Kikongo and Tsiluba. Postcolonial studies, it is worth noting in
passing, has been criticized for its over-reliance on European languages – indeed, one critic has recently argued that a negative
side-effect of the ascendancy of postcolonial studies over more traditional forms of scholarship ('Orientalist', 'Africanist' and so on) has
been the devaluation in 'Western' academia of competence in non-
metropolitan languages.[15] The point I want to emphasize here, before
offering further clarification of the issue in the next chapter, is that my
approach to *Heart of Darkness* fits it into a historical context that
remains primarily British/European and North American. I am dealing only with parts of the historical story.

Thirdly, I want to say a little more about the motivations of imperialism. In the Introduction I cited the definition offered by Williams
and Chrisman of colonialism as 'a particular phase in the history
of imperialism, which is now best understood as the globalization of
the capitalist mode of production, its penetration of previously non-
capitalist regions of the world, and destruction of pre- or non-capitalist
forms of social organization', and this certainly provides a legitimate
way of looking at what happened in the CFS. Prominent among
imperialists' motives was undoubtedly the allure of wealth, which
for Leopold, as Ascherson argues, was potentially a means of consoli-
dating the position of the monarchy. 'Other monarchs', he notes,
'watched the birth of modern ... capitalism with mixed feelings of

suspicion, incomprehension and contempt. Leopold understood that the private fortunes of a King remained as much a measure of his power to act freely as they had been in the Middle Ages. . . . Leopold had discovered a way to reverse the historical victory of the middle classes over their kings: a new path to absolutism.'[16]

There is a danger, however, of making the pursuit of profit and power through empire sound more measured and rational than it actually was. The fact that Leopold, whose inherited fortune was vast, came so close to bankrupting himself and was saved by the unforeseen and unforeseeable benefits of the rubber boom shows how financially risky a pursuit imperialism could be, and shows too that the choice of the Congo region in particular as his target was not based on any sound sense of its economic viability. This is made clearer still by the way he spent a significant part of his enormous profits on whimsical projects – monuments, new wings on his palaces, a Japanese tower and a Chinese pavilion – which, as Hochschild puts it, 'would earn him a place less in the history books than in the guidebooks'.[17] Indeed, Leopold's flights of fancy proved alienating to the Belgian government and populace, whose disapproval was bound to shake his grip on power in the long term. Reflecting in 1908 on the achievements of Leopold's Crown Foundation (the Fondation de la Couronne), the Belgian prime minister, Auguste Beernaert, remarked bluntly: 'In Africa: nothing. In Belgium, nothing but lavish projects.'[18] Regal idiosyncracies aside, public antipathy and/or apathy towards empire was common in other imperial centres too: to take one small example, the day after a debate in the French National Assembly in 1914 about an important new set of policies for Algeria, a newspaper in Algiers carried the headline: 'Only 587 dé-putés missing' – which is to say only ten had turned up.[19]

Imperialists' arguments for imperialism included the economic, of course, but were not limited to that sphere. Leopold, as we have already seen, pontificated freely on the work of civilization, and in a typical speech said:

> I am pleased to think that our agents, nearly all of whom are volunteers drawn from the ranks of the Belgian army, have always present in their minds a strong sense of the career of honour in which they are engaged, and are animated with a pure feeling of patriotism; not sparing their own blood, they will the more spare the blood of the natives, who will see in them the all-powerful protectors of their lives and their property, benevolent teachers of whom they have so great a need.
>   Our only programme . . . is the work of moral and material regener-ation, and we must do this among a population whose degeneration in

its inherited conditions it is difficult to measure. The many horrors and atrocitites which disgrace humanity give way little by little before our intervention...

Our progress...will soon introduce into the vast region of the Congo all the blessings of Christian civilization.[20]

In Leopold's case it seems indisputable that the use of such rhetoric to justify his imperial schemes was frequently manipulative and insincere. The hypocrisy of his remarks about 'sparing the blood of the natives' is breathtaking, and it is impossible to believe, for instance, that he cared about the slave trade, except insofar as it interfered with his own plans. His relations with the so-called Arab traders led by Tippu Tip in East Africa, who sold men and ivory further east, are one indication of this. (The word 'Arab,' incidentally, is misleading in that, although a good number of the slaves ended up in the Arab world, most of the traders with whom Europeans and the victims of the trade fought in Africa were Swahili-speaking Africans. Some of them were partly of Arab descent.) Initial contact with the traders was collaborative to a degree – for example, Stanley, acting in Leopold's name, appointed Tippu Tip as district governor of the Stanley Falls area in 1887. But the relationship was always marked by suspicion and rivalry, and from 1890 agents of the CFS launched into a series of confrontations in which they confiscated ivory from Arab traders, leading to a running war between the two factions from 1892 to 1894.[21]

In the case of the 'Arab' slave traders, as in others, Leopold proved adept in his speeches at mobilizing stock elements of contemporary colonial discourse in which others may have believed more fully: the notion of self-sacrificing service to one's country and humankind; the notion that the colonizers' ultimate duty/goal was to educate and improve the 'natives', morally, materially and culturally; and Christian evangelism. Like Kurtz's report, those speeches gave 'the notion of an exotic Immensity ruled by an august Benevolence', and there were few 'practical hints to interrupt the magic current of phrases'.[22] European civilization was assumed to be the highpoint of human 'progress', and to set standards by which other cultures were simply not civilized at all. Central to all of this was not only ethnocentricity but the profound racism that allowed the imperialists to treat the 'natives' as less than human, and that relied on and consolidated a notion of race whose shaky foundation I analyse in chapter 3. Common to all of these topoi was the metaphorics of darkness and light; and though Stanley's use of 'dark continent' in his title of 1878 may have been the first printed use of the phrase, it was far from novel. The title *Heart of Darkness* would have resonated, then, against specific phrases such as Stanley's, or Schweinfurth's *In the Heart of Africa*, or Leopold's phrase about 'the darkness enshrouding entire populations', or the name of one Christian mission, 'Heart of Africa',[23] and these in turn were part of that wider metaphorical net, its threads stretching between the physical and the metaphysical.

The brief description of 'colonial discourse' that I have just offered is intended to give a broad sense of some of its more common traits, which a literary text such as *Heart of Darkness* may or may not share. Even for that limited purpose a little more needs to be said about the very notion of 'discourse'. Its use in postcolonial studies is greatly influenced by the work of Michel Foucault, for whom it designated broad systems or spheres of representation and attendant practices making it possible (for those socially placed to do so) to make sense of the world in a certain way and to orient the world accordingly, while in effect making it impossible or illegitimate to apprehend or organize in certain other ways. According to Foucault, discourse is always a matter of power as well as knowledge.[24]

The precise scope and force of Foucault's term, suggestive though it may be, and the uses to which it has been put, have been the subject of some controversy. In the present context the most notable example has been debate about Said's *Orientalism*, a work that has played a pivotal role in shaping postcolonial studies. Foucault's influence can be seen in a passage such as the following:

> The representations of Orientalism in European culture amount to what we can call a discursive consistency, one that has not only history but material (and institutional) presence to show for itself. As I said in connection with Renan [for Said, a key figure in nineteenth-century Orientalism], such a consistency was a form of cultural praxis, a system of opportunities for making statements about the Orient. My whole point about this system is not that it is a misrepresentation of some Oriental essence – in which I do not for a moment believe – but that it operates as representations usually do, for a purpose, according to a tendency, in a specific historical, intellectual, and even economic setting.[25]

The argument about the way that representations 'operate', or are used, in specific historical circumstances is clearly an important one to postcolonial studies, but the philosophical underpinnings of the argument here are insecure. In the course of his book, Said seems to hesitate between the view that 'Orientalist' scholarship misrepresents the 'Orient' and the view that any such notion of misrepresentation is untenable – as may be implied when he links misrepresentation to the implausible notion of 'some Oriental essence'. At times, then, it seems that 'discourse' is understood wholly to *determine* consciousness; relatedly, the term 'truth' tends to appear in inverted commas, as it does in Said's lead-up to this passage, but their significance is far from clear since – as Chris Prendergast points out in an insightful discussion of *Orientalism* – a conventional distinction between truth and falsehood remains in play nonetheless.[26]

In the Afterword I will return to some of the epistemological issues that arise here, and for now want just to make some relatively straightforward points about the pertinence of the notion of 'colonial discourse' to Leopold's case and others. The first is that, in view of the questions already raised about the partial irrationality and riskiness of Leopold's pursuit of an empire, it is clear that his motives and practices, including his rivalry with other European leaders, need to be understood not just in terms of brute force and the mechanics of economic production and exploitation, but also in terms of the fantasmatic attractions of power. Imperialists' violent actions in the real world, to put it another way, were driven partly by the imperial fantasy world; and they were consolidated and contested, as my epigraphs from Conrad and Djebar both suggest in their different ways, in the sphere of representations as well as on the ground. It is such factors that make a certain notion of colonial discourse a potentially useful one, in my view, and make literature's role as a form of (imaginative engagement with) colonial discourse seem worthy of serious attention.

The example of Leopold's own *uses* of colonial discourse also makes it clear, I think, that any general model of the relationship between discourse, consciousness and imperial politics needs to be fairly flexible and variegated. Leopold may indeed have been a hypocrite, but even in his case the issue is more complex than that: he doubtless believed some of the things that he said, and many of the explorers, missionaries, soldiers, geographers and humanitarians that he gathered together at his great geographical conference certainly had plans and goals that they sincerely believed in. This in itself is no defence of those plans and goals, of course, but in assessing them now it cannot be assumed that they coalesced into a single brutally coherent project, and, more importantly, it must be recognized that some of them – anti-slavery campaigns, for example – truly were legitimate. In practice, as Fanon emphasized repeatedly, colonialism created a polarization of colonizer and colonized that for the most part made nuances of attitude among the colonizers politically irrelevant from the point of view of the colonized; and no doubt numerous different attitudes and practices contributed in their different ways to the devastating dominance that the colonizers achieved, at least for a time.[27] Nevertheless, there is, again, a danger of making the colonial project, or colonial discourse, sound more concerted and homogeneous than it was. In practice, numerous different discourses, generated from or in response to the imperial powers, helped variously to constitute, support or undermine different colonial projects. When one looks at photos of the *Roi des Belges* or 'King of the Belgians', the unimpressive 'twopenny-half-penny river-steamboat with a penny whistle attached' on which Conrad travelled the Congo, the imperial project of which they provide a synecdochic snapshot suddenly appears less potent and more precarious than one would believe from the robust rhetoric of a Leopold.[28] One could very well object that it was concerted *enough*, and horribly potent, but, all the same, to understand how different people reacted differently to imperialists' designs, or how the varied forms of colonialism meant and became different things in their encounters with different cultures, or how the era of colonial settlement came (more or less) to an end, one needs to understand that, between rhetoric or discourse and consciousness, and between theory and practice, there is always some sort of gap.

2

Racism, Realism and the Question of Historical Context

Is *Heart of Darkness* racist? It is true that you do not have to go far into the story to find racist discourse, and I will begin by giving just a couple of brief, and perhaps familiar, examples. One, cited by Achebe in his famous speech, is a passage near the beginning where Marlow describes his journey along the coast before reaching the river, and says:

> 'Now and then a boat from the shore gave one a momentary contact with reality. It was paddled by black fellows. You could see from afar the white of their eyeballs glistening. They shouted, sang; their bodies streamed with perspiration; they had faces like grotesque masks – these chaps; but they had bone, muscle, a wild vitality, an intense energy of movement, that was as natural and true as the surf along their coast. They wanted no excuse for being there.' (p. 30)

Clearly, this representation resonates with stereotyped characteristics of the 'native', especially in its emphasis on physical difference, including the glistening eyeballs and muscularity of the 'black fellows', their grotesque physiognomies, their sweat and their sheer physicality, itself associated with the 'natural' and the 'wild'. Marlow later remarks that 'Going up that river was like travelling back to the earliest beginnings of the world' (another indication of 'primitiveness'), then says:

> 'suddenly, as we struggled round a bend, there would be a glimpse of rush walls, of peaked grass-roofs, a burst of yells, a whirl of black limbs, a mass of hands clapping, of feet stamping, of bodies swaying, of

eyes rolling, under the droop of heavy and motionless foliage. The steamer toiled along slowly on the edge of a black and incomprehensible frenzy. The prehistoric man was cursing us, praying to us, welcoming us – who could tell? We were cut off from the comprehension of our surroundings; we glided past like phantoms, wondering and secretly appalled, as sane men would be before an enthusiastic outbreak in a madhouse.' (p. 62)

Here one could again point to the circulation of racial stereotypes; to the imperial symbolism of the difficult progress made by the steamer (as emblem of 'Western' civilization) through the jungle; and to the confusion of, or slippage between, cultural difference and a fantasmatic chronological difference, such that the 'native' is represented as backward, as situated and perhaps arrested at some earlier, prehistoric and precultural point on a developmental scale with White Europeans at its (or as its) highest point.

Does the presence of many comparable passages in *Heart of Darkness* prove the racism *of* the text as a whole – prove, in other words, that Conrad's story is racist? Postcolonial critics have hesitated over this question and have answered it in different ways. This chapter hopes to cast light on both the form and the foundation of this ongoing history of critical hesitation and disagreement.

Plausibility

One of the first reasons for the critic to hesitate is that Marlow's remarks could be explained in terms of realism. Someone in Marlow's position might indeed have seen muscly and incomprehensible men with glistening eyeballs, or more accurately might, partly because of his prejudices and fears, have perceived them in such a way. Cedric Watts makes this argument in response to Achebe, stating that 'Conrad is offering an entirely plausible rendering of the responses of a British traveller of *c.*1890 to the strange and bewildering experiences offered by the Congo. The passage is patently justified on realistic grounds.'[1]

The force of this argument as a response to Achebe may be diminished if one thinks further about these notions of the 'realistic' and the 'plausible'. A classic theoretical critique of the latter concept was offered by Gérard Genette in his essay 'Vraisemblance et motivation'. (The dictionary translation of *vraisemblance* tends to be 'verisimilitude', but the English term is less flexible and more technical than the French; the adjective *vraisemblable* can be rendered as 'plausible', 'probable' or 'convincing'.) When as readers we assess whether a literary representation is *vraisemblable* we are in part measuring it, Genette argues, against a commonsensical and intuitive set of beliefs and values; and if it measures up, and in that sense we decide to accept it as 'realistic', as a reliable picture of the real world, it thereby seems to endorse those beliefs and values. Yet according to Genette there are numerous reasons why one might take a sceptical view of this process:

1 'Common sense' and intuition are neither ideologically neutral nor wholly reliable. This becomes obvious when one remembers that it once appeared a matter of simple intuition and self-evidence that the earth was flat; or indeed when one thinks of the still widespread aberrations of racist thought. Racists presumably feel intuitively the truth of their racist beliefs.

2 The supposed authority of the 'endorsement' offered by the representation depends on its offering a 'true' 'picture' of the world, yet its objectivity is always and inevitably compromised by the very selectivity and subjectivity that make the words cohere into such a 'picture'. By the same token that picture is subtly infused with values, making it amenable to particular value-judgements.

3 The relation of the *vraisemblable* to the real is complicated by the fact that *vraisemblance* is in part irreducibly and specifically literary. Here the French term's flexibility is crucial in that it points in one direction towards probability (something that might be calculated neutrally on an empirical basis) and in another direction towards the conventions of literary realism. In a realist narrative a succession of coincidences is likely to be judged 'implausible' or 'unrealistic' even if it is not impossible – and is in that sense conceivably real. So *vraisemblance* can be said to serve a regulatory function that makes 'realism' narrower than the 'real': this is why fact is stranger than (realist) fiction. For Genette, the criteria of *vraisemblance*, especially in the seventeenth-century literature from which his two primary examples are drawn, are closely linked with those of *bienséance*, a term used to describe traditional limits of taste or propriety in drama and literature: both concepts involve, and fuse, notions of probability and of obligation, of the habitual and the socially acceptable, within a specifically literary framework.

4 Within this framework, the criteria of *vraisemblance* thus mean that readers (and writers) may tie literary value not only to 'probability' or 'plausibility', but also to a certain model of psychological 'coherence' or 'consistency': if a character in a fiction acts 'out of character', this may appear 'implausible', whereas it is perfectly plausible to assert that real individuals occasionally act out of charac-

ter. On another level, *vraisemblance* is thus intimately involved not only with our desire for plausibility in literature, but also with our whole untrustworthy *sense* of probability, of what constitutes a consistent or coherent pattern of behaviour, and what constitutes the 'character' of a person, rather than of a fictional character. Genette goes on to draw attention to a circularity in commonsensical understandings of motive and behaviour, such that one might in the same movement find in Marlow traits typical of 'the seaman', and also 'explain' or account for his behaviour in terms of his (seaman's or seaman-like) character. In this way, one appears to reconfirm simultaneously the accuracy of the representation and one's grasp of personality. At this point, a further circularity emerges: fiction may play a normative role in relation to our judgements of other people; and the standards by which those judgements are made may themselves derive in part from fiction. In relation to *Heart of Darkness*, for example, even a reader much less well-informed than Watts might feel that she or he can grasp intuitively the 'likely' responses of a British traveller in about 1890; and to a significant degree it is surely a tradition of literary representations that has shaped, directly or indirectly, that intuition.

Genette points out, moreover, that the criteria of psychological 'coherence' that realism could be said to deploy are not only relatively narrow but unstable, not to say incoherent. He draws attention to the expediency with which Balzac (habitually treated as an archetypal realist writer) provides motives for his characters' behaviour, constantly nudging the reader along with ad hoc generalizations and miniature, short-lived psychological models ('She was one of those women who . . .' and so on). Genette remarks:

> Since pretty much any feeling or attitude can serve equally well, in terms of novelistic psychology, to account for [*justifier*] almost any given act, the factors 'determining' behaviour almost never actually determine it; and it would seem that Balzac, aware of and disconcerted by the compromising freedom he thus possesses, tries to disguise it behind a somewhat random repetition of connectives – *because, for, so* – . . . which are scattered so abundantly through the text that to my mind they end up emphasizing the very thing they wish to mask: the arbitrariness of the story [*l'arbitraire du récit*].[2]

He goes on to explain further this notion of the story's arbitrary nature:

> These *retrograde* determinations constitute precisely what I have called the arbitrariness of the story, which does not really mean indeterminacy

but the determination of the means by the ends and, to put it more bluntly, *of causes by effects.*[3]

To put this another way, the realist narrative is constructed teleologically: that is to say, earlier events are coloured or given their shape by later ones, to which they thus seem to lead inexorably and inevitably. This is characteristic of much narrative (for example in the creation of suspense) but clearly uncharacteristic of reality. According to Genette, readers become caught up in the game of pretending that the characters are real and *have* their own motivations, and so are drawn into an 'illusion' whereby realistic fiction, as a mode of making sense of the world, masks its own conventionality (which is to say its respect of generic/ideological norms) and is accepted as a trustworthy reflection of a world that is imagined to make sense on its own:

> Motivation therefore creates the appearance and alibi of causality that finalistic determination – which in fiction is the rule – bestows upon itself: the *because* whose job it is to make you forget the *why* and so to naturalize, or to realize, the fiction (meaning to allow it to pass for real) by concealing its deliberateness [and] its artificiality: in short, its fictionality. The reversal of determination that transforms the (artificial) relation between means and ends into a (natural) relation of cause and effect is the very instrument of this process, clearly necessary for current patterns of consumption which demand that fiction be taken as an illusion, albeit perhaps imperfect or half-hearted, of reality.[4]

There are, I think, certain problems with this characterization of fiction and of realism, to which I will return later. For now, my point is to show how Genette's arguments, and particularly his discussion of the way that motivations may 'justify' characters' behaviour, suggest that Watts's article may beg the question that Achebe raised. The 'justification' for Marlow's comments found in realism or the *vraisemblable* is a literary or generic one; Achebe's question, however, may raise questions about the ideology of realism as such. Genette, like many other theorists, is suspicious that, if we accept the putative 'illusion' that the realist text represents the world 'as it really is', we are being misled epistemologically – because really, in Prendergast's phrase, 'The language of mimesis re-presents not the world but the world as already organized in discourse' – and so ideologically, insofar as a commonsensical and restrictive view of the world is delivered to us with all the authority of the unmediated 'real'.[5] Genette encourages the critic to stop pretending that it is the fictional reality that has shaped the story-telling, rather than vice-versa, to stop playing the game of psychologizing, and so to break out of this circle and to analyse the unfolding of the story in 'functional' terms. 'Function', he points out, is not the same as 'intention'; rather, it should be conceived of *structurally*, as the organizing principle of the narrative. It might also be conceived of *socially*, which is to say in terms of the social function of literature ('No literary story is *only* a story', he remarks in passing).[6] According to Genette, in other words, critics should account for the presence of a given element in the text not in terms of the text's 'internal' dynamics – that is, by reference to the fictional universe in which things 'exist' and 'happen' – but in terms of its function within the text as a sense-making construct.

If, then, one wanted to offer a *functional* explanation of why Conrad's text refers to 'glistening eyeballs', one would do so not by saying that the eyeballs 'really' were glistening when Marlow saw them, or by saying that 'he' projects his own preconceptions onto the 'black fellows', but rather by considering how these words *work*, or *how* they *make sense* and what sort of sense they make, for the narrative as such and for the reader. Realist narrative, it has been argued, obeys an implicit law such that descriptions must not burden readers with pointless or incongruous information, information that would fall beneath what Stephen Heath calls the 'threshold of functional relevance'.[7] In many contexts, to describe characters' eyeballs may indeed seem gratuitous and irrelevant; and if the allusion does not seem so here, that is arguably not only because it may connote a (perceived) threat, but also because it gains a supplement of sense as part of description that insists upon fetishized physical qualities including 'colour'. The way that the reader processes such 'information' needs to be understood, then, at once in relation to narrative convention and in terms of a wider world of representations.

Modernism and the representation of representations

So far I have used the term realism and Genette's theory of *vraisemblance* fairly flexibly, partly in order to cast light on some of the conventions on which the cognitive processing of fiction in general seems to rely. The justifications for this should become clearer in the course of the book, but at this point I want to say a little more about certain literary-historical distinctions that I have neglected up until now.

It should be recognized that the 'realism' or *'vraisemblance'* of *Heart of Darkness*, a text that may be broadly 'realistic' but is not typically 'realist', may be different from that of the seventeenth- and nineteenth-century literature discussed by Genette. Indeed, it could be argued that it corresponds much more closely to the definition of 'modernism' that he offers in passing: modernism as Genette sees it is characterized by 'the distrust of *vraisemblances*', and he remarks that the 'opposite' of seventeenth-century literary works in which the criteria of *vraisemblance* are accepted implicitly are 'works that are most emancipated from any allegiance to *public opinion*'. In such works, he goes on,

> the story [*récit*] no longer concerns itself with corresponding to a system of general truths; it is drawn from a particular truth, or from the depths of the imagination. The radical originality and the independence of this sort of attitude situate it, ideologically, at the other end of the spectrum from the servility of *vraisemblance*. Nonetheless, the two approaches have something in common, namely their shared elimination of commentary and justification.[8]

The classic seventeenth-century text, according to Genette, has no need of an omniscient narrator to guide and coerce the reader, because so much may be left to common sense, assumed and unsaid. The modernist text has no place for one, its particularity lying in its refusal of over-general models and received opinion – and perhaps also, by extension, of over-simple psychologizing models of cause and effect. For Genette, this means that the modernist text – as *distinct* from the realist text – offers the reader something other than conservative reassurance.

Heart of Darkness fits Genette's model of modernism in that it lacks an omniscient narrator and offers in Marlow a narrator who is, in his particularity, hard to fathom and to categorize and at times hard to understand. Marlow's perspective is a personal one, marked – and marked as such for the reader, one might argue – by his many hesitations and equivocations, and by the same exorbitancy of language that helps mark the text as a whole as literature rather than reportage. The frame of reference through which Marlow perceives and makes sense of his experiences is, as Robert Hampson has pointed out, both distinctly his rather than Conrad's (in that Marlow, unlike Conrad, does not recognize Cyrillic script, for instance) and recognizably European;[9] and though some of Marlow's particularities may be shared by, and thus perhaps invisible to, much of his audience and indeed Conrad, Marlow goes so far as to draw attention to his own unreliability as a narrator. His comment about his 'momentary contact with reality', for example, is one sign that his relation to the reality of Africa is, or was, oblique and at times almost delirious: he was trapped, he notes in the same passage, within 'a mournful and senseless delusion' (p. 30). Still more explicitly, he calls into doubt his own ability to represent his experiences adequately, to himself or to his audience, when he says:

> 'Kurtz . . . was just a word for me. I did not see the man in the name any more than you do. Do you see him? Do you see the story? Do you see anything? It seems to me I am trying to tell you a dream – making a vain attempt, because no relation of a dream can convey the dream-sensation, that commingling of absurdity, surprise, and bewilderment in a tremor of struggling revolt, that notion of being captured by the incredible which is of the very essence of dreams . . . .'
> He was silent for a while.
> 'No, it is impossible; it is impossible to convey the life-sensation of any given epoch of one's existence.' (p. 50)

In this passage as in others – characterized by idiosyncratic punctuation that conveys Marlow's pauses and switches of narrative pace – it is clear too that Marlow is only the secondary narrator of the story, his speech reported, as the inverted commas indicate, by a primary narrator who is one of the nameless members of Marlow's first audience. These men, the narrator tells us, were 'tolerant of each other's yarns – and even convictions' (p. 16). He also remarks that as a seaman-storyteller Marlow was 'not typical', except in 'his propensity to spin yarns' (p. 18). Perhaps mockingly, he describes Marlow's story-telling posture as akin to 'the pose of a Buddha preaching in European clothes and without a lotus-flower' (p. 20), just before handing the bulk of narration to Marlow with the comment, 'it was only after a long silence, when he said, in a hesitating voice, "I suppose you fellows remember I did once turn fresh-water sailor for a bit," that we knew we were fated, before the ebb began to run, to hear about one of Marlow's inconclusive experiences' (p. 21). Taken together, these remarks seem to imply, first, that Marlow's views, which the narrator does not necessarily share, may be both idiosyncratic and unclear; secondly, that, in his propensity to 'spin yarns', Marlow may have followed narrative patterns and used attention-seeking strategies that further distance his narrative, in immeasurable ways, from the (remembered) events; and, finally, that the narrator, too, has his own personal perspective, shares Marlow's propensity to spin a yarn, and, through placing inverted commas around Marlow's story, is making perhaps implausible demands on, or claims for, his own powers of memory as he 'quotes' him. The primary narrator too may, then, be thought of as unreliable. Indeed, his own perspective on the story seems to blur in the opening pages, after he has reported his thoughts on the 'great knights-errant of the sea' (p. 17). Only retrospectively, when Marlow suddenly comments 'you say Knights?' (p. 19), can we as readers deduce that these were remarks spoken aloud, and so an important cue for Marlow's tale.

To summarize, it seems that an 'image of Africa' (to borrow Achebe's phrase) reaches Marlow's audience filtered through the mist of incomprehension and prejudice within which he first perceived 'Africa', through his memory, through the narrative structures and expressive limitations of the seaman's yarn, and in response to the particular conversational context in which the tale is told; they reach *us* only after further filtering via the narrator, who has his own prejudices, opinions and even, one might speculate, purposes. It could be argued, then, that in view of these complexities it is implausible to claim that this representation tries to pass itself off as an unmediated reality; one might even argue, on the contrary, that it constantly *reminds* us that 'The language of mimesis re-presents not the world but the world as already organized in discourse', to repeat Prendergast's phrase. For Hampson, correspondingly, '*Heart of Darkness* . . . does not offer a representation of Africa: it offers a representation of representations of Africa.'[10] One might compare Genette's remark that the next step 'beyond' classic realism (in relation to a gradation of forms of *vraisemblance*, more, perhaps, than in terms of literary history or sophistication) takes the shape of texts in which 'the dramatic action will slip into the background, and the *récit* will be overtaken in importance by the *discours* – which is the prelude to the crumbling of the novel as a genre, and the arrival of *literature*, in the modern sense of the word.'[11] (Genette uses 'récit' to mean the content of the story and 'discours' for the telling of the story.) In these terms Marlow's narratorial voice, at once digressive and attention-grabbing, helps make *Heart of Darkness* a paradigmatic work of modernist literature.

Frames of reference (i): the world in the text

Where does this leave us in relation to Achebe? In fact, he foresees such arguments about the complex framing of Conrad's story and its performance of unreliability, and is not persuaded by them. He writes:

> It might be contended, of course, that the attitude to the African in *Heart of Darkness* is not Conrad's but that of his fictional narrator, Marlow, and that far from endorsing it Conrad might indeed be hold-

ing it up to irony and criticism. Certainly Conrad appears to go to considerable pains to set up layers of insulation between himself and the moral universe of his story. He has, for example, a narrator behind a narrator.... But if Conrad's intention is to draw a cordon sanitaire between himself and the moral and psychological *malaise* of his narrator his care seems to me totally wasted because he neglects to hint, clearly and adequately, at an alternative frame of reference by which we may judge the actions and opinions of his characters.[12]

Much hinges here on what one means by a 'frame of reference', and what qualifies as a 'hint'. In response to Achebe, it might be argued that the same narratorial particularity through which Conrad has, in Genette's terms, avoided the false promises of narratorial omniscience, of ready generalization and of common sense – the very characteristic of the text that *makes* it, for Genette, non-conservative – makes it impossible for the text to provide anything as (artificially) coherent as the phrase 'frame of reference' suggests. One might argue, in other words, that the particularity and unreliability of Marlow's perspective discourage the reader from extrapolating from it, or for finding in it support for racist opinions; or that (to introduce a term that I will examine in detail in the next chapter) they prevent the reader from *identifying* with Marlow. But one might start, more modestly, by asking whether the opinions expressed by Marlow and other characters fall, as Achebe implies, squarely or consistently within a single frame of reference.

The answer to this would again depend on the standard by which a judgement was made; one might argue, for instance, that all of the opinions expressed in the text were 'European' in important respects. This is not to say, however, that all those opinions are fundamentally imperialist and/or racist; and it is perhaps worth noting here that, although racism will be central to my discussions here and in the next two chapters – and was chosen as a focus partly because of its continuing pertinence – racism was never a monopoly of European imperialists', and its place varied within different forms and instances of colonial discourse. Even passages such as those quoted at the start of this chapter, which are among those that may sound most offensive to the modern ear, contain tensions and shifts of connotation that not only complicate the reader's understanding of Marlow as a character, but more specifically, and more importantly in the present context, complicate his – and our – relationship to his uncomprehending and condescending remarks, whose place within a certain racist and imperialist ideology might otherwise seem beyond doubt. Many accomplished critical responses to the text and to Achebe have followed this

line of argument, of which this subsection will provide a brief overview. Readers familiar with this material should skip ahead.

Even in the first passage I quoted, any presumption of imperial
mastery and mission may be undermined by the sense that Marlow is
disorientated, his comprehension of the situation limited, and the
purpose of his journey not clear-cut. His remark that the 'black
fellows ... wanted no excuse for being there' seems to imply that he
and his fellow-travellers do not belong in Africa, and that their own
right to be there and reasons for being there are not secure. Comparably, even as the second passage seems on one level to imply that
the gulf between the 'civilized' man and the 'native' is unbridgeable,
on another it creates possible points of comparison, contact and
even kinship. Marlow's equivocation in this respect could be perceived in his use of 'fellows' or in the hesitancy signalled by the
punctuation and the uncertain register of the phrase 'they had faces
like grotesque masks – these chaps.' Indeed, just after the second
passage Marlow addresses directly (but still equivocally) this question
of kinship:

> 'you know, that was the worst of it – this suspicion of their not being
> inhuman. It would come slowly to one. They howled, and leaped, and
> spun, and made horrid faces; but what thrilled you was just the thought
> of their humanity – like yours – the thought of your remote kinship
> with this wild and passionate uproar.' (p. 63)

Achebe feels that the underlying sentiment here is 'There go I but for
the grace of God', and that Marlow's metanarrative comments are
underpinned by stark oppositions whereby Africa is assumed (and
shown) to be 'the antithesis of Europe and therefore of civilization'.[13]
Such oppositions could be said to constitute a profound 'frame of
reference'; and there are, as one might expect, numerous moments
when the 'black fellows' and the jungle are associated with darkness.
However, there are moments too when the poles of the dualism are
reversed, so to speak: for example, in the first narrator's extended
treatment of the gloom of London and 'the west' (p. 16) in the story's
opening pages, and the repeated association of the Thames with
darkness in the closing lines; in Marlow's opening remark, 'And this
also has been one of the dark places of the earth' (p. 18); and at the
moment when, after arriving at Kurtz's camp, Marlow comments that
he now found himself in 'some lightless region of subtle horrors,
where pure, uncomplicated savagery was a positive relief, being
something that had a right to exist – obviously – in the sunshine'
(p. 95).

Marlow uses comparisons and points of reference that could be said to convey his (to a degree, inevitable) ethnocentricity and incomprehension, but could also be seen as 'a narrative strategy designed to undermine the ethnocentricity of his audience', as Hampson puts it.[14] In another striking reversal of the commonplaces of imperialist discourse, for instance, he reminds his audience of a time when 'I was loafing about, hindering you fellows in your work and invading your homes, just as though I had got a heavenly mission to civilise you' (p. 21); and later, explicitly unsettling the standard connotations of a familiar exotic image, muses that the 'far-off drums' that he heard may have had 'as profound a meaning as the sound of bells in a Christian country' (p. 39). Indeed, as Hampson points out elsewhere, it is conceivable that the drums were being used precisely to announce a Christian service.[15] On another occasion, Marlow remembers, he explicitly made the mental leap of putting himself in the position of the 'cannibals' who were among his crew, and perceived – 'in a new light, as it were' – both how unappetizing the pilgrims looked, and that contrary to his prejudiced expectations the 'cannibals' had exercised 'restraint' in not attacking them (p. 71). Conversely, much of his own behaviour, let alone that of Kurtz, remains obscure to him: 'I don't know why we behaved like lunatics', he remarks (p. 53), a comment one might compare with that later 'madhouse' image (p. 62).

On this basis one could argue that the text allows the imperial encounter to be understood in terms more complex than the meeting of Light with Darkness, or of civilization with nature, and more complex than the unchallenged imposition, or imitation, of European norms. There are intimations that the Europeans and the Africans are caught in a circular dynamic of mutual incomprehension in which each projects prejudices onto the other, a process that Christopher Miller terms 'mutual fetishization'.[16] There are signs too that the Europeans are influenced by the Africans, as well as vice-versa. Kurtz's behaviour is the clearest instance of this, but there are also indications that Marlow himself has been altered; it seems that the process Bhabha describes as 'hybridization' is taking place, whereby the apparently polarized identities of the colonizer and the colonized become destabilized.[17]

One of the most remarkable reversals of perspective occurs near the beginning of the story, when Marlow explains his longstanding urge to explore:

'Now when I was a little chap I had a passion for maps. . . . At that time there were many blank spaces on the earth, and when I saw one that looked particularly inviting on a map (but they all look that) I would put my finger on it and say, When I grow up I will go there.... I have been in some of them, and ... well, we won't talk about that. But there was one yet – the biggest, the most blank, so to speak – that I had a hankering after.

'True, by this time it was not a blank space any more. It had got filled since my boyhood with rivers and lakes and names. It had ceased to be a blank space of delightful mystery – a white patch for a boy to dream gloriously over. It had become a place of darkness.' (pp. 21–2)

This notion that European exploration had filled that 'blank space' with darkness, rather than bringing enlightenment to the Dark Continent, turns on its head one of the standard tropes of imperialist discourse.[18] It is consistent, it turns out, with many of the remarks that Marlow makes elsewhere in the novel about the motives and the effects of the Europeans' behaviour there. One response to the perception of kinship might have been – and historically sometimes was – the attempt to move 'primitive' peoples forward along the timescale of civilizational development, so to speak, but nothing in *Heart of Darkness* suggests that any such 'progress' was being made in the CFS; Marlow certainly does not seem to think so, and the very inconclusiveness of Marlow's story, noted by the first narrator at the start, distinguishes it formally from the straightforward teleology of a certain imperial narrative of illumination and improvement.

None of this is to say, of course, that Marlow's own frame of reference is explicitly or consistently or 'consciously' anti-imperialist, or that his criticisms can be assumed to be general. Again, the text is full of equivocations and slippages. Just before these reminiscences about his map-reading, for example, he had elaborated his idea that England was once a 'dark place' for its Roman conquerors:

'these chaps were not much account, really. They were no colonists; their administration was merely a squeeze, and nothing more, I suspect. They were conquerors, and for that you want only brute force – nothing to boast of, when you have it, since your strength is just an accident arising from the weakness of others. They grabbed what they could get for the sake of what was to be got. It was just robbery with violence, aggravated murder on a great scale, and men going at it blind – as is very proper for those who tackle a darkness. The conquest of the earth, which mostly means the taking it away from those who have a different complexion or slightly flatter noses than ourselves, is not a pretty thing when you look into it too much. What redeems it is the idea only. An idea at the back of it; not a sentimental pretence but an idea; and an unselfish belief in the idea – something you can set up, and bow down before, and offer a sacrifice to ...' (p. 20)

In this sharply critical passage it remains ambiguous how far Marlow's misgivings about what he refers to later as 'the philanthropic pretence of the whole concern' (p. 46) amount to a criticism of colonialism as such, and how far they concern only the misapplication of colonial principles. There seems to be a distinction here between conquest and colonialism, the latter redeemed by an 'idea'. As Hampson points out, however, 'Marlow's assertion of the redeeming "idea" behind imperialism leads him into a figurative language which subverts the idea he has been asserting. . . . Indeed, it might be argued that it is this image that prompts the story that follows rather than any search to express the redeeming "idea".'[19] Marlow knows the unedifying ending of his story, so whereas at first sight it may seem that the 'idea' of colonialism, its rational underpinning, redeems it, and will be the subject of the story, it may seem retrospectively that the story is more about the aberrations of imperial discourse that encourage a Kurtz to see himself as someone before whom others should 'bow down', and about how the idea of an idea itself becomes fetishized and irrational, so that it ends up as 'something you can set up, and bow down before, and offer a sacrifice to . . .'. As Joseph Bristow argues, *Heart of Darkness* depicts a world in which rational acquisition becomes irrational hoarding, economic routine becomes ritual, indirect violence becomes overt barbarism, and 'The "idea", therefore, has no rationale. It simply exists for itself.'[20] For Bristow, the figure of Kurtz serves precisely to reveal that imperialism has no ethical basis.

To other critics, however, it seems that Marlow (and the reader) are drawn into a form of complicity with Kurtz. Discussing the ending of the book in this light, Benita Parry writes:

> what the fiction validates is Marlow's conviction that the choice is between a rigorous adherence to ethnic identity, which carries the freight of remaining ignorant of the foreign, or embracing the unknown and compromising racial integrity.
> . . . Marlow, who had accepted the cannibal helmsman as a partner and acknowledged the 'claims of distant kinship' in his dying look, can sacrifice this obligation to the greater loyalty owing a man who has disobeyed every tenet of this creed but to whom he is bound through the umbilical cord of his culture, and in this he demonstrates an act of solidarity with a world whose values he suspects and whose practices he disavows.[21]

This solidarity is a matter of gender as well as ethnicity; not only does the text seem to signal some sort of male homosocial bond both between Marlow and Kurtz and between Marlow and his listeners, but it also indicates more or less explicitly that this bond excludes women.[22] Before departing on his adventure, Marlow goes to see his 'excellent aunt', and is discomfited by her naïve declarations of faith in the civilizing mission of the Company, and her readiness to use the imperial vocabulary of enlightenment:

> 'I was going to take charge of a twopenny-half-penny river-steamboat with a penny whistle attached! It appeared, however, I was also one of the Workers, with a capital – you know. Something like an emissary of light, something like a lower sort of apostle. There had been a lot of such rot let loose in print and talk just about that time, and the excellent woman, living right in the rush of all that humbug, got carried off her feet. She talked about "weaning those ignorant millions from their horrid ways," till, upon my word, she made me quite uncomfortable.' (p. 28)

Marlow remarks to his (male) audience that he 'ventured to hint that the Company was run for profit', and goes on:

> 'It's queer how out of touch with truth women are. They live in a world of their own, and there had never been anything like it, and never can be. It is too beautiful altogether, and if they were to set it up it would go to pieces before the first sunset.' (p. 28)

This comment is echoed in a more aggressive and disturbing form later in the story when Marlow's narrative temporarily breaks down, as he explains that, in his final meeting with the Intended, he 'laid the ghost of his [Kurtz's] gifts at last with a lie' (p. 80). The two women provide another way of describing the adventure's 'frame': it is the aunt who launches Marlow upon his journey, and it is his lie to the Intended about Kurtz's final words that marks its close. Marlow's conviction that women are 'out of it' becomes self-fulfilling: he explains his decision to lie in terms of his belief that she would be unable to bear the 'darkness', which both women are protected/prevented from seeing. On one level the aunt in particular needs, in Marlow's view, to be left innocent of the violence that subtends the colonial enterprise; and on another level there is a sense in which civilization seems necessarily to be built on particular forms of oppression and suppression, of which women may be both victims and perpetrators.[23] In relation to gender too, then, it could be argued that, after many hesitations, the ending of *Heart of Darkness* 'reinstates the discourse of imperialism but reinstates it as a lie', as Hampson puts it.[24]

Frames of reference (ii): the text in the world

The criticism on which I have drawn up till now works from and in support of various theoretical positions (narratological, feminist, postcolonial and so on), but it has turned mainly on 'internal' textual evidence, focusing on what I have called 'the world in the text'. Hampson's argument about the relation of *Heart of Darkness* to the 'lie' of imperialism, however, moves outside this frame by instructively contrasting Conrad's story, which was first published chapter by chapter in *Blackwood's Magazine* between February and April 1899, with an article called 'Life and death in the River Niger'. The latter, a piece of reportage about a steamer journey up the Niger, appeared in the same issue as the third and final instalment. Hampson's comparison reveals how extensively Conrad's text departs from the conventional tropes and structures of the imperialist travelogue: the form of 'Life and death in the River Niger' is much simpler, displaying less 'verbal self-consciousness' than Conrad's text and using a single, authoritative narratorial voice; relatedly, in terms of 'content' it shows a more profound lack of interest in Africans, accepts uncritically the commercial framework of imperial exploration and assumes unequivocally that the imperial enterprise is justified and progressive.[25]

A comparable critical move is made by Andrea White in her book *Joseph Conrad and the Adventure Tradition*, where she argues that *Heart of Darkness* needs to be understood in relation to the 'adventure story' genre to which it could be said to belong. That genre, she argues, would have encouraged Conrad's readers to approach the text with specific assumptions and reading 'strategies': to return to an earlier issue, these assumptions might have included the norms of *vraisemblance* specific to and characteristic of the adventure genre (for, as Genette notes, these norms vary by genre, and through history). White, offering a kind of social-functional analysis, concludes that, viewed in this context,

> Marlow is not so much Conrad's spokesman as a strategic innovation that served his purposes in disrupting the generic adventure story and its essentially dangerous monolithic illusions. This use increases the dialogic possibilities and allows the story to be the site of struggle between disparate languages and outlooks. As Mikhail Bakhtin observed, that very dialogic quality ensures that no one voice necessarily emerges the absolute victor, and is itself a subversion in this discourse that had always sought to champion the imperial subject. (p. 177)

Similarly one might also attempt to position Conrad generically as a 'romantic' novelist: it is not the term most often applied to him now, but, in a review of 1923, Mary Austin could speak of him as 'at the very top of the list of romantic novelists' and 'the great master of English Romanticism' – phrases which appear all the more striking when one finds that Stanley, writing to James Osgood in search of an American publisher/distributor for his book *Coomassie and Magdala: The Story of Two British Campaigns in Africa*, tried to sell it by saying: 'The book is interesting and though reporting absolute facts only reads like a Romance.'[26]

Such arguments about the perhaps unfamiliar generic conventions through which *Heart of Darkness* was once read serve as a reminder that Achebe's questions about the reader's 'frame of reference' need to be addressed not only in terms of the text's internal dynamics and 'dialogic possibilities' but also in relation to the frames of reference available to readers historically. Achebe's implicit understanding of this issue is, I think, that 'white racism' has always overridden all other considerations and continues to do so, connecting the text with the world and unifying past and present (White) readers in their attitude to both. Thus, after making his statement that Conrad was a racist, he says:

> That this simple truth is glossed over in criticisms of his work is due to the fact that white racism against Africa is such a normal way of thinking that its manifestations go completely unremarked. Students of *Heart of Darkness* will often tell you that Conrad is concerned not so much with Africa as with the deterioration of one European mind caused by solitude and sickness. They will point out to you that Conrad is, if anything, less charitable to the Europeans in the story than he is to the natives, that the point of the story is to ridicule Europe's civilizing mission in Africa. A Conrad student informed me in Scotland that Africa is merely a setting for the disintegration of the mind of Mr Kurtz.
>
> Which is partly the point. Africa as setting and backdrop which eliminates the African as human factor. Africa as a metaphysical battle-field devoid of all recognizable humanity, into which the European wanders at his peril. Can nobody see the preposterous and perverse arrogance in thus reducing Africa to the role of props for the break-up of one petty European mind?[27]

Achebe is doubtless right that, to many readers, the setting for the story has appeared to be a vague and perhaps metaphorical 'Africa', exploited by a vague and perhaps metaphorical 'Company'. Part of Achebe's charge, echoed by various postcolonial critics, is that such vagueness and such metaphoricity in themselves amount to a form of racism and contribute to the ongoing and active history of Eurocentricity and racial discrimination. Achebe, who remarks in the introduction to *Hopes and Impediments* that 'Conrad casually wrote words that continue to give morale to the barricades of racism', contends specifically that the 'age-long attitude' embodied in *Heart of Darkness*'s use of Africa as undifferentiated backdrop has fostered and continues to foster 'the dehumanization of Africa and Africans'.[28] Achebe's claim works on two levels, then: on one level, *Conrad* (or 'the text') is guilty of a sort of racism of omission or abstraction, such that the colonial reality on which the action rests comes to seem unimportant; and on another level, Conrad's text will encourage readings and actions that similarly degrade Africa and Africans. But I want to suggest, in response to these claims, that the argument made by Achebe is itself too abstract, and assumes too much about the place and fate of the text in the world. More precisely, I want to show that Achebe's 'omission' argument is ahistorical, in that it ignores crucial elements of the original historical context that made the setting of *Heart of Darkness* not only specific but readily recognizable to its intended readers.

* * * * *

When Conrad travelled to the Congo in 1890, little was known in Europe about King Leopold's manoeuvrings, the history of which I sketched out in chapter 1. There had been some public criticism of his discrimination against foreign merchants, but otherwise his methods had gone largely unchallenged. In the year of Conrad's journey, however, one George Washington Williams wrote the first wide-ranging and radical critique of the CFS. He had travelled to the Congo from the United States to explore the feasibility of entrusting the work of civilization there to Black Americans (of whom he was one); appalled by what he saw, he sat at Stanley Falls and wrote an open letter to Leopold in which he detailed the many abuses of Leopold's regime as he saw them: its violence, cruelty and deceitfulness in dealing with 'natives', Stanley's tyranny, continued slave-trading, the practice of concubinage with local women and the lack of educational/philanthropic work.[29]

Williams's document prompted hostile responses from Stanley and others, but it also planted the seed of further protests, such that the Congo became, at least in passing, a matter of debate for the Aborigines' Protection Society in Britain, and in the Belgian parliament in June 1891. From 1891 to 1894, Leopold's bloody war against Tippu Tip's slave traders led to further press coverage of the region. A man named Arthur Hodister, whom Sherry claims as the original of Kurtz, was an early victim of the fighting, and it was reported in *The Times* that after Hodister and his comrades were killed their heads were stuck on poles and their bodies eaten.[30] Towards the end of the war, pointedly and patriotically negative attention was turned against the Belgians by the British when an important British trader in the region, Charles Stokes, was summarily executed after being charged with supplying arms to the Belgians' enemies. Initially the incident was kept secret, but it leaked into the press in 1895.

Other relatively solitary voices were raised in Europe and North America during this period: an American Baptist missionary called Murphy spoke out against the abuses of the 'rubber system' in 1895; an Englishman, Parminter, who had worked for the same Belgian company as Conrad between 1883 and 1895, gave an interview to Reuters in which he recounted seeing a Belgian officer returning from an expedition with 'a number of ears fastened together on a string'; and Sjöblom, a Swedish missionary who had arrived in the CFS in 1892, fuelled journalistic interest in the issue not only in Sweden but also in France, Belgium and Britain by writing critical articles for a Swedish Baptist paper, and sending reports in English to the Congo Balolo Mission in London.[31] The ripples of journalistic interest spread: as Sven Lindqvist recounts, Sjöblom's activities led to a small comment in the monthly magazine *Regions Beyond* in May 1896: 'We want more ... than investigation; the crying need is for redress' – and this remark in turn was picked up in a sharp article, 'Civilization in Africa', by Charles Dilke, an ex-Cabinet secretary, published in July 1896 in the magazine *Cosmopolis*.[32] That same year an army officer called Philip Salusbury published an article in the *United Service Magazine* condemning the 'barbarous conditions' of Leopold's regime – a condemnation all the more striking as its author had volunteered in 1894 for Leopold's army in the Congo, the Force Publique.[33] The growth of bad publicity surrounding the CFS was a worry for Leopold, and in September 1896 he instituted a 'Commission for the Protection of the Natives'. It was another smoke-screen, but the gesture helped silence some of his critics and seemingly satisfied the British Foreign Office, which for some time had been receiving reliable reports of Belgian atrocities but was anxious not to intervene directly.[34]

In the very month that Dilke's article appeared in *Cosmopolis*, Conrad wrote and submitted to the same journal his first fictional treatment of the Congo. The story 'An outpost of progress' lavishes a savage irony on Carlier and Kayerts, the Company agents who are its protagonists. We read, for example, that:

They... found some old copies of a home paper. That print discussed what it was pleased to call 'Our Colonial Expansion' in high-flown language. It spoke much of the rights and duties of civilization, of the sacredness of the civilizing work, and extolled the merits of those who went about bringing light and faith and commerce to the dark places of the earth. Carlier and Kayerts read, wondered, and began to think better of themselves.[35]

The story was duly published in the journal in 1897, in the jubilee issue celebrating Victoria's sixtieth anniversary on the throne and generally joining in the patriotic chorus rejoicing the sacred work of civilization.

If one is interested in the kind of work that fiction performs, or can be expected to perform, in such a context, it is striking that Conrad's story could be juxtaposed with comparable material by the editors of *Cosmopolis*. What to make of this is not clear, however: as we will see, its acceptance into such a journal could be seen variously to offer an endorsement or an indictment of Conrad's relatively oblique representation of the historical material that was his starting point. Either way, even if for some readers the particular or primary object of Conrad's implied criticism may have remained obscure, the characters' names offered a fairly broad hint, and for most readers it must have taken its place in a series of texts and speeches which, over the next couple of years, continued to give public consciousness of Leopold's Congo nudges and jolts. Glave's diary of his hideous experiences in the CFS was published in extracts in *Century Magazine* from 1896 to 1897, and in May 1897 Sjöblom went to London and spoke to the Aborigines Protection Society, of which Dilke was chairman. Sjöblom's visit received widespread publicity, and the ensuing debate in the press, together with the fact that, for the first time, the question of the Congo was raised in the British parliament,[36] forced further action from Leopold, who in June and July went in person to Stockholm and London to counter the accusations being made against him and his agents. For this reason and others, including the jubilee celebrations, it seems that the protest in England (if not in Sweden) lost much of its impetus at around this time; and in 1898 most of the publicity given to the CFS was, according to Lindqvist, favourable, with reports in the illustrated magazines on the opening of Leopold's impressive new railway.

It was in this context, when public awareness of the situation in the CFS was fairly widespread in England, but levels of public *concern* had seemingly dropped, that Conrad started to write *Heart of Darkness*. Lindqvist goes further in specifying the immediate context in which Conrad began to write his story, making two points. First, Kitchener's return in Autumn 1898 was similarly triumphant to that of Stanley: he claimed to have 'saved' Sudan, and naturally did not draw attention to the brutality of his methods, which included annihilating his opponents from the safe distance of gunboats, and killing off the wounded. This may well have reminded Conrad of Stanley's escapades in the Congo.[37] Secondly, Lindqvist notes that Conrad's favourite paper, the *Saturday Review*, reported on 17 December 1898 a speech about the CFS by Courtney, chair of the Royal Statistical Society, which drew on Glave and argued that:

> The Belgians have replaced the slavery they found by a system of servitude at least as objectionable. Of what certain Belgians can do in the way of barbarity Englishmen are painfully aware. Mr Courtney mentions an instance of a Captain Rom, who ornamented his flowerbeds with heads of twenty-one natives killed in a punitive expedition. This is the Belgian idea of the most effectual method of promoting civilization in the Congo.[38]

According to Lindqvist it was the next day, Sunday 18 December 1898, that Conrad started writing *Heart of Darkness*.[39]

After its initial publication in *Blackwood's Magazine* in 1899, *Heart of Darkness* was republished as the second story in the collection *Youth* in 1902. Contemporary reviews of that collection tended to focus on 'Youth', but one exception was the anonymous review (by Edward Garnett) that appeared in *Academy and Literature* on 6 December 1902 – a review of which Conrad himself approved – which stated:

> 'Heart of Darkness,' to present its theme bluntly, is an impression, taken from life, of the conquest by the European whites of a certain portion of Africa, an impression in particular of the civilising methods of a certain great European Trading Company face to face with the 'nigger.' We say this much because the English reader likes to know where he is going before he takes art seriously, and we add that he will find the human life, black and white, in 'Heart of Darkness' an uncommonly and uncannily serious affair.... The stillness of the sombre African forests, the glare of sunshine, the feeling of dawn, of noon, of night on the tropical rivers, the isolation of the unnerved, degenerating whites staring all day and every day at the Heart of Darkness which is alike meaningless and threatening to their own creed and conceptions of life, the helpless bewilderment of the unhappy savages in the grasp of their flabby and rapacious conquerors – all this is a page torn from the annals of the Dark Continent – a page which has been hitherto carefully blurred and kept away from European eyes.[40]

These remarks seem to indicate not only Garnett's own familiarity with the situation in the CFS, but also, more importantly, his assumption that his reader too will be familiar with it: his way of talking about it, which may now seem slightly oblique in its refusal to name the CFS, seemed to him 'blunt'. On this evidence it would appear that Garnett considered *Heart of Darkness* to provide not only a form of testimony about an actual historical situation, but also, prospectively, an encouragement to take seriously a political problem that had started to slip from view.

To return to Achebe's criticism of Conrad's vagueness, if Conrad did not name the CFS, it was, on one level, because in 1899 he did not need to. It is not Conrad's fault if most readers in the 1970s (when Achebe was writing) failed to recognize the contemporary significance of its setting, or if academic criticism has passed through phases during which historical questions of that sort were widely held to be relatively insignificant. That in Conrad's day the Congo was readily recognizable in his text is evident from another unsigned review, which notes in passing that *Heart of Darkness* 'deals with life on the Congo and the Belgian ivory-hunt' and recommends that it be read attentively.[41]

Re-reading it attentively now, with an awareness of the history that I have sketched out, one finds that the opening pages are packed with precise indications of its historical context, and numerous allusions to specific topics within the ongoing Congo debates. Marlow's own introduction to his story consists in speculations on the motives of a hypothetical Roman commander in England, expressed in ironic terms that are already reminiscent of the Stanley controversies:

> 'Imagine him here – the very end of the world . . . They must have been dying like flies here. Oh yes – he did it. Did it very well, too, no doubt, and without thinking much about it either, except afterwards to brag of what he had gone through in his time, perhaps. They were men enough to face the darkness. And perhaps he was cheered by keeping his eye on a chance of promotion to the fleet at Ravenna by-and-by, if he had good friends in Rome and survived the awful climate.' (p. 19)

Just after this, Marlow makes the speech in which he describes 'conquest of the earth' as 'robbery with violence, aggravated murder on the grand scale', then goes on to explain his motives for embarking on his trip up a 'mighty big river', depicted on a map which had once been blank but was now 'a place of darkness'. At this point the contextual references become more exact: 'Then', he remarks, 'I remembered there was a big concern, a Company for trade on that river. . . . You understand it was a Continental concern, that Trading Society' (p. 22). He indicates that he crossed the Channel to meet his prospective employers (p. 24); they speak French (p. 25) and use francs (p. 32), but it is clear that they are not French from his reference to 'a French steamer' (p. 29), from his remark 'the French had one of their wars going on thereabouts' (p. 30) when they suddenly encounter a man-of-war (a reference to the French annexation of Dahomey in 1890), and from his allusion, near the end of the story, to 'their infamous cookery' (p. 114). The territory of the country in question is coloured yellow on the map, the standard cartographic colour for Belgian possessions in that era; and in their territory, which they believe will 'make no end of coin' (p. 24), they are using chain-gangs to build a railway (pp. 32–5) and collecting ivory (p. 37ff).

In the course of the first fifteen or so pages, then, and at intervals throughout the text, the identity of Marlow's employers is made all but explicit; and the negative connotations around their imperialist enterprise accumulate rapidly, carried in the references to the 'whited sepulchre' (p. 24), to Marlow's sense that there is 'some conspiracy' around their 'trade secrets' (p. 25), and to the Company's indifference to the suffering and death of the men associated with their activities (pp. 29–35; the term 'men', he insists, applies to the natives and the imperialists alike). The grandiose and hypocritical rhetoric surrounding these activities is also, as I have already noted, mocked (p. 28), and the 'philanthropic pretence of the whole concern' declared 'unreal' (p. 46).

The setting of the novel is quickly established, in other words, as something much more precise and concrete than a metaphysical 'Africa'. Critics attentive to the text's historical content have picked up numerous still more specific references, most of which would have been less arcane and more resonant in their day, and all of which show how closely Conrad's text engages with the CFS and the discourses surrounding it. Watts, for example, sees in the reference to 'Workers, with a capital' an allusion to Carlyle, who was associated with such rhetoric, and whose work *Past and Present* of 1843 Stanley would quote in justifying Leopold's activities; Hampson suggests that Marlow's use of 'apostle' in the same passage may have been inspired by the French press, in which Pierre de Brazza (Stanley's French rival in the exploration and colonization of the Congo) had been described as an 'apostle of liberty' in 1882; Parry points out that the *Times*'s evocation of 'unspeakable riches' is echoed ironically in the text's evocation of 'unspeakable rites'; Ledger points out that:

Marlow's directory of the heroes of the British Empire includes a mention of John Franklin (1786–1847), who commanded an expedition from London in 1845 to discover a north-west passage permitting navigation between the North Atlantic and the North Pacific. Marlow reflects that his ships, the 'Erebus' and 'Terror', never returned from the voyage (they became ice-bound in the Arctic, and all the men perished). What he fails to mention, though, is the exact way in which the explorers died. The full significance of the reference to Franklin, which late-twentieth-century readers can so easily miss, lies in the fact that it was subsequently claimed that the last surviviors on the 'Erebus' and 'Terror' had resorted to cannibalism in a desperate but unsuccessful attempt to stay alive.

And Hawkins, quoting the passage where Marlow explains how the crew was paid 'every week three pieces of brass wire, each about nine inches long; and the theory was they were to buy their provisions with that currency in river-side villages. You can see how *that* worked' (p. 70), explains: 'Conrad here presents a picturesque detail that seems absurd but in fact shows the absence in the Congo of a standard monetary system, a necessity for free trade and the development of a consumer population paid for its work. It is another example of Leopold's imperial inefficiency.'[42] One might also hear an echo of the Stokes affair in a passage where Marlow overhears a conversation:

> 'Who was it they were talking about? I gathered in snatches that this was some man supposed to be in Kurtz's district, and of whom the manager did not approve. "We will not be free from unfair competition till one of these fellows is hanged for an example," he said. "Certainly," grunted the other; "get him hanged! Why not? Anything – anything can be done in this country. That's what I say; nobody here, you understand, *here*, can endanger your position. And why? You stand the climate – you outlast them all. The danger is in Europe; but there before I left I took care to–" They moved off and whispered, then their voices rose again. "The extraordinary series of delays is not my fault. I did my possible."' (pp. 57–8)

Again, the resonance here depends not only on the event recounted, but also on the sense of evasiveness and unscrupulousness that is conveyed – reinforced by the reminder, in the shape of the Gallicism 'I did my possible' (= 'I did my best'), that French is the medium of this exchange. And to take one final example from later in the book, Kurtz, we are told, 'desired to have kings meet him at railway-stations on his return from some ghastly Nowhere' (p. 110).

One might still wish to ask, of course, why, if the reference to the CFS was so obvious, it was not explicit. There are several ways of responding to this. One is to note that 'explicitness' is to some degree amenable to historicization in the same way as 'abstraction' or as the criteria by which one judges a hint 'clear' or 'adequate', in that the perception of what is 'in' the text and what is not is itself historically variable. It may be, as Cellard argues in a rather different context, that 'to assert that "it" is not there because it has not been said (or written) explicitly... is to react as a post-1960 reader and not as a reader would have reacted' when the work was written.[43] This argument does not really answer the initial question, however, to which another response is that the decision not to name Belgium or the CFS could have been in some sense strategic. Miller considers this possibility, writing, 'Concern for propriety of course accounts to some extent for this "repression of the referent": so that *Heart of Darkness* would not become a mere political tract (perhaps banned in Belgium), Africa becomes the "heart of darkness"'.[44] This point, it may be noted in passing, may be used to qualify Cellard's, insofar as naming and not-naming have never amounted to exactly the same thing for the censor wishing to gauge a text's political implications; conversely, Cellard's argument suggests that Miller's use of the term 'repression' is somewhat tendentious, and moreover that Miller is actually talking about certain signifiers, rather than a referent.

Conrad's 'concern for propriety' could have had various motives and effects. It may be viewed (as Miller indicates) as a pre-emptive response on Conrad's part to the risk of offical censorship or censure, or as his attempt to avoid the sort of mental defences erected by readers against literature that could be dismissed as a 'mere political tract' – especially, perhaps, by readers of *Blackwood's Magazine*, who were drawn primarily from the army, the administration, the gentry, the clergy and the teaching profession, were predominantly conservative, male, and indeed imperialist, and were accustomed to a particular focus on the colonial world.[45] Or, relatedly but perhaps less charitably, it may be viewed as Conrad's attempt to position himself as a writer of *literature* specifically, which would be consonant with Genette's remarks about the characteristics of modern 'literature', with Nadelhaft's remark that, 'Looking as he did for acceptance as a great writer, Conrad struggled regularly against his tendency to explore his personal history', and with McDonald's Bourdieusian analysis of the literary field in the 1890s, wherein, he argues, 'As a prospective "man of letters"... Conrad had... a special [but not necessarily fully conscious] interest in insisting on his purist disinterestedness.'[46] There again, it could be seen as Conrad's means of playing with the perverse attraction of the 'repressed' or the unsaid, in order to focus attention all the more firmly on the real identities that the text 'hides' (or pretends to hide). Finally, to re-enter the level of fictional analysis, it could be interpreted as Conrad's depiction of Marlow's negotiation of many of these same prospective obstacles and inducements to comprehension. Marlow's audience, too, as we are reminded when one of his listeners growls at him that he should 'try to be civil' (p. 60), cannot be assumed to be unconditionally receptive to his story. The fact that the 'primitive' qualities of the Congo seen in *Heart of Darkness* seem more pronounced than they 'really' would have been in 1890 can be addressed in similar terms, as can the use within the narrative of terms (concerning 'barbarism' and so on) that the modern reader is likely to find rebarbative, and the use of other, broader elements of imperial discourse: Hawkins, pursuing this line of argument in some detail, speculates that, 'While Conrad himself may not have approved of either efficiency or the "idea", he knew these popular values could be used to condemn the Congo.'[47]

Like any writer Conrad was forced, then, to navigate his way through the various interlocking conventions that established loose parameters for the literary and the political, and for the ways in which writers and readers might link the two spheres. An instructive point of comparison in this regard is his curious novel *The Inheritors*, written in collaboration with Ford M. Hueffer (who later changed his name to Ford Madox Ford). They began work in 1899, with Hueffer, who was apparently inspired by *Heart of Darkness*, doing most of the writing. The finished work was published in June 1901, and Hueffer later described it as 'a political work, rather allegorically backing Mr Balfour in the then Government; the villain was to be Joseph Chamberlain who had made the [Boer] War. The sub-villain was to be Leopold II, King of the Belgians, the foul – and incidentally lecherous – beast who had created the Congo Free State in order to grease the wheels of his harems with the blood of murdered negroes.'[48] One of the protagonists, the Duc de Mersch, is indeed unmistakeably based upon Leopold: he is 'the titular ruler of some little spot of a Teutonic grand-duchy', is described as 'a philanthropist on megalomaniac lines', has an ambitious and costly plan to build a railway to facilitate his 'corporate exploitation' in his territory overseas, and has a lavish beard – which, as every newspaper caricature made clear, Leopold did too.[49]

The Inheritors is a disconcerting read. A haze of partial comprehension seems to surround the narrator, Granger, an aspiring writer. His efforts to position himself amidst the political machinations in which he becomes embroiled are dangerously incompetent, and he is driven along by a mix of cynical and self-centred impulses which make him both untrustworthy and unlikeable. Another character, Callan, is also a writer; unlike Granger he manages to write an honest exposé of the Duc de Mersch's schemes, but he too, in his pomposity, is less than sympathetic. The reader may well believe Granger when he remarks, on reading some of Callan's fiction, 'I fathomed a sort of plot. It dealt in fratricide with a touch of adultery; a Great Moral Purpose loomed in the background. It would have been a dully readable novel but for that; as it was, it was intolerable.'[50] *The Inheritors* is a political novel that prefigures, reflexively and with a fair degree of scepticism, the pitfalls of the genre, including the anxiety that a Great Moral Purpose may consign a work of fiction to unreadability.

Topical though it may have been, the action of *The Inheritors* is not only refracted through the prism of science-fiction (Granger is in love with a woman from another dimension) but also geographically displaced and so, in a sense, 'metaphorized'. Consequently it sits differently in relation to the sorts of issue raised by Achebe, in that Africa does not feature within the fictional world at all, and its counterpart, the metaphorical 'Greenland' that is the object of the Duc's plans, may as well be a wholly fictional place. *Heart of Darkness* by contrast, though it makes various omissions and some minor modifications in relation to geo-historical reality, introduces no such purely fictional elements, no imaginary aliases or alibis. None of this is to say, of course, that it is about Africa or Africans in the way Achebe might wish, or indeed in the way that Achebe's own fiction is. Clearly, the reader will not learn anything much about African cultures or even the landscape from Conrad's text. But, to return to an issue raised in the Introduction, the fact that *Heart of Darkness* is about one thing and not about something else does not in itself constitute much of an argument against it; and if, as Lindqvist has argued, the first wave of protests against the CFS in Britain had petered out so easily, just at the time that Conrad was writing, Conrad would arguably have been justified in feeling that, in this instance, the role of the fiction writer wishing to intervene responsibly through his or her work consisted not in establishing the 'facts' of the 'case' against Leopold's Congo – sufficient facts were, after all, available, if contested by Leopold's apologists – but in making them stick in people's minds, and in giving them emotional weight.[51]

Conrad himself appears to embrace such a perspective in his preface to a new edition of *Youth* of 1917, where he writes:

'Heart of Darkness'... received a certain amount of notice from the first; and of its origins this much may be said: it is well known that curious men go prying into all sorts of places (where they have no business) and come out of them with all kinds of spoil. This story, and one other... are all the spoil I brought out from the centre of Africa, where, really, I had no sort of business...

'Heart of Darkness' is experience... it is experience pushed a little (and only a very little) beyond the actual facts of the case for the perfectly legitimate, I believe, purpose of bringing it home to the minds and bosoms of the readers.... That sombre theme had to be given a sinister resonance, a tonality of its own, a continued vibration that, I hoped, would hang in the air and dwell on the ear after the last note had been struck. (p. 11)

Certain early reviews (not necessarily typical ones) took a similar line: Hugh Clifford in *The Spectator* of 29 November 1902, for example, wrote: '"The Heart of Darkness", the story which holds the central place in this enthralling book,... is a sombre study of the Congo – the scene is obviously intended for the Congo, though no names are mentioned – in which, while the inefficiency of certain types of European "administrators" is mercilessly gibbeted, the power of the wilderness, of contact with barbarism and elemental men and facts, to effect the demoralisation of the white man is conveyed with marvellous force.' The latter theme had been covered before, he noted, but 'never, beyond all question, has any author till now succeeded in bringing the reason, and the ghastly unreason, of it all home to sheltered folk as does Mr Conrad in this wonderful, this magnificent, this terrible study.' Comparably, a review in the *New York Times Saturday Review of Books and Art* on 4 April 1903 remarked that, 'Like certain caricatures that in their fidelity to the main facts make ordinary portraiture unconvincing, these grotesque figures drive home to the imagination.'[52]

An argument akin to these is powerfully presented by the anthropologist Michael Taussig, who sees in *Heart of Darkness* 'a combined action of reduction and revelation – the hermeneutics of suspicion and of revelation in an act of mythic subversion inspired by the mythology of imperialism itself.' He goes on:

Naturalism and realism as in the aesthetic form of much political as well as social science writing cannot engage with the great mythologies of politics in this nonreductive way, and yet it is the great mythologies that count precisely because they work best when not dressed up as such but in their guise and in the interstices of the real and the natural. To see the myth in the natural and the real in magic, to demythologize history and to reenchant its reified representation; that is a first step. To reproduce the natural and the real without this recognition may be to fasten ever more firmly the hold of the mythic.

Yet might not a mythic derealization of the real run the risk of being overpowered by the mythology it is using? Is there not the distinct desire in *Heart of Darkness* for Kurtz's greatness, horrible as it is? Is not horror made beautiful and primitivism exoticized throughout this book, which Ian Watt calls the enduring and most powerful literary indictment of imperialism? Is not the entire thing overly misty?

But maybe that's the point: the mythic subversion of myth, in this case of the modern imperialist myth, requires leaving the ambiguities intact – the greatness of the horror that is Kurtz, the mistiness of terror, the aesthetics of violence, and the complex of desire and repression that primitivism constantly arouses.[53]

If one approaches *Heart of Darkness* in this way, Achebe's argument might almost be reversed. Rather than seeing the vague geopolitical material as the text's way of getting onto metaphysical questions, one could consider the vaguely metaphysical material as a way of making the geopolitical issues seem not, or not just, more palatable, but more resonant and more pressing.

Effectiveness

In a way Taussig offers another version of the idea that *Heart of Darkness* is a representation of representations, though he gives it a new spin and a new sense of urgency. His response to the text seems to me very suggestive as one account of fiction's work, not least because of the twists of uncertainty within his argument. In the end, however, even *his* rapid oscillation between different perspectives may stop too soon. Taussig wants to recruit the text, finally, to the cause of the 'mythic subversion of myth', but I think that the ambiguities of which he speaks – to which, indeed, his notion of subversion is tied – may prevent this. It may not be possible, in other words, to label 'subversion' of this sort subversive in the way Taussig wishes. I will explore this issue in theoretical terms in the Conclusion. For now, to end my present discussion of *Heart of Darkness*, I want to think further in historical terms about the 'strategic' aspects of Conrad's handling of his colonial material.

The first question here concerns the way 'geopolitical issues' are construed by Conrad's text in relation to the wider European and North American debates to which I have alluded. Those debates, as Achebe indicates, were restricted in their ideological and political scope; almost invariably they avoided or, more accurately, totally failed to perceive 'the ultimate question of equality between white people and black people', and scarcely ever considered the possibility that Africans might own African land.[54] Consequently, only for relatively few participants in those debates was imperialism as such at stake (William Morris was one of the exceptions). The point in relation to *Heart of Darkness* is not only that a radically anti-imperial position was at this juncture all but unthinkable in Europe, or that espousing such a position would in any case have been of dubious strategic value, but also, more specifically – and more disorientatingly, in terms of a generalized anti-imperial discourse – that the takeover of the CFS by the Belgian government, which is to say the *beginning* of a properly Belgian empire, seemed to many of Leopold's European, Scandinavian and North American critics to be the best hope, at least in the first instance, of ending or limiting the abuses perpetrated within his private domain.[55] Like the East India Company, the monopolistic English trading concern that came to serve as the cutting edge of the British empire in India, Leopold's companies operated outside the political constraints of the nation-state,[56] in which such critics seemingly put their faith.

In practice, the impact of Leopold's eventual handover was limited, and Ndaywel è Nziem comments plainly: 'Even if juridically it went through two distinct phases, 1885 to 1908 (Congo Free State) and 1908 to 1960 (Belgian Congo), in reality what the country experienced was a single undifferentiated period of colonization.'[57] In a sense the fundamental unimportance from the Congolese perspective of the change of regime mirrors the indifference of many Europeans to the horrendous suffering created by Leopold's regime; among his European opponents the primary issue was often that of making trading arrangements more equitable from a strictly European perspective, or even of making them more efficient from a Belgian perspective.[58] Within Belgium, in other words, some of the opposition to Leopold's regime hinged on the anxiety that the rate and nature of exploitation of the territory would debilitate its natural resources and deplete – which is to say, exterminate – its labour force to the point where the Congo was no longer lucrative. Indeed, it was possible to voice opposition to Leopold's methods even without challenging the assumption that trading companies, rather than the state, remained the most suitable candidates to rule or to manage somewhere like the CFS, on the grounds that they had the strongest *interest* in keeping the natives healthy. The anxiety about the 'inefficiency' of certain methods could be voiced, in other words, from within discourses that were fundamentally concerned only with long-term Belgian economic 'health', fundamentally indifferent to the Congolese, and either pro-or anti-colonial.

To the extent that it may echo some of these ideas, *Heart of Darkness* may be condemned as pusillanimous, or praised as tactically astute (in appealing to the widest possible anti-Leopold constituency) and/or viewed as fundamentally hesitant about the choice between the devil and the deep blue sea. From one perspective, Conrad's focus on Belgian abuses could be seen as too narrow, rather than insufficiently specific: Marlow's remark, for instance, that 'some real work is done' in the 'red' (i.e. British) colonial territories, seems to create a dubious distinction between good and bad imperialism, and to ignore the murderous inequalities that were (and are), as Fanon argued so strongly, inherent in imperialism as such. Whether we should see *Conrad* as invoking a distinction between good and bad imperialism remains uncertain, of course, for all the same reasons that the racism of the text is hard to pin down: again, Marlow (whose remark about 'real work' might even be read as ironic) is distinct from Conrad; and, once again, either one of them could be seen as having taken a *strategic* decision to focus on the CFS and exempt the British empire from explicit criticism, or to expose it only to implicit criticism (for example, when Marlow tells us that 'All Europe contributed to the making of Kurtz' (p. 83)). Watts makes this sort of argument, writing that:

> Our easily-made inferences root Marlow's 'autobiography' in the topical, enabling it to be read as a denunciation of particular evils which flourished at a particular time in a particular place; while his degree of obliqueness, the apparent reticence, by inducing our imagination to flicker initially over a wider geographical and temporal range, extends the tale's moral and political subversiveness.[59]

A further question that arises once the text is viewed as subversive is how successful its (hypothetical) 'strategies' were. The points I made at the end of the previous section about the relation between the geopolitical and the 'metaphysical' material are most fruitfully considered, I would argue, as speculations not on Conrad's intentions but on the 'work' that the text might have done or may do. That work is firstly the work of signification, one might say, but there is only so much scope for considering that process in isolation and/or on the basis of the sort of textual/generic comparisons made by Hampson and White, instructive though those are. Once a book such as *Heart of Darkness* is viewed as being, at least in part, an intervention in a political debate, it seems inevitable that we should want to quantify

its effectiveness – and so, perhaps, to decide which of the pro- or anti-
Conrad perspectives sketched out above is (politically) the correct
one. All of this implies – and it is a point to which I will return –
that there is something fundamentally unconvincing about discussing
'subversiveness' with reference only to textual evidence. The critic
may describe the 'distance' or difference between a text such as *Heart
of Darkness* and other texts or other forms of discourse, but to
describe it as *subversive* of the latter can only, I think, mean that it
is subversive of those discourses for *someone* (consciously or not) or
was subversive of certain specific discourses for certain people at a
given point in history.

It is tempting, I think, for anyone wishing to position Conrad as an
anti-imperialist to overstate the subversive impact of his writing. His
three fictional 'interventions' in the Congo debates can certainly be
made to appear timely, not only, as we have already seen, in relation
to their moment of conception and publication, but also in that it was
shortly after the publication of *Youth* in 1902 that the Congo debate
really took off, becoming a prominent topic in the British parliament
in 1903. The literary variations between 'An outpost of progress',
Heart of Darkness and *The Inheritors* could also be viewed positively
in this light; the odd science-fiction elements of *The Inheritors*, unique
in Conrad's work, constituted not just a textual experiment, so to
speak, but also, in practice, an experiment in reaching and addressing
a different audience. It is clear, however, that other factors were vastly
more important in producing real political momentum towards the
ultimate transformation of Leopold's Congo into the Belgian Congo,
a process begun in 1906 and completed in 1908. The historian trying
to understand this episode fully would need to consider a broad
international context. I do not have the space here to discuss it at
length or to assess the relative importance of different factors within
it, and will simply note briefly that these included:

- Congolese resistance to the Belgians: on this topic, Ndaywel è
  Nziem writes of the major mutinies in 1895, 1897 and 1900: 'In
  colonial historiography, these different episodes are termed "Bate-
  tela revolts". In reality, they were part of a single continuing war
  of resistance, wherein those who had been defeated and integrated
  into the victor's army accepted their new weapons then turned
  again on their enemy. Throughout the East of the country these
  first "Congo rebellions" threw the colonial project into disarray
  for a decade.' He notes poignantly, however, that one of the great
  disadvantages faced by the Congolese was that it was impossible for them to understand the nature and scale of European

ambitions, so they would assume that they would be undisturbed if they moved away instead of fighting, or that after winning a battle they could then return safely to their villages.[60]

- In Belgium, the anxieties to which I have already alluded about long-term 'inefficiency' and sheer exhaustion of resources, and the growing unpopularity of Leopold, partly because of his scandalous private life and his willingness to deal with Tippu Tip. Even in later stages of the debates and the profit-making, the Belgian government wanted Belgium's budget kept separate from that of the colony, in case the latter became a drain again. The new Charter assured this separation in its first article.

- The change in the climate of opinion towards imperialism, in Britain and elsewhere, prompted by the South African or Boer War of 1899 to 1902, during which the British suffered severe defeats before their eventual victory, and the murderous mistreatment of Boer prisoners by the British caused an international scandal.

- The extraordinarily sustained and vigorous work of Edmund Dene Morel, who dedicated himself full-time to campaigning against abuses in the Congo from 1901 until long after the official transfer of power. Morel was certainly the single most important figure in the British context, and worked to boost the growing impetus of the international debate specifically on free trade, especially in view of the imitation by other countries of methods used in the CFS. As Morel wrote in one of his many publications, *King Leopold's Rule in Africa* of 1904: 'The movement for reform ... inaugurated by the Aborigines Protection Society in 1896, made slow but appreciable progress in the education of public opinion. Towards the close of 1901 it received an impetus through the representations sent to the Foreign Office by fifteen British Chambers of Commerce, protesting against the treatment of British merchants in the French Congo. It became apparent to the Chambers more closely interested in the subject, that the hardships undergone by certain British firms in the French Congo were wholly attributable to the theoretical adoption by France of the system of State appropriation, or State-delegated appropriation of the land and the raw material yielded by the land, which is the bedrock of Congo State methods, and which France had applied to the French Congo in an evil moment.'[61] Leopold became worried that England was going to convene a second Berlin conference to review the application of the Berlin act; France and USA appeared favourable to this plan, which might have led to annexation of the CFS by one of the act's signatories.

- The work of Roger Casement, whom Conrad had met in Matadi in 1890 and whose criticisms of Leopold's regime culminated in a damning report commissioned by the British government and published in 1904, when Casement was British consul. The fact that Casement was given this role indicates that Foreign Office policy had shifted since the 1890s to a more confrontational position: Casement should be understood, in this context, in part as an instrument of the Foreign Office. Leopold's reaction to the Casement report was a poorly judged damage-limitation exercise, which backfired when the Commission of Inquiry, constituted for the occasion and composed of a Belgian, an Italian and a Swiss, was horrified by what it witnessed on its research trip and in November 1905 produced newly authoritative evidence of the appalling practices that were widespread in the CFS.
- The launch by Morel, with Casement's support, of the Congo Reform Association (CRA), and associated direct political campaigning in Britain, the US, and elsewhere. Among those drawn into the campaign were two well-known literary figures, Mark Twain – who in 1905 published *King Leopold's Soliloquy*, donating the proceedings from its many reprintings to the CRA – and Conan Doyle, who brought the debate to the attention of prominent friends, including Kipling, Whitelaw Reid (the American ambassador), President Taft, Prince Henry of Prussia, and the Prince of Wales. Conan Doyle's booklet *The Crime of the Congo*, published in September 1909, was translated into French and German.[62]

Conrad was invited by Casement to contribute to his crucial report; he declined, but agreed to write a letter for Morel to use in *King Leopold's Rule in Africa*, which Morel incorporated as follows:

> I do not think I can more fittingly close this review of the famous Belgian debate than by giving the following quotation – which I am permitted to do – from a letter written a few weeks ago by Mr Joseph Conrad to a personal friend. In it the well-known author, who has lived in the Upper Congo, expresses in a few admirable sentences the feeling which all who have studied King Leopold's rule in Africa share with him:-
> 'It is an extraordinary thing that the conscience of Europe, which seventy years ago put down the slave trade on humanitarian grounds, tolerates the Congo State to-day. It is as if the moral clock had been put back many hours. And yet nowadays, if I were to overwork my horse so as to destroy its happiness or physical well-being, I should be hauled before a magistrate. It seems to me that the black man – say of Upoto – is deserving of as much humanitarian regard as any animal, since he has

nerves, feels pain, can be made physically miserable. But, as a matter of fact, his happiness and misery are much more complex than the misery or happiness of animals, and deserving of greater regard. He shares with us the consciousness of the universe in which we live – no small burden.

. . .'The slave trade was an old-established form of commercial activity; it was not the monopoly of one small country, established to the disadvantage of the rest of the civilized world in defiance of international treaties and in brazen disregard of humanitarian declarations. But the Congo State, created yesterday, is all that, and yet it exists. It is very mysterious.'[63]

Of course, one could say of Conrad, as one could say of anyone, that he could have done more: Brantlinger, for one, is critical of Conrad on these grounds, remarking, with reference to Twain and Conan Doyle, that 'Other prominent novelists who had never been to the Congo contributed as much or more' to the work of the Congo Reform Association.[64] But if one is intent on comparing the three novelists, then the dates of Conrad's contributions – to the debates, if not to the association – seem to bespeak a certain prescience and a certain courage; compared with Conan Doyle in particular, Conrad wrote from a relatively isolated and uninfluential position, at earlier and more crucial points. None of the three made a contribution to compare with that of Morel or Casement, however, and it is surprising, I think, that a recent teaching edition of *Heart of Darkness*, published by the University of South Africa in 1999, contains a section entitled 'Four great reformers: Morel, Casement, Mark Twain and Conrad'.[65] For the postcolonial literary critic liable to overestimate the anti-colonial, or indeed colonial, efficacy of European/American writing, it is sobering to note that Conrad is not mentioned at all in Cookey's detailed 1968 study of *Britain and the Congo Question*, or in Ndaywel è Nziem's recent 800–page *Histoire générale du Congo*, and that, in the book by the Congolese author, Casement and Morel too are very peripheral figures. If one is attempting to understand as far as possible and in the broadest and least Eurocentric perspective how colonialism and anti-colonialism in the Congo, or even reform in Belgium, came about, the exercise of chastising or praising Conrad for the 'size' of his contribution seems like a red herring, and means judging literature against a particular political scale by whose standards it will always appear trivial – as indeed will such a judgement itself.

Perhaps it bears repeating that, within a framework where literature, or some literature, does appear worthy of attention, interest in

'Conrad' is primarily interest in his writing. If Joseph Conrad had not written about the Congo at all (if he had written only on other topics, or had been a composer, say), the question of the extent of his contribution to the Congo debates would not arise. For the critic, then, as I asserted in the Introduction, any sort of political assessment should surely centre on the relation between the *text* (rather than the author) and the political discourses with which it is, or was, involved. Addressed in these terms, however, the nature of the contribution becomes, as we have seen, much harder to gauge, and its 'size' can only be guessed at. For one thing, the evidence that can be gleaned from elements of the text's context (the sort of evidence I have already examined) tends to lead back into inconclusive issues of interpretation. To return to an earlier example, one can only speculate on the political implications or ramifications of publishing 'An outpost of progress' in the jubilee issue of *Cosmopolis*, or *Heart of Darkness* in *Blackwood's Magazine*. On the one hand, as I suggested earlier, one might admire Conrad's craftiness in reaching an audience eminently in need of subversion. Conrad seems to make a hint along these lines in a letter to his friend the Scottish aristocrat and socialist R. B. Cunninghame Graham, asking: 'why preach to the already converted?'[66] On the other hand, one might assume, with Andrea White, that 'the context [of publication] probably served to encourage generic expectations and predispose readers to read the story within the tradition being celebrated by the other articles in *Maga*, rather than against it.'[67]

In weighing these alternative assessments one may turn to the critical tradition for evidence, but familiar problems of textual indeterminacy soon resurface. Strange equivocations can be found even within a single review, which again could be taken to show either the success or the failure of the text's subversive thrust: a reviewer in the *Manchester Guardian*, for example, wrote:

> It must not be supposed that Mr Conrad makes attack upon colonisation, expansion, even upon Imperialism. In no one is the essence of the adventurous spirit more instinctive. But cheap ideals, platitudes of civilisation are shrivelled up in the heat of such experiences. The end of this story brings us back to the familiar, reassuring region of common emotions, to the grief and constancy of the woman who had loved Kurtz and idealises his memory. It shows us how far we have travelled.[68]

Does the opening disclaimer imply that Conrad's putative attack on (Belgian) imperialism has made itself felt to this critic, or that it has not? There is no clear answer to this, not least because of the need to reckon with the generic conventions and mediations of criticism itself; it may be plausible, then, to treat that opening remark as irony or litotes. Certainly it is striking that most of the contemporary and early reviews of *Heart of Darkness* give almost no sense of the story's political engagement, discussing instead the recurring nautical themes, man's soul, and Conrad's style, but this does not necessarily tell us that the political aspects of the text failed to register, or even that they failed to register consciously. Rather, it may tell us something about the implicit definition of the task of the critic or reviewer at that time. A French editor of Conrad, Deurbergue, generalizes about turn-of-the-century critical practice in the following terms:

> Rather than considering themselves as interpreters mediating between the artist and his audience, most critics seemed anxious above all to protect the latter from the suspect designs of the former. . . . The potential reader (perhaps particularly the potential female reader?) projected by these reviews was clearly imagined to be anxious, intellectually timid, emotionally immature and of a nervous disposition – a sort of bloodless philistine who had to be reassured about his, or her, place in society and in the universe. Consequently any art that was not purely decorative, or conducive to a flight into the imaginary, that is to say any grown-up art, was treated as if it were the strongest eau de vie, one which, if taken in less than cautious doses, was likely to be fatal to the patient.[69]

Described in these terms, the reader bears a remarkable similarity to the Intended – and, one might add, is no less fictional a character.[70]

Successive generations of critics, defining themselves in part against their predecessors, have imagined the reader in different ways, of course, and have attached varying degrees of importance to the reader, the author, and the text's 'effects'. There is only a very limited amount that any single fictional text can do to influence this process; and, in any case, the text is no more (or less) 'responsible' for those critical 'readings' that have taken it to condone or ignore imperialism than for those that have perceived it as anti-colonial. Hampson is quite right, then, to point out that Achebe does not give sufficient weight to the issue of the text's institutionalization, a process that has seen the text depoliticized and repoliticized at different points in history (and in critical history more narrowly), and one that raises the question of how depoliticized readings might be related to the wider imperialism of, or pockets of anti-imperialism within, academia, journalism and society at large. As Hampson points out, 'the text is now supplemented (literally, in the case of the Norton edition) by Achebe's exposure of its racist attitudes',[71] and today one would be hard pressed, I think, to find a Conrad student who would wish to question the *significance* of the issues raised by Achebe. Moreover, one cannot assume that readers who are outside any academic institution and disinclined to read prefaces and footnotes invariably imbibe the text's ideological toxins passively; such readers too may happen to be informed about the novel's historical background, and they too may also be critical, oblique or creative in their responses to the text (an issue discussed further in chapter 5).

If, then, the ultimate failure of any attempt to quantify the *impact* of such a text is as inevitable as the urge to do so, it is partly because the evidence that one needs happens to be unavailable, and partly because the available evidence happens to be murky. But it is also, I want to suggest by way of a provisional conclusion, something to do with the nature of literature as such and the critical work that has helped to create and define that 'nature', issues that I will continue to explore in the rest of the book. At this stage it can already be seen that if, for example, one accepts (as all critics do) the distinction of author from narrator within fiction as a general rule, then any work of fiction, even if it is less self-conscious than *Heart of Darkness*, will be able to evade the kind of postcolonial 'reading' that aims to *determine* absolutely and polemically that text's degree of complicity with colonial (and/or sexist or racist) discourse, because in all cases it will be possible to argue that the representation of that 'discourse' must be interpreted as distinct from the discourse itself. It seems that to ignore Conrad's 'meticulous staging' of his story, as Said refers to it, or, beyond that, to ignore that what Achebe called 'layers of insulation' do not just wrap but *constitute* the story, is to neglect at once one of the forms of attention constitutive of literary criticism, and a fundamental part of Conrad's fiction *as such*.[72]

This is not to dismiss the kind of misgivings expressed by Achebe, or to exempt fiction from the political questions he wishes to raise; it is merely to stress once again that for the literary critic such questions are properly addressed to the text rather than the author, and that the text, as the literary critic 'constructs' or understands it, cannot answer. To talk of a text as 'racist' tends logically to lead, I have argued, to explicit or implicit speculations on its impact, at which point one necessarily enters a partly pragmatic realm where historical and contingent factors are likely to play a more significant role than the text 'itself' in determining whether, *in effect*, that text has worked in complicity with or in resistance to reactionary discourses. One cannot enter such a realm through the kind of immanent critical approach that is most (and, in literary-critical terms, properly) attentive to textuality, irony, framing, 'voice', and so on; indeed attention to such literary specificities, as they have been constituted within a certain literary and literary-critical tradition (a point to which I return in the Conclusion), introduces a certain indeterminacy into the literary work's relation to its own socio-historical context. Once one enters the sphere where impact might be assessed, on the other hand, and is faced with the propagation of imperialist discourses and practices, and other forms of violence and inequality, it can seem trivial and trivializing to dwell on the particularities of literary structure, or to spend one's time on fiction at all.

Conrad's references to his stories as his own 'spoil' or 'loot' from Africa perhaps give ironic expression to his own anxiety on this account, and form a backdrop to his attempts to persuade others that his motivation for writing about the Congo was, at least in part, political. Watt reports that in January 1898 Arthur Symons, in discussing Conrad's *The Nigger of the Narcissus* and Kipling's *Captain Courageous*, had complained: 'Where is the idea of which such things as these should be but servants? . . . everything else is there, but that, these brilliant writers have forgotten to put it in.'[73] Responding to this in a letter to William Blackwood, editor of *Blackwood's Magazine*, Conrad wrote, about his next project:

> The title I am thinking of is 'Heart of Darkness' but the narrative is not gloomy. The criminality of inefficiency and pure selfishness when tackling the civilizing work in Africa is a justifiable idea. The subject is of our time distinctly – though not topically treated.[74]

Once again, numerous questions of interpretation open up alongside those concerning the limits of Conrad's political consciousness: his implausible statement that the story is 'not gloomy' may make us think that these remarks too are 'strategic', designed to reassure an editor who may have been placated by the idea that the story was not gloomy, not topical, and was driven along by a 'justifiable idea'. That Conrad was not in truth unduly optimistic about the likely impact of his work, however, or about how well it would be understood, can be surmised from another letter, of February 1899. After a favourable response from Cunninghame Graham to the first part of *Heart of Darkness*, he wrote:

> There are two more instalments in which the idea is so wrapped up in secondary notions that you, – even you! – may miss it. And also you must remember that I do not start with an abstract notion. I start with

definite images and as their rendering is true some little effect is produced. So far the note struck chimes in with your convictions, – *mais après*? There is an *après*. But I think that if you look a little into the episodes you will find in them the right intention, though I fear nothing that is practically effective.[75]

By this time, then, the 'justifiable idea', so distinct at the start of the story, has become 'wrapped up in secondary notions'. Does this matter? For whom are they secondary? I have argued here that, when one looks at *Heart of Darkness* in its historical context, one can speculate plausibly that, in both intention and effect, it is indeed 'justifiable' against such criticisms as Achebe's. The lingering fear among critics and novelists alike that all this amounts to 'nothing that is practically effective' is unlikely to disappear, however; and the critical defence of this text, or any literature, on such grounds may be in part a result of literary critics' own search for a nobly and directly political 'saving idea' to justify their activities.

3

'Race', Reading and Identification

I will begin this chapter with quotations from two critics, Edward Said and Roland Barthes, who made their mark at different moments in the recent history of literary criticism and theory. In *Culture and Imperialism* Said writes of Camus:

> Camus is a novelist from whose work the facts of imperial actuality, so clearly there to be noted, have dropped away; . . . a detachable *ethos* has remained, an ethos suggesting universality and humanism, deeply at odds with the descriptions of geographical locale plainly given in the fiction. . . .
>
> His clean style, the anguished moral dilemmas he lays bare, the harrowing personal fates of his characters, which he treats with such fineness and regulated irony – all these draw on and in fact revive the history of French domination in Algeria, with a circumspect precision and a remarkable lack of remorse or compassion.
>
> Once again the interrelationship between geography and the political contest must be reanimated exactly where, in the novels, Camus covers it with a superstructure celebrated by Sartre as providing 'a climate of the absurd'.

The contrast with Barthes's description of Camus in *Writing Degree Zero*, published forty years earlier, could scarcely be more pronounced:

> Proportionately speaking, writing at the zero degree is basically in the indicative mood, or if you like, amodal; it would be accurate to say that it is a journalist's writing, if it were not precisely the case that journalism develops, in general, optative or imperative (that is, emotive) forms. The new neutral writing takes its place in the midst of all that

shouting and all those judgements, without becoming involved in any of them; it consists precisely in their absence. But this absence is complete, it implies no refuge, no secret; one cannot therefore say that it is an impassive mode of writing; rather, that it is innocent. The aim here is to go beyond Literature by entrusting one's fate to a sort of basic speech, equally far from living languages and from literary language proper. This transparent form of speech, initiated by Camus's *Outsider*, achieves a style of absence which is almost an ideal absence of style; writing is then reduced to a sort of negative mode in which the social or mythical characters of a language are abolished in favour of a neutral and inert state of form; thus thought remains wholly responsible, without being overlaid by a secondary commitment of form to a History not its own.[1]

Where Barthes sees in *The Outsider* neutrality and innocence, Said perceives concealment and complicity. For Barthes, who coins the term *écriture blanche* to describe Camus's style (rendered as 'colourless writing' in the English translation), *The Outsider* represents a kind of ideal blankness; for Said, this seeming blankness is, one might say, secretly White, that adjective resonating through the history of imperial domination that the novel tacitly legitimates.

In parallel with postcolonial work on Conrad, a growing body of critical writing has developed that draws attention to Camus's engagement and non-engagement with 'the facts of imperial actuality', in the light of which Barthes's approach may now seem unsatisfactory.[2] It is apparently oblivious, for instance, to the circulation of stereotyped representations of 'the Arab' within the text: 'Arabs' (I will explain the inverted commas shortly) are constructed in the book as a somewhat threatening presence, as unpredictable and inscrutable. This starts when Raymond tells Meursault that he has been followed all day by 'a group of Arabs' (43/67), and Meursault in turn describes them to Marie as 'Arabs [who] had something against Raymond' (50/79).[3] The fact that the Arabs – or at least some of the Arabs – carry a knife reinforces Meursault's and the reader's perception of potential violence, and perhaps connotes primitiveness and treachery. One might argue, then, that the reader is being fed a (perverse) form of 'comforting myth', and allowed to feel overhastily that he or she has grasped all that is necessary – *functionally*, in Genette's terms, and perhaps more widely – about the socio-historical setting. The 'Arabs' are almost completely unindividuated: despite being told that Raymond's mistress's name indicates to Meursault that she is 'Moorish', for instance, we are never told her name; and with regard to the group of Arab men we are told only that one is her brother. Nor is the dead man named in the course of the trial, during which no Arab witnesses are called. One might argue, then, that Barthes's approach echoes Camus's own *under* representation of native Algerians, and that both, more profoundly, converge with and sustain the 'structure of feeling', and ultimately the ideological dispositions, on which colonialism was founded. On another level, both could be criticized for reinforcing the notion that the proper trajectory of literature/criticism carries us beyond such 'background' issues as the geographical and historical setting and towards more rarefied philosophical or theoretical questions. For Said, as for Achebe, this notion is closely related to (and helps promote) a more general assumption that these people and their country are unimportant in themselves.

Though Barthes must surely be seen in this instance, if not in all of his work, as having endorsed a mode of reading that is indifferent to historical context and of which Said is critical, Said's own passing reference to Barthes's notion of *écriture blanche* is curiously neutral.[4] In a passage comparing Camus with Orwell, he writes: 'Both were famous for the clarity of their style – we should recall Roland Barthes's description of Camus's style... as *écriture blanche* – as well as the unaffected clarity of their political formulations.'[5] Barthes, the eminent literary theorist and critic, escapes criticism. This may be a sign that Said's criticism is directed at the text 'itself' rather than its readers, yet his remarks on this point are, as we have seen, somewhat equivocal: after all, he says that descriptions of geographical locale, 'at odds' with the vague universalism characterizing the prevailing ethos in which the book has been read, are 'plainly given' in the text, and that certain 'facts of imperial actuality' are 'there to be noted'. It is not clear, in other words, to what extent the 'text itself' is held responsible for the ways in which it has been read.[6]

Some of the interpretative moves that one might make at this point are closely akin to those I made in the last chapter. Again, a critic is likely to point out there is a highly distinctive narrative voice, and a personal narrator who cannot be assumed to be a spokesperson for the author; so, again, it could be argued that it is impossible to state with certainty that any racist assumptions and attitudes are Camus's, rather than just Meursault's, and the critic might justify their presence in the text in terms of realism and the *vraisemblable*, and/or of a distanced and perhaps distancing representation of those attitudes as such. It should also be noticed, again, that the sort of critical attention brought to the text has its own history, and that the way the text has actually been read (particularly, perhaps, by those involved with literary criticism) has doubtless varied not just from person to person but also from place to place, and with the passage of time.

In this chapter I want both to examine some further specific issues of historicization, and to extend my consideration of general theoretical questions concerning reading as such, and 'realism' as a reading practice. I will focus particularly on the notion of identification, one of the most flexible and apparently useful notions available to the critic wanting – or, as I have suggested, forced – to speculate on the way that a text is (likely to be) read, and on the way that the text 'works' and affects its readership.

One way of trying to decide whether *The Outsider* is *effectively* racist, it would seem, is to ascertain whether the text impels the reader to identify with Meursault. If an identification with Meursault appears to be timeless and universal, this may support the view that the book itself is to blame for the way that the 'facts of imperial actuality' have, in practice, 'fallen away' for most of its readers. O'Brien describes such an identification as a 'stock response'; and Sartre, in an an early critical article on the novel, states that, in general, 'the reader begins his reading by identifying with the hero of the novel', before complaining that, in fictions such as *The Outsider*, artists provide us with 'convenient fictions to keep us satisfied', where figures such as Meursault are embodiments of:

> pure gazes that escape the human condition and can thereby inspect it. In the eyes of these angels, the human world is a *given* reality. They can say that it is this or that and that it could be otherwise; human ends are contingent: they are simple facts which the angels regard as we regard the ends of bees and ants.... However, by forcing the reader to identify with an inhuman hero, we make him or her soar like a bird above the human condition; he escapes, he loses sight of that prime necessity of the universe he is contemplating: the fact that man is inside it.[7]

Despite the various contrasts between the remarks made by Sartre and Said (and despite Said's slight misrepresentation of Sartre's perspective), the two critics appear to share certain assumptions. Both assume, it seems, that the novel's highest level of significance, and its fundamental aims, lie at the level of the universal, as one sees in their references to the 'human condition', the universe, the absurd, universality and humanism. I would suggest – more tentatively in relation to Said than to Sartre – that they further assume that the reader is invited or even compelled to see things from the perspective of, or to *identify* with, Meursault – Meursault as (pseudo-)universal representative – and that this is how the text does its ideological work. To Said, one might say, it seems that Meursault – to whom he refers, for good reasons, as a 'French' character – is presented as a representative of humankind, but actually stands as a representative of a 'Greater France' both fantasmatic and real, of which Algeria was a part.[8] It will be particularly important, then, to consider the likely historical effect of Camus's story on its primary readership in metropolitan France, the imperial centre from which Algeria was governed.

This chapter will test three levels of objection to the assumption that the reader (French/universal) will, or would, identify with the ('French'/universal) character Meursault. These are, first, that Meursault should not be thought of as French; secondly, that the text does not offer to its readers the sort of character with whom they can identify; and, thirdly, that the very notion of 'identification' is misleading as a way of describing the relation of the reader to this text, and perhaps to any fictional narrative.

Frenchness

First, then, Meursault's Frenchness. As I have already pointed out, Said remarks that 'the facts of imperial actuality' are 'clearly there to be noted' in a text where 'descriptions of geographical locale' are 'plainly given'. In other words, it could be said that the text itself tells the reader that the story takes place in a country other than metropolitan France; and, more importantly, it could be said that various aspects of Meursault's behaviour, far from being readily assimilable into the (French) 'universal' by French readers, may well have seemed characteristically North African and his identity distinctly 'un-French'.[9] There is evidence for this on various levels. First, the social group to which Meursault belongs, that of colonial settlers, defined *itself* partly in contradistinction from the metropolitan French, to whom the members of that group felt a certain allegiance, but of whose physical, cultural and psychological distance they were also keenly aware. This is clear in *The Outsider*, not least when Meursault describes Paris to Marie: 'It's dirty. Full of pigeons and dark courtyards. The people have all got white skin' (45/70). The relation of Meursault's social group to the metropolis is complicated by the fact that, as the surnames of various characters in *The Outsider* remind us (Pérez, Salamano, Marie Cardona), a large section of Algeria's European population was not of French origin.[10] To put it another way, the White section of the population was itself culturally diverse and sometimes fractured: the Jews of Algeria acquired French citizenship only in 1870, thanks to the Crémieux Decree, and Derrida remarks in

The Monolingualism of the Other that, when it was withdrawn again in October 1940, this occurred not 'under the Occupation', as people tend to describe it, but was 'the doing of the French alone'.[11]

Issues of allegiance and identification are also doubtless in play when it strikes Meursault that his sentence is ascribed to 'so vague an entity as the French people' (105/167). They also surface repeatedly in Camus's autobiographically inspired *The First Man*, which was incomplete at the time of his death in a car crash in 1960. The later text uses a wide range of overlapping ethnic/religious/national markers. In talking about the young men of Algeria going off to fight in the First World War, for instance, its narrator/protagonist, Jacques, refers to 'waves of Arab and French Algerians', at which point there seems to be a cross-racial solidarity among Algerians, distinguished from the metropolitan French.[12] Elsewhere in *The First Man* he alludes to 'a Westerner of great sensitivity and culture';[13] observes that 'all of them, especially the men, insisted like all Mediterraneans on white shirts and pressed trousers' (an unusual use of the notion of 'Mediterraneanness', generally used to signal a mythical community including native North Africans, but which seems to have a specifically European resonance here);[14] notes at one point that 'Pierre's street, which led to the market, was dotted with dustbins that famished Arabs or Moors [*Mauresques*], or sometimes an old Spanish tramp, had pried open at dawn';[15] and refers to himself and his schoolmates as 'African children'.[16] Schools, incidentally, imposed French norms: as Derrida notes, Arabic could be studied only as an optional 'foreign' language, whereas Latin was compulsory. But for *all* Algerian schoolchildren, France and even French were alien in certain respects, according to Derrida, who writes: 'The *metropole*, the Capital-City-Mother-Fatherland, the city of the mother tongue: that was a place which represented a faraway country, without being one, near but far away, not foreign, for that would be too simple, but strange, fantastic, and phantom-like [*fantomal*].'[17]

Derrida's text is just one example of the ample non-fictional documentation of this sense of cultural distance between the metropolitan French and the settlers in Algeria. Camus himself raises the issue in his essays, for example when he comments:

> it may be the moment to destroy a few prejudices. To start with, by reminding the French that Algeria exists. By that I mean that it exists outside France and that its particular problems have a particular colour and scale. It is impossible, consequently, to think you can resolve those problems by following the example of metropolitan France.[18]

Further extra-literary evidence comes from Bourdieu's sociological research a few years later:

> The 'Pied Noir' defines himself in opposition to his concept of the *Francaoui*....On the one hand you have generosity, virility, and the cult of the body, i.e. a cult of pleasure, strength and physical beauty, whose temple is the beach; on the other, meanness, impotence, intellectualism, asceticism, etc. But then in contrast to that, he also defines himself against the 'Arab' who in his eyes incarnates a life of instinct, ignorance, routine etc. Whence a self-definition that is fundamentally contradictory.[19]

Indeed, as we have already seen, the real social 'group' to which the fictional Meursault feels himself to belong had more than these two ways of defining itself differentially – and so both courted more 'contradictions' and offered more fluid ways of eluding them than Bourdieu's description implies.

As far as the historical reception of *The Outsider* is concerned, it is important, of course, to consider how the cultural difference or distinctness of North African society was felt in metropolitan France. Sartre's contemporary reaction to the novel gives some idea of this, and of the exotic associations of Algeria in the French imagination at the time: phrases that leap out from his review essay of February 1943 include:

> *The Outsider* was barely off the press when it began to arouse the widest interest. People told each other that it was 'the best book since the armistice'. Amidst the literary productions of its time, this novel was, itself, an outsider. It came to us from the other side of the line, from across the sea.... The turn of his reasoning, the clarity of his ideas, the cut of his essayistic style, and a certain kind of solar, ceremonious and sad sombreness, all indicate a classic temperament, a man of the Mediterranean.... When you start reading the book you feel as if rather than reading a novel you are listening to an Arab's monotonous, nasal chanting.[20]

This final, startlingly patronizing point perhaps indicates that, from a French perspective, 'Arabes' and *pieds noirs* appeared more culturally similar, and more mutually influencing, than the latter liked to think – as the very term *pied noir* may suggest.

A curious light is cast on this question of the French perception of North African characteristics by Fanon's *The Wretched of the Earth*, which contains a polemical summary of colonial stereotypes of native Algerians. Fanon reports that colonial observers of the 'Algerian' had purportedly discerned an 'inability...to analyse a situation or to organize a mental panorama...a complete or almost complete lack of emotivity...a tendency to accidents and pithiatic reactions', and had noted that 'verbal expression is reduced to a minimum.'[21] They also claimed quite specifically that:

> *The Algerian kills savagely:* first, the favourite weapon is the knife ...The savagery of the Algerian manifests itself especially in the multiplicity of wounds he inflicts, some of these being made pointlessly after the victim's death....
> *The Algerian kills for no reason:* very frequently magistrates and policemen are taken aback by the motives for a murder, prompted by nothing more than a gesture, an allusion, an ambiguous remark...the cause or the motive that they look for as a justification and basis for such murders turns out to be desperately trivial. Which often gives the impression that the social group conceals the real motives.
> ...The Algerian is resistant to any inner life. There is no inner life where the North African is concerned. Instead, the North African gets rid of his worries by throwing himself on the people around him. He does not analyse.[22]

Though some of these remarks activate specifically 'Arab' stereotypes, much of this description is, I think, strikingly apt for Meursault, right down to the banal motivation for his crime and the extra shots he fires into his victim's body. The remarkable degree of coincidence between Fanon's description of the stereotyped non-White Algerian and Camus's portrait of Meursault (who may thus start to appear oddly 'representative' of a broader social group at some imaginary level) would seem to lend support to the idea that it is a mistake to assume that patterns of identification (and non-identification) between the White metropolitan French and White settlers would always have been predictably 'racial'.

Describing 'race'

Before going on to the second possible level of objection to the idea that the reader in general, and the French reader in particular, necessarily identifies/identified with Meursault, it should be pointed out that the import of the various pieces (and genres) of evidence adduced so far is debatable. It may be true that the multiple, mobile and inconsistent ways of conceiving of settler identity, and of any wider 'Algerian' identity, disturbed any basis on which the French might identify with Meursault or any inhabitant of Algeria, or vice-versa. It may be, indeed, that one is dealing here with patterns of mutual historical influence and actual transformations in people's consciousness; Fanon furnishes further evidence here, arguing that colonial stereotypes had the power to become self-fulfilling in an ambivalent process whereby the Algerian identified with the European's image of him, and that the European conversely 'seemed to be paying homage – an equally ambivalent homage – to the violent, passionate, brutal, jealous, proud, arrogant Algerian who stakes his life on a word or on some detail.' And he continues: 'It should be noted in passing that in their confrontations with the French from France, the Europeans of Algeria are more and more inclined to identify with this image of the Algerian, in opposition to the Frenchman.'[23]

Questions could be raised, however, about the reliability of the historical witnesses on whom I have called. The particularities of Fanon's rhetoric, and indeed of his own processes of identification in Algeria, are pertinent here, but I will leave discussion of them until the Afterword. Camus, for his part, was quite explicit in his journalism about how isolated he felt in his opinions; and in his autobiographical fiction he would not have felt obliged to meet historical standards of accuracy. In *The First Man* he doubtless aimed to represent a real community, but he surely also aimed to reshape it. Above all, one must bear in mind that the imaginary realm within which these colonial stereotypes circulated occulted the reality of colonial relations at least as often as it reflected them accurately, and even as it continued to influence them. Considering Fanon's summary of those stereotypes in this light, weighing up what it conceals as well as reveals, one may find, in the remark that the 'real motives' may be concealed in/by the social group, an echo of Said's comments on Camus – a member of the same colonial group as Meursault: applied to *The Outsider*, this might suggest precisely that, behind the seemingly random and individual violence of Meursault's act (which would invite a 'universalizing' existentialist interpretation), and beyond a certain metropolitan imaginary where *everyone* in North Africa was tainted with 'motiveless' violence, there was the systematic violence of one particular social group's domination of another.

The fact is, then, that the forms of fluidity and 'hybridity' that can be found within Algerian identity may not have counted for much in practice, and may not count for all that much in the face of Said's political criticism of Camus's works, in that there are fundamental respects in which the division between the settler – or, more precisely, the French/European settler from a Christian background – and other populations was utterly entrenched. Indeed, a certain mobility of identification and of description, in Camus's texts and outside them, may have been made possible by the very fixity of group identity on another level, the level on which Meursault comes to side with Raymond against his 'Mauresque' and her Arab protectors, despite having good reasons not to. From Said's perspective, the crucial question would seem to be, again, whether the construction of the text is such that Meursault is likely to carry the reader with him.

A discussion of comparable elements of mobility and fixity underlying those last two 'ethnic' labels, 'Arabes' and 'Mauresques', will help, I hope, to answer this question. Both are used in *The Outsider*, where one reads: 'Near the coffin there was an Arab nurse [*une infirmière arabe*] in a white overall, with a brightly coloured scarf on her head' (12/14), then, later, about a different woman, Raymond's mistress: 'When he told me the woman's name, I realized she was Moorish [*Quand il m'a dit le nom de la femme, j'ai vu que c'était une Mauresque*]' (36/54). Clearly the solidarity between Meursault and Raymond could be analysed in part as a matter of gender, but what I want to stress here is the play of 'racial' distinctions in their relations and in the text. As 'racial' or ethnic markers, it should be noted, the terms 'Arabe' and 'Mauresque' offer no reliable information. It is quite possible that the 'Arab nurse' is ethnically Berber (as her colourful headscarf may suggest) rather than Arab: the text does not permit us to make this distinction. It is for this reason that I have tended to place 'Arabe' in inverted commas: the term's primary force is often connotational rather than denotational, in English as in French. The invocation of the 'Arab' threat by Leopold and other European powers in the course of the 'Scramble for Africa' was another example of this.

The problem here is not fundamentally one of insufficiently fine racial distinctions. Indeed, making a distinction between Arabs and Berbers in a North-African context creates problems of its own, both because French colonial uses of that distinction could be seen as an instance of 'divide and conquer', and because, derived etymologically from the Greek *barbaroi* via Semitic and Arabic *brabra* (linked with the English 'barbarian'), 'Berber' is at root pejorative. Moreover, it is evident from the peculiarities of the term 'Mauresque' ('Moorish'), which might seem to avoid such negative connotations, that there are profound problems of reference, rather than issues of imprecision or inadvertent rudeness. According to the *Robert* dictionary, 'Mauresque' has been used as a noun meaning 'Moorish woman' since 1611, and the adjective 'maure' since the mid-fifteenth century to mean 'Arab, Muslim', or, more specifically 'Hispano-Moorish' – i.e. 'Moorish' in what we might consider the precise modern sense of that word, where it would refer to the Muslim people of both Arab and

Berber descent who conquered Spain. The term is also used, however, to refer to the inhabitants of ancient Mauretania (corresponding to parts of modern Morocco and Algeria), and to some inhabitants of modern Mauritania. Furthermore the adjective 'maure' is used, the *Robert* indicates, in relation to 'western Africa' more widely: one may speak of 'the Moors of Senegal [*les Maures du Sénégal*]' and 'the Moors of the Sudan [*les Maures du Soudan*]'. But modern Sudan is of course in East Africa; so this must, confusingly, be an allusion to the former French colony called 'Soudan' which fell largely within what is now Mali.[24] The term's etymology offers only irony to those seeking stable ground beneath these shifts and confusions: according to one source, 'maure' can be traced back to a Phoenician word for 'Westerners'.[25]

There is, clearly, a persistent slippage here, as terms such as Arab, Berber, Moor (*Maure/Mauresque*) and Muslim have become repeatedly recharged and displaced under the pressure both of historical change and of a continuing history of racial identification and 'othering'. On one level the word 'Arab' in my first example of the 'Arab nurse in a white overall' tells us very little, then, in that it leaves us with a degree of uncertainty about the nurse's ethnic background, her religion (it is possible that she is Jewish, say), and indeed her colour in any chromatic sense (in which sense Meursault himself, it will be remembered, thinks of himself as non-white). But on another level, in terms of both the fictional world and the dialectic between representations and the world they represent, the (non-)description of the nurse leaves us in no doubt that she is being marked as non-White, as different, in a moment that provides a prime example not just of the differential construction of meaning but also of the differential construction of 'race'.

* * * * *

At this point, I think it is worth offering a brief excursus on the subject of 'race' and racism. The *Oxford English Dictionary* defines racism as a 'belief in the superiority of a particular race leading to prejudice and antagonism towards people of other races' or 'the theory that distinctive human characteristics and abilities are determined by race.' 'Racist' is first used as a noun in 1932 as a synonym for 'racialist', itself first used in 1917 and defined by the *OED* as 'a partisan of racialism; an advocate of racial theory'. 'Racialism' is defined as 'belief in the superiority of a particular race leading to prejudice and antagonism towards people of other races, especially those in close proximity who may be felt as a threat to one's cultural and racial integrity or economic well-being'; 'racism' may be

a synonym, or may mean 'the theory that distinctive human characteristics and abilities are determined by race.' 'Racism' was first
used in this sense in 1932; 'racist' as an adjective was first used in
1938.

Perhaps 'racism' can be said to have existed 'since time immemor-
ial', in the words of a recent study, but the statement is anachronistic
insofar as the term as such and the history that have given it its
contemporary sense are relatively modern. It was during the nineteenth century that the major racial theories were developed, dividing
and hierarchizing human beings by skin colour and other physio-
logical traits. Key figures included Cuvier, who postulated the existence of three major 'races', white, yellow and black; and Herbert
Spencer, who played a major role in the development of 'social
Darwinism' as a justification of unchecked competition, class stratifi-
cation and imperialism. As Ashcroft, Griffiths and Tiffin note, 'Although race is not specifically an invention of imperialism, it quickly
became one of imperialism's most supportive ideas, because the idea
of superiority that generated the emergence of race as a concept
adapted easily to both impulses of the imperial mission: dominance
and enlightenment.'[26]

The notion of 'race' today finds no serious apologists. A recent
scientific work on genetic variation, *The History and Geography of
Human Genes*, begins with a subsection entitled 'Scientific failure of
the concept of human races', in which the authors state:

> The classification into races has proved to be a futile exercise for
> reasons that were already clear to Darwin. Human races are still
> extremely unstable entities in the hands of modern taxonomists, who
> define from 2 to 60 or more races...To some extent, this latitude
> depends on the personal preference of taxonomists, who may choose
> to be 'lumpers' or 'splitters.' Although [*sic*] there is no doubt that there
> is only one human species, there are clearly no objective reasons for
> stopping at any particular level of taxonomic splitting....
>
> There is great genetic variation in all populations, even in small ones.
> This individual variation has accumulated over very long periods, be-
> cause most polymorphisms observed in humans antedate the separation
> into continents, and perhaps even the origin of the species, less than half
> a million years ago. The same polymorphisms are found in most popu-
> lations, but at different frequencies in each, because the geographic
> differentiation of humans is recent, having taken perhaps one-third or
> less of the time the species has been in existence. There has therefore
> been too little time for the accumulation of a substantial divergence. The
> difference between groups is therefore small when compared with that
> within the major groups, or even within a single population....

The major stereotypes, all based on skin colour, hair colour and form, and facial traits, reflect superficial differences that are not confirmed by deeper analysis with more reliable genetic traits and whose origin dates from recent evolution mostly under the effect of climate and perhaps of sexual selection...

The claims of a genetic basis for a general superiority of one population over another are not supported by any of our findings. Superiority is a political and socioeconomic concept, tied to events of recent political, military, and economic history and to cultural traditions of countries or groups. This superiority is rapidly transient, as history shows, whereas the average genotype does not change rapidly.[27]

Various points arise here. One is that any notion of 'mixed' race is misleading in that it posits the idea of there being 'pure' races in the first place: as is stated elsewhere in the same passage, because there was already considerable migration even at the time of *homo erectus* (the immediate predecessor of our species), 'Whatever genetic boundaries may have developed, given the strong mobility of human individuals and populations, there probably never were any sharp ones, or if there were, they were blurred by later movements.' The 'confusion' about the reference of the term 'Moor' is not, then, an accidental or unusual one, but rather provides at once a window onto the racial 'mixity' that is actually the norm, and an instance of the historical determination to categorize people 'racially' in ways that disguise and deny it. One might make a closely comparable point about 'hybridity', which risks being misleading insofar as it implicitly accepts certain assumptions about the existence and nature of the non-hybrid, or alternatively becomes so generalized a model of human interaction as to provide no insights specific to the colonial and 'postcolonial' situations to which it has been widely applied.[28]

Even the above scientific declaration concerning the failure of any (would-be) scientific concept of race is arguably not radical and/or careful enough. On one level, the problem is contingent on the circumstances under which the research has been and is carried out: Native American activists, among others, have voiced suspicion of the ultimate goals and uses of genetic research of the sort carried out by Cavalli-Sforza's team.[29] On another level, the very terms in which Cavalli-Sforza expresses his points risk blurring the most fundamental implications of his own conclusions. For one thing, the notion of 'superiority' raises questions of cultural relativism that are perhaps skated over too quickly here. For another, the idea that racial classifications are 'still extremely unstable' is misleading both in its implication that racial classifications might ever not be unstable, and in underplaying, despite the intensifying adverb, the absolute arbitrariness, in this instance, of classification as such. To be fair, the authors do state that their own taxonomic choice is 'completely arbitrary'; the fact is, any choice would be. One can, then, go beyond Cavalli-Sforza's succinct statement in a recent interview, 'Those differences that we *see* are a misleading sample of the differences that actually exist', or Bill Clinton's comment, drawing on Cavalli-Sforza's work in response to the first complete draft produced by the human genome project, 'One of the great truths to emerge . . . is that in genetic terms, all human beings, regardless of race, are more than 99.9 per cent the same.'[30] From a racial(ist) perspective, after all, the 0.1 per cent might, I suppose, be the all important part, and I would argue:

- that, in reality, there *are* only 'racial' *differences* and there are no *races*. In other words, there is, in the extra-linguistic world, a limited spectrum of genetic variations in humans and there are *no* prelinguistic categories or divisions that subdivide this spectrum (rather than an 'unstable' number of such categories);
- that the history of the word 'race' means that it cannot be used without profoundly misleading connotations, and so is best avoided;
- that, in view of the history of racial thought, including scientific thought, and its relation to inequality, no one should be surprised if people are suspicious of the motives and uses of any science that creates or works with 'racial' categories, in however large or small a number; and
- that in theory, at least, the most radical point about the differences/similarities we 'see' is not whether they are a small or large part of the total range of genetic differences/similarities, but that this 'seeing' – unlike genetic differences 'as such', the scientific concern that is at once more concrete and more abstract – is *not* wholly extra-linguistic, and not exempt from socio-historical determinations.

The example of skin pigmentation should help to clarify this. In North Africa many Berbers, one of the non-White groups to whom the nurse in *The Outsider* might belong, are fair-skinned – fairer-skinned, in fact, than many White French people. Any two skin colours (in the chromatic rather than the racist sense) could be described as the same, or as different, depending on context and the criteria by which they were judged: thus any given person's skin could be said to be the same colour, or different colours at different points in time, as cells are renewed. Difference and sameness, to make the point abstractly, are themselves defined differentially. The issue here is not just, then, that 'white' is not actually the colour of any human skin, but that it provides a fundamentally pseudo-biological (pseudo-chromatic and pseudo-authoritative) means of 'describing' a difference that discourse on skin colour actually helps to create. In other words, the fact that the sighted 'see' skin colour is, in the present context, only trivially a biological fact; what matters is that, in practice, our perception of *significant* differences in pigmentation both presupposes and perpetuates the way we 'make sense' of skin colour. The idea that differences simply 'exist' is already problematic from this perspective, insofar as it may lead one to think of 'seeing' as too neutral an activity, when it is actually always caught up in a process of sense-making.

A small 'mind experiment' may help support the last point. If you bring to mind a fairly large group of people you know from varied ethnic backgrounds, you almost certainly cannot remember them without in some sense remembering their skin colour. But not only is it unlikely that you remember it accurately as a *colour* (in the sense that you could re-create it, given the means); more tellingly, in support of the point about 'seeing', it is highly unlikely that you remember the colour of everyone's eyes (though you will be more likely to remember it in cases where it runs counter to expectations about 'colouring' more generally). This is not because eyes are smaller and less visible than the skin – you would probably remember a lip-ring or a small facial tattoo – but, I would suggest, because eye colour does so much less cultural work.

The recollection of eye colour is, I might add finally, a topic that has already been addressed in literary criticism. It has been pointed out that the colour of Emma Bovary's eyes could be said to change in the course of Flaubert's novel; it is described variously as black, brown and blue. One could, of course, attempt to recuperate these variations within the framework of realism and the *vraisemblable* in terms of different characters' perceptions in changing light, communicated via the free indirect discourse for which the novel is famous. One might also, however, more pragmatically, say that it simply does not matter, and that no one except a critic would ever notice such a thing.[31] What I am suggesting is that the reader is unlikely to remember any description specifically of eye *colour* (and indeed, the use of 'noir', meaning black or dark, is arguably not an 'attempt' to 'describe' eye colour at all) because it does so little sense-making work, beyond its ability in a given context, surrounded by and bolstered with other adjectives and adverbs, to create, for the reader, Emma's beauty, and a sense of her allure for other characters.

The purpose of this last literary detour is to reintroduce the argument that the notion of 'functionality', used earlier in relation to *vraisemblance*, can be related to processes of cognition broader than those involved in reading a 'realistic' piece of fiction. The repeated allusions to 'racial' types in *The Outsider could* be said to 'show' (realistically) that the notion of race is significant for Meursault and those around him (as it was for Marlow), and perhaps for those he 'represents'; but if these references, particularly the unobtrusive adjective 'arabe', are not found jarring, this is because they are similarly significant for the reader, as they doubtless were for Camus or Conrad. The conventions governing the reader's relationship to the text at such points are by no means purely literary or formal; race is significant here *both* in the sense that 'race' carries social signification within the fictional/real world, *and* simultaneously in that it is functionally relevant within the narrative. That these two orders of significance coincide and shade into one another allows one to glimpse how narrative structures and systems of reference may correspond to and seemingly passively endorse social constructions of racial difference, thus 'drawing on and reviving' imperial discourse, in Said's terms (or 'naturalizing' cultural differences, in Barthes's).

To assert this does not commit one to any view on the *extent* of literature's responsibility in the construction of the imperial discourse of which this racial/racist discourse is an element; but it does commit one to the view that literature is not 'innocent' of such responsibility. Moreover, even if one concedes that its role may be relatively small (Said may overstate it, but it cannot really be measured), this is not to say that it is logically secondary. The example of 'Arabe'/'Mauresque' makes this clear, I think, because the terms' instabilities indicate that in such an instance there is no stable prediscursive reality, or even a stable discursive order, for the text secondarily to represent. Racial/racist discourse disguises this, however, and must have played its part historically in channelling the responses of the book's readers. In view of all this, it would be, I think, not just implausible but also theoretically weak to claim that there is a consistent critical 'displaying' of racism, even if *theoretically* it is always possible, as we have seen, to open a space between the text as such and the racism it represents.

Meursault's character

Irrespective of issues of ethnic allegiance, the reader's potential identification with Meursault might appear to be discouraged by the sort of character that Meursault is. The most obvious point in this connection is that Meursault is odd and frequently unsympathetic, and he hardly strengthens his claim on the reader's affections by falling in with the obnoxious Raymond. We may even consider him sociopathic: the *Collins* dictionary defines a sociopath as 'a person afflicted with a personality disorder characterized by a tendency to commit antisocial and sometimes violent acts and a failure to feel guilt for such acts.' Evidence that this is not a bad description of Meursault is sufficiently apparent that it seems unnecessary to cite it here.

Various counter-examples indicate, however, that Meursault is more fully 'socialized' and less exceptional than is generally acknowledged – partly because he shows some sympathetic (and ordinary) characteristics, partly because others too can be insensitive, and partly because, as O'Brien points out, he is, like anyone else, capable of lying. At the very start, for instance, the reader's impression of brutality comes partly from the telegram ('Mother passed away. Funeral tomorrow. Condolences' (9/9)) rather than from Meursault; and, when he arrives in Marengo, he wants to see his mother immediately but is forced by the concierge to meet the director ('I wanted to see mother straight away. But the caretaker told me I had to meet the warden' (10 /11)). Similarly, his boss seems to resent the fact that he is taking time off work, though Meursault notes that this could scarcely be refused 'under the circumstances [*avec une excuse pareille*]'; and, when he is in prison and the topic of his mother is brought up by the lawyer, he remarks: 'He asked me if I'd felt any grief on that day. This question really surprised me and I thought how embarrassed I'd have been if I'd had to ask it' (64–5/101–2). Despite this he also notes that he would like to be friends with the lawyer [*'je désirais sa sympathie'*, 65/103], 'not so that he'd defend me better, but, so to speak, in a natural way [*non pour être mieux défendu, mais, si je puis dire, naturellement*]' (65/103).

As with Marlow in *Heart of Darkness*, then, the presentation of Meursault within *The Outsider* could be said to make room for relatively complex responses. Although Meursault's is the only narrative voice, moreover, the fictional world does not provide unambiguous endorsement of his views. To take the example of racism once more, the text makes it possible to perceive as such Meursault's or Raymond's arguably racist preconceptions about the threat posed by the 'Arabs', in that there is no firm evidence that they are truly threatening. Of the men outside his block he notes: 'They were looking at us in silence, but in their own particular way, as if we were nothing more than blocks of stone or dead trees' (50/79); and, when he looks back after leaving with Raymond and Marie, he remarks: 'They were still in the same place and looking with the same indifference at the spot where we'd just been' (50/79). These descriptions, with their emphasis on the Arabs' indifference, leave open the possibility of assuming that much of the aggression is projected by Raymond and then Meursault.[32] There are similar ambiguities in the beach scene: Raymond immediately identifies one of the Arabs on the beach as the brother of his mistress, but the fact that Meursault has just described them as 'right at the far end of the beach and a long way from where we were' (54/86), and as wearing nondescript overalls, may make us sceptical about Raymond's reliability. In the fight, Raymond strikes the first blow. When he and Meursault return, the Arabs appear 'completely calm and almost pleased [*tout à fait calmes et presque contents*]' (56/89), according to Meursault; and, when Meursault returns alone, the man apparently draws his knife only in self-defence, and does not use it.

The obvious counter-argument to these last points is the same one that I made concerning the use of 'Arab' – namely that the potential distance between Meursault and the reader does little to impose itself, so to speak. I now want to explore another means by which such distance might be created or emphasized, and identification consequently discouraged, shifting focus from the constitution of Meursault as an *individual* character to his *constitution* as a character at all. Although it may seem, on the basis of my discussion so far, that Barthes is wrong to view Camus's text, and probably any text, as 'neutral' in the way he does, it may be objected that I have missed the point of Barthes's comments about Camus's *writing*, in that my account, part speculative and part historical, of the relationship between the reader, the world and the 'fictional world' has needed to discuss Meursault as if he were a real person. It may be objected, in other words, that my assumptions about the reader's assumptions concerning the mimetic qualities of the text take for granted the predominance of a 'realist' mode of reading from which Barthes was keen to distance himself. At this juncture, then, I want to consider an aspect of the text that seems to undercut its realism.

One of the operations that readers would normally expect to perform in making sense of a first-person narrative in 'realist' mode would be to locate the character/narrator in time, and in relation to the events narrated. The famous first line of the novel ('Mother died today [*Aujourd'hui, maman est morte*]' (9/9)) seems to make this easy.[33] Throughout the next five chapters, although Meursault's tenses, and his temporal perspective, keep taking small jumps, the reader can still make sense of them fairly easily, unifying them into a single, though mobile, narratorial point of view. *Discours* and *récit* remain close in time, as it were: in the second paragraph Meursault tells us: 'I'll catch the two o'clock bus [*Je prendrai l'autobus à deux heures*]' (9/9); already in the third, he explains: 'I caught the two o'clock bus [*J'ai pris l'autobus à deux heures*]' (9/10). He stays in the perfect tense (and on the same time plane, so to speak) for the rest of the first chapter; chapter 2 begins in the same tense, and from 'today' again ('I had trouble getting up because I was tired from my day yesterday [*J'ai eu de la peine à me lever parce que j'étais fatigué de ma journée d'hier*]' (23/33)); the narrative then moves on to the next day, and we are told that he and Marie spent the night together; chapter 3 begins: 'I worked hard at the office today [*Aujourd'hui j'ai beaucoup travaillé au bureau*]' (29/43); then chapter 4 introduces a slightly greater temporal distance, starting: 'I worked hard all week [*J'ai bien travaillé toute la semaine*]' (37/57), before reducing that distance through later references to 'yesterday' and 'this morning' (38/58).

The ending of chapter 6, however, which is also the ending of the first of the book's two parts, renders Meursault's position in time, and in relation to the narrative, more enigmatic. It reads: 'I fired four more times at a lifeless body and the bullets sank in without leaving a mark. And it was like giving four sharp knocks at the door of unhappiness [*Alors, j'ai tiré encore quatre fois sur un corps inerte où les balles s'enfonçaient sans qu'il y parût. Et c'était comme quatre coups brefs que je frappais sur la porte du malheur*]' (60/95). These are sentences whose hitherto uncharacteristic portentousness suggests that the narrator transcends the time of the story, in the sense that he knows what will happen later. The narration, in other words, seems teleological in a way it had seemed specifically not to be up until this point.

The second part of the book is initially narrated from a similarly greater temporal distance, which reaches an extreme when we read: 'The first few months were bad. . . . I was tormented with desire for a woman. That was natural, I was a young man [*Les premiers mois ont été durs. . . . Par exemple, j'étais tourmenté par le désir d'une femme. C'était naturel, j'étais jeune*]' (76/120–1). There are several other examples of retrospection of this sort: chapter 2 of part II begins, for instance: 'There are some things I've never liked talking about. When I went to prison, I realized after a few days that I wouldn't like talking about this part of my life. || Later on, I didn't see any point in being so reluctant any more [*Il y a des choses dont je n'ai jamais aimé parler. Quand je suis entré en prison, j'ai compris au bout de quelques jours que je n'aimerais pas parler de cette partie de ma vie. || Plus tard, je n'ai plus trouvé d'importance à ces répugnances*]' (71/113); shortly afterwards, after hearing of Marie's visit, we read: 'It was soon after that that she wrote to me. And it was from that point on that the things I've never liked talking about began [*C'est peu après qu'elle m'a écrit. Et c'est à partir de ce moment qu'ont commencé les choses dont je n'ai jamais aimé parler*]' (75/119) – a somewhat different use of the compound tense which again suggests that the past is being viewed from a more distant, continuing present, with the benefit of sense-making hindsight. Elsewhere the temporal distance is narrower, and we are even returned to the present in chapter 5, which begins: 'For the third time, I've refused to see the chaplain. I have nothing to say to him [*Pour la troisième fois, j'ai refusé de recevoir l'aumônier. Je n'ai rien à lui dire*]' (104/165). The narration then slips back into the imperfect tense; the chapter consists largely of Meursault's account of what he thought while in prison, but also provides a commentary on this as if from some outside situation. We read, for instance: 'If I ever got out of this prison, I'd go and watch all the executions. I was wrong, I think, to consider this possibility [*Si jamais je sortais de cette prison, j'irais voir toutes les exécutions capitales. J'avais tort, je crois, de penser à cette possibilité*]' (106/168).

Critics who have noticed these complexities have attempted to explain them in terms of intricate narrative/psychological models, one of the most adroit of which is elaborated by Fitch when he argues that the narrative perspective of the book as a whole is unified in relation to Meursault's frame of mind after his time in prison.[34] It is dizzying, however, to try to reconcile the complex, highly crafted and very self-conscious narrative performance the text would then be with the very psychological models that permit such an interpretation. Ultimately, I would argue, we are forced to accept that the jumps and slippages in temporal perspective are such that our attempts to unify them mimetically and trace them back to a single, temporally identifiable source all remain unsatisfactory.

This raises questions about the constitution of our sense, back within the realist problematic, of there being a 'real' character 'behind' the text to whom the conflicting signals would point, and whom we can judge. Shuttling between the realist and anti-realist constructions of the text, one might find paradoxical encouragement for a more formal, self-reflexive reading in the way that our problems in this respect are prefigured within the narrative through other characters' difficulties in getting to grips with Meursault.[35] More particularly, both lawyers use metaphors of reading to describe their understanding of him: the prosecution refers to 'the horror that I feel looking at a face in which I can read nothing that is not monstrous [*l'horreur que je ressens devant un visage d'homme où je ne lis rien*]

que de monstrueux]' (99/157), and the defence responds: 'I too...
have peered into this man's soul, but unlike my eminent colleague
from the State Prosecutor's office, I did find something there and in
fact I read it like an open book [*Moi aussi... je me suis penché sur
cette âme, mais, contrairement à l'éminent représentant du ministère
public, j'ai trouvé quelque chose et je puis dire que j'y ai lu à livre
ouvert]*' (100/159). This process of 'reading', it should be noted,
involves actively *re-creating* Meursault, imaginarily writing (or rewriting) him as a coherent character who will be acceptable to his
audience. Meursault finds this odd, especially when his lawyer speaks
of him in the first person: 'I thought my lawyer's speech was never
going to end. At one point though I listened because he said, "It's true
that I killed a man." Then he went on like that, saying "I" every time
he meant me' (100/158–9). When he asks a policeman why the lawyer
is doing this, he is assured that it is conventional.[36]

Conventional realist readings of *The Outsider* have tended to see in
the second half of the book a parody and implied critique of the
operation of a law court, whose decision hinges, anomalously, on
Meursault's behaviour at the funeral and with Marie rather than on
his crime. From a historicizing perspective, these readings themselves
open the text to the criticism that it is unrealistic: even in 1942, in
fact, one French reviewer complained that Camus had 'repeatedly
sacrificed *vraisemblance* in the course of the trial scene. It would
never be altogether plausible for someone to be given a death sentence
if the crime was a matter of members of the underworld [*gens du
milieu*] getting even. And when the victim is an Arab, it is all the more
incredible.'[37] Similarly, O'Brien argued in 1970 that it is highly implausible that the defence does not play on the settlers' fear of 'the
Arab', and that Meursault is condemned. The text misrepresents the
extent to which a 'racial' solidarity would have overridden a more
abstract, universal standard of justice (as it did, one might say, for
Meursault in his dealings with Raymond, and in a way for Marlow in
his dealings with Kurtz and the Intended); it misrepresents, in other
words, the colonial 'clubbishness' of the court, to which (if one again
moves paradoxically between levels of analysis) Meursault could be
said to draw attention when he remarks: 'I noticed at this point that
everyone was meeting and welcoming everyone else and chatting
away, as if this were some sort of club where people were happy to
find themselves amongst their own sort of people [*comme dans un
club où l'on est heureux de se retrouver entre gens du même monde]*'
(82/130). O'Brien's point, though, is that 'What appears to the reader
as a contemptuous attack on the court is not in fact an attack at all: on
the contrary, by suggesting that the court is impartial between Arab

and Frenchman, it implicitly denies the colonial reality and the colonial fiction.'[38]

The text's potential disruption of realist modes of reading may make it possible to argue, however, that the court scene bears within it a form of 'criticism', at a level at once more fundamental and more obscure. Rather than suggesting that Meursault is 'actually' not such a bad type, or even that he is in some respects typical of the White settler (not least in his relation to colonial law), the text could be said to block our attempts to create for 'him' a coherent and consistent *character*, and to explain or understand him in terms of a character-*type* with a comprehensible inner life. As the prosecuting lawyer implies, Meursault is two-dimensional. This sort of analysis, which stresses the ultimate lack of 'characteristics' of the fictional character, returns us to a perspective close to that of Barthes, who writes:

> If writing is really neutral, and if language, instead of being a cumbersome and recalcitrant act, reaches the state of a pure equation, which is no more tangible than an algebra when it confronts the hollow that is man, then Literature is vanquished, the problematics of humankind is uncovered and presented without any colouring, the writer becomes irretrievably honest.[39]

So the critical point here would be the one discussed earlier in relation to *vraisemblance*: namely that notions of character-type and the models of predictability which we project into the 'hollow that is man', and which are crucial to a trial of this sort, are partly derived from and perpetuated by fiction. Meursault's lawyer, it should be remembered, encourages him *not* to tell the truth: the court room is an arena governed not by truth but by notions of the plausible and the *vraisemblable* that in part remain irreducibly literary. Via Barthes rather than Said, then, one might arrive at the same conclusion reached earlier: what seems merely descriptive may contain a normative thrust. Read in this way, *The Outsider* fractures the realist paradigm in a way that *Heart of Darkness*, for all its narratorial uncertainty, does not, and could be said to encourage suspicion concerning the congruence between the models of human behaviour/ character used in a trial – or for that matter in the racist psychological works discussed by Fanon – and those models used and promoted in fiction.

*****

It seems, then, that there are respects in which Said's and Barthes's approaches are not incompatible, converging in their concern with the way we use fictions and narrative tropes to make sense of the world. Nevertheless, there remain respects in which the sort of close analysis in which I have engaged to establish this convergence, and Barthes's approach in itself, may be irrelevant to the concerns voiced by Achebe and Said, or even complicitous with the types of colonial blindness to which they draw attention. Said's account of how literary texts do political work sometimes seems cursory – his phrase 'draw on and in fact revive' in this chapter's first quotation is a case in point – and, as I have been trying to show, it is difficult to make political mud stick to the surface of the literary text once slippery facets of its literariness and particularity have been brought to the fore. The text, moreover, can always be said to offer the reader multiple and mobile sites of possible identification – a process that is seemingly unbounded by the reader's 'identity' and unimpeded by 'contradiction' of the sort perceived by Bourdieu in the identity of the *pied noir*. Yet to the extent that all these lines of approach seek to contribute, explicitly or implicitly, to an account of what it is to read the text, it is impossible to ignore the fact that in this particular case many of the details on which I have dwelt in critical slow-motion – especially the more 'formal' points concerning the construction of perspective and character – seem effectively to have vanished when the narrative has been run at a conventional speed, leaving many readers with a perhaps strangely sympathetic impression of Meursault. The sense-making process whereby we constitute an 'image' of a 'character', and perhaps identify with him or her, is, it would seem, so fundamental to the conventions allowing us to 'read' not just fiction but the world that the sorts of incoherence and cultural dissonance in *The Outsider* to which I have drawn attention are unlikely to slow the reader's momentum through the text, any more than are putative inconsistencies in the description of Emma Bovary's eye colour.

It again seems reasonable to conclude that *The Outsider* can justifiably be criticized for failing to distance the reader when, for instance, it engages the facile mechanisms of the stereotype and the fleeting racial reference. At this point in my argument it is also all the more clear that, as was noted in relation to *Heart of Darkness*, any single text's power to create such distance is fundamentally limited. From a certain critical perspective *The Outsider* makes it *impossible* to take Meursault's perspective as a real one, let alone a reliable one; but, from another perspective, it is impossible to read the text, unless reading means something other than 'making sense of', *without* considering him 'real' within the fictional world, and without making sense of that fictional world in terms that necessarily extend beyond the conventions of fiction-reading as such, leading into and out of the world with which the text thus stands in dialectic.[40] Strikingly, Barthes himself appears to recognize that what he considers the ideal blankness of a literary text – its detachment from 'History', and its realization of 'a neutral and inert state of form' – is in fact a fiction: later in his essay on *écriture blanche* he writes:

> Unfortunately, nothing is more unreliable than *écriture blanche*; mechanical habits develop in the very place where freedom existed, a network of set forms hems in more and more the initial freshness that discourse has, writing appears afresh in lieu of an indefinite language.[41]

The mechanical habits or *automatismes* in question are, I think, precisely those constituting what I have called a realist mode of reading; and, contrary to Barthes's wishes in certain utopian moments, this would not appear to be something the reader can simply abandon. An analysis of the complex 'formal' qualities of *The Outsider*, for instance, cannot but refer to 'content', and necessarily moves ceaselessly between the text 'itself' and the fictional world, revealing that the text is fundamentally and constitutively dependent on the very norms of ('realist') reading and representation it can be said to transgress. To put it another way, Barthes's statement imagines a wholly fictional moment at which the autonomy of writing is absolute, prior to the rushing in of worldly convention, yet that autonomy itself can only be understood as convention, and as partial. The 'liberty' whose inevitable loss concerns Barthes here is thus, I would suggest, comparably abstract and fictional; Barthes's separation of ('blank') writing and the real is finally not only politically problematic for the way it 'neutralizes' Camus's writing, but also theoretically flawed for implying that we might ever in reading make a choice between thinking of Meursault as a person and thinking of 'him' as merely a sequence of signifiers.

To think of reading as somehow suspended between these two poles has ramifications for the question of readerly 'identification', in that it implies that all readers of fiction have a certain tacit mastery of quite complex conventions. What follows is the third of my three levels of potential objection to the assumption that the reader of *The Outsider* will always 'identify' with the character Meursault, and it will consist in a brief and tentative account of what I see as problems with the notion of 'identification' as such, as a way of describing the relation of the reader to any fictional narrative, irrespective of the objective or imagined existence of common ground between them.

Against identification

Although the notion of identification, understood broadly, can be placed within a long history of critical and philosophical thought, only from the mid-nineteenth century was the term as such used to describe 'the becoming or making oneself one with another in feeling, interest or action', in the words of the *Oxford English Dictionary*. In the book that introduced the concept of 'personal identification' with a fictional character (the first usage cited in the *OED*), Robert Aris Willmott, a renowned pulpit orator, both hymned and warned against the 'spell' that literature casts. 'There is one pleasure of literature that fades almost as quickly as it blooms', he wrote: 'I mean the intensity of belief in what we read...The sense of reality gives the charm. Introduce judgement, and the spell is broken.' The spell, he notes, may affect anyone, and its effects may be damaging. He goes on to discuss figures including Montaigne, Pope, and Locke who said that they would read anything, and admonishes:

> The example is dangerous. A discursive student is almost certain to fall into bad company. Homes of entertainment, scientific and romantic, are always open to a man who is trying to escape from his thoughts. But a shelter from the tempest is dearly bought in the house of the plague. Ten minutes with a French novel, or a German rationalist, have sent a reader away with a fever for life.[42]

Literature and other types of writing, Willmott suggests, can contaminate and bewitch; and the most likely victims of literature in particular are children and others who lack the defences provided by 'Taste' or education and so lack 'independence' of mind and of judgement – those, in other words, who, like Emma Bovary, lack 'critical distance' on the fiction that they consume.

From the first, the concept of 'identification' as applied to fictional narratives – in novels, on the stage, or, later, on cinema, TV and computer screens – is built on the assumption that fictional worlds constitute an alternative 'reality' in which the reader 'believes'; and, from the first, it is associated with danger. Anxieties on this score have been expressed in a wide range of critical contexts. Sartre, it will be remembered, voiced his concern that *The Outsider* offers the reader 'convenient fictions to keep us satisfied' by offering one of those 'pure gazes that escape the human condition and can thereby inspect it', and that, in this way, the reader is forced to 'identify with an inhuman hero'. Žižek warns against the ideological lure for the viewer of conventional narrative film, such that, in his words:

> before s/he identifies with the persons from diegetic reality, the viewer *identifies with him- or herself as pure gaze* – that is, with the abstract point which gazes upon a screen. This ideal point provides a pure form of ideology in so far as it pretends to float freely in an empty space ... The illusion involved in our identification with a pure gaze is ... cunning: while we perceive ourselves as external bystanders stealing a furtive glance into some majestic Mystery which is indifferent to us, we are blinded that the entire spectacle of Mystery is staged *with an eye to our gaze*: to attract and fascinate our gaze – here, the Other deceives us in so far as it induces us to believe that we were *not* chosen; here, it is the true addressee him/herself who mistakes his/her position for that of an accidental bystander.[43]

George Steiner gives the issue a different spin in his essay 'To civilize our gentlemen' of 1965, where he discusses the very basis of research and teaching in the humanities (in terms that appear, incidentally, remarkably prescient in their analysis of issues that led to the emergence of postcolonial literary studies, among other things). Steiner discusses the sense of disciplinary uncertainty produced by historical changes including the shifting relation of modern literary studies to nationalism, the modern recognition that different forms of English are legitimate, the proliferation of non-metropolitan literatures, and the growing doubts of many professional critics about the moral force once assumed to inhere in literature. Expressing this loss of confidence, and the good reasons for it, Steiner writes:

> We have little proof that a tradition of literary studies in fact makes a man more humane. What is worse – a certain body of evidence points the other way. ... Unlike Matthew Arnold and unlike Dr Leavis, I find myself unable to assert confidently that the humanities humanize. Indeed, I would go further: it is at least conceivable that the focusing of consciousness on a written text which is the substance of our training and pursuit diminishes the sharpness and readiness of our actual moral response. Because we are trained to give psychological and moral credence to the imaginary, to the character in a play or novel, to the condition of spirit we gather from a poem, we may find it more difficult to identify with the real world, to take the world of actual experience to heart – 'to heart' is a suggestive phrase. The capacity for imaginative reflex, for moral risk in any human being is not limitless; on the contrary, it can be rapidly absorbed by fictions, and thus the cry in the poem may come to sound louder, more urgent, more real than the

cry in the street outside. The death in the novel may strike us more
potently than the death in the next room. Thus there may be a covert,
betraying link between the cultivation of aesthetic response and the
potential of personal inhumanity. What then are we doing when we
study and teach literature?[44]

Each of my three examples clearly deserves to be discussed in its own
right. My aim for now, though, is merely to support the claim that a
notion of the dangers of identification resurfaces across highly dispar-
ate critical discourses. The question arises of whether, beneath the
disparities, there is a steady core of assumptions about the seductions
of fiction and the consequent purposes and duties of criticism, in
response to which I wish to argue for a certain scepticism about
'identification' as a recurring topos of criticism, and as the site of a
persistent anxiety about the way in which 'other' people read.
    This scepticism should certainly extend, in my view, to the uses
made of Freudian psychoanalysis in many theoretical treatments of
the topic. The reasons for this, which I cannot develop fully here,
would hinge on the following three observations:

1 Even those working within the discourse of psychoanalysis,
starting with Freud himself, see Freud's definition of 'identification'
as somewhat vague and unsatisfactory. Laplanche and Pontalis note
that identification cuts across a whole series of other concepts, from
psychology and everyday speech, including imitation, empathy, sympathy, mental contagion, projection, and so on.[45] The point here is
not just that the term is overflexible but that it might be viewed as
erasing the distinctions between various more or less voluntary or
involuntary responses, for which other more precise terms are available.
2 Insofar as 'identification' *is* defined in Freud, it seems to pertain
primarily to hysteria (e.g. a child coughing when her or his parent is
sick) and/or to fundamental processes through which a young child
constructs an identity. A sense of 'identification' as both inevitable
and potentially pathological may indeed be shared by Freud and
various other more recent critics, but the process we refer to as
'identifying' with a fictional character would seem to be at a significant distance from the constitutive/pathological forms of psychic
incorporation discussed by Freud. *The Outsider* may help clarify
this point. As we have seen, Meursault is struck by his lawyer's
rhetorical identification with the crime, and elsewhere in the story,
remembering a journalist who caught his attention in the court room,
he explains, 'I had the peculiar impression of being watched by myself

[*j'ai eu l'impression bizarre d'être regardé par moi-même*]' (83/132).
Several *different* levels of 'identification' are thus brought into play.
Part of what makes Meursault seem odd and slightly asocial is his
failure to understand at once that the lawyer's 'identification' is indeed
rhetorical; this is the sort of thing, in fact, that encourages the reader to
consider the possibility that Meursault's imagined identification with
the journalist was for him momentarily 'real' or total – which is to say,
perhaps, pathological. Neither instance bears much resemblance to the
reader's own relation to all of this; any readerly 'identification' with
Meursault is not deliberate in the manner of the lawyer's, but nor,
unlike Meursault's uncanny relation to the journalist, is it wholly
uncontrolled. Moreover, it does not necessarily depend on any active
liking for or sympathy with Meursault as a 'person', does not mean
experiencing the same emotions he experiences or fails to experience,
and certainly need not imply any impulse on the reader's part to imitate
him. The pleasure we can gain from reading about Meursault's predicament in the court room, even where it may appear to hinge on our
being 'involved' through a process we might call, again, 'identification', clearly depends on a fundamental separateness and distinctness
of perspective – a prior, radical 'non-identification', as it were.

   3 The politically conservative aspect of the anxiety about the reactions of 'others' (to books or anything else) may be present in Freud's
theory not, as it were, incidentally, but at a more fundamental level of
his conceptualization of the psyche and of identification specifically. It
is in the work on mass psychology that Freud went furthest in elabor-
ating the notion of identification; and in that work, as Rena Grant has
argued, 'The famous Freudian pessimism seems to take on...an
almost hysterical quality...; it is quite clear that Freud is repelled
by idea of the group.'[46] Paul Connerton has argued in this connection
that Freud's *Group Psychology and the Analysis of the Ego* (1921)
needs to be understood in relation to, and indeed as part of, 'a new
genre of conservative political analysis' – the analysis of crowd or
mass behaviour – that flourished in the late nineteenth century in the
face of revolutionary masses.[47] Freud, he argues, confuses two senses
of 'regression' (everyday and technical) in the interests of conservative
political polemic. According to Freud, when an individual becomes
part of a crowd, 'his liability to affect becomes extraordinarily inten-
sified, while his intellectual ability is markedly reduced'; crowds/
masses are 'extraordinarily credulous', have 'no critical faculty',
'demand illusions', 'constantly give what is unreal precedence over
what is real' and are 'almost as strongly influenced by what is untrue
as by what is true'. A mass, he suggests, 'thinks in images...whose
agreement with reality is never checked by a reasonable agency.'[48]

If these same terms could describe the female readership of *Madame Bovary* imagined by critics and censors in the mid-nineteenth century, or the feared teenage cinema audience of *A Clockwork Orange* in the late twentieth, this is, I am suggesting, more than coincidence. Rather, the various examples may be linked by a continuous but largely disavowed history, within which the dangerous mesmerism of fiction has been too readily assumed and repeatedly overstated. Willmott's remarks about the effects of French novels now sound somewhat implausible, of course, not to say hysterical; it is hard to imagine anyone today making such an argument, which clearly falls outside the norms of contemporary literary-critical discourse. Yet the kind of point Willmott was making would, translated into contemporary vocabulary, sound much less implausible if it were made today in relation to a film, video or videogame, and it may be made from a 'progressive' political perspective as easily as from a conservative one. To take one recent example, bell hooks writes in the introduction to *Reel to real: race, sex and class at the movies*:

> Whether we like it or not, cinema assumes a pedagogical role in the lives of many people . . . Most of us, no matter how sophisticated our strategies of critique and intervention, are usually seduced, at least for a time, by the images we see on the screen. They have power over us and we have no power over them.[49]

The inclusive 'we' used by Willmott, Sartre, Žižek, Steiner and hooks alike in describing 'reading' is, at least at moments, necessarily fissured by the very premise of their arguments.[50] Critics, like censors, find themselves obliged to use a differential model of 'reading' in speculating on the (perhaps unconscious) effects of fictional narratives on readers who, unlike themselves, are assumed to lack the immunity of critical 'distance'. Both the political pedigree and the theoretical basis of that model are questionable, and their arguments might be contextualized within a history of critical topoi on the dangers of the wrong sort of reading (or 'reading'). If anxieties about the seductive contamination of fiction now take hold more firmly in relation to filmic narratives, say, than the literary narratives that were once their primary focus, I am inclined to think that this has less to do with inherent differences between the various media of representation than with their social conditions of circulation and with the history of critical/censorious discourse that has attended and regulated their reception.[51]

Contrary to Sartre's statement, *The Outsider* cannot *force* us to 'identify' with Meursault, and not just because Meursault may be so constructed, historically and formally, as to discourage identification, but because no text has that power. Although, on one level, my argument about the dynamics of racial othering within *The Outsider* emphasized not just a mimetic relationship but certain forms of representational continuity between the fictional and real world, on another level, the break between reality and the fictional representation is sharp enough that readers' refusal to be knocked off their stride by the novel's anti-mimetic quirks of perspective should be taken as a sign of fundamental competence rather than incompetence in the art of reading.

The process often described as 'identifying' with characters in a narrative may indeed be inextricable from the conventions of reading (or making sense of, and gaining pleasure from) fictional narratives in various media, but, if one wishes to understand what exactly that process is, it is surely crucial that the 'belief' in fiction to which Willmott alludes is not for anyone, or for anyone who is not profoundly and exceptionally mistaken, a real belief. The anthropomorphism of Žižek's description of the ideal point that 'pretends' to float freely, and may also be cunning, is misleading, then, not only in that it attributes to film a kind of pernicious agency, but also in that it too is part of a vocabulary of illusion (a vocabulary we saw earlier in the work of Genette). What sort of 'illusion' is one dealing with, one must ask, when no one falls for it, or if *really* to fall for it is psychotic?[52] In other words, it is as misleading to take literally the notion of film or literature as 'illusion' as the notion of literature as 'spell'. The fiction that Meursault is a real person is necessarily *entertained* by the reader in reading, but that entertainment, so to speak, and the experience of 'identifying' with Meursault, is indissociable from the awareness that Meursault is fictional. Such awareness, I am arguing, should be considered primarily neither in temporal terms – that is, as existing before and after reading, say, or at moments when implausibility bursts the fictional bubble – nor as a faculty with which critics are particularly well-endowed, but as fundamental to and immanent in the experience of the reading of fiction as it is currently practised. Whatever ideological work fiction may do, it does not do it by 'pretending' to be real.

4

Representation, Representativity and 'Minor' Literatures

> – *Nice, very nice, this song*, répétait Jock. *Is it folklore?*
> – Folklore toi-même, dit Tarik.
>
> Chraïbi, L'Inspecteur Ali[1]

As we have seen, much of the work of postcolonial studies with regard to writers such as Conrad or Camus has consisted in re-establishing links between their writing and the colonial context from which it emerged, but from which a certain history of reception had detached it. When it comes to 'postcolonial' or 'minor' literature, as I suggested in the Introduction, the history of reception is very different.

The term 'postcolonial literature' is, of course, used in different ways, and is subject to the same sorts of variance and confusion around the notion of the postcolonial that I discussed in the Introduction, including issues of identity (*who* qualifies as a postcolonial writer?) and chronology (should 'postcolonial' describe only the post-independence era?). As in the Introduction, I should state at once that I do not want to promote any particular definition of that term; rather, in this chapter I want to analyse what is at stake in the field of reception to which the label points, a field of which a certain variance and confusion may be characteristic. What appears to be at stake are both literary and political issues of representation, which seemingly take on a particular urgency in the context of anti-colonial activism and/or the writer's position as the 'representative' of a 'minority'. I propose to explore these issues primarily through the notion of 'representativity', a term I will seek to clarify shortly but whose very slipperiness will carry the argument beyond what may initially appear a rather narrow literary-critical concern within postcolonial studies, and towards broader issues, including the study of literature in general, the question of 'language politics', and the status of 'minorities' in society.

An important element of the history of reception that I want to discuss is the sort of anthology that groups together a certain number of writers from a former colony. One such collection, an anthology of North African writing in French (the *Anthologie des écrivains maghrébins d'expression française*), was published in 1964, just two years after Algerian independence, edited and introduced by the eminent Tunisian writer Albert Memmi. It was the first such anthology to be published in France, he noted in his introduction, though comparable anthologies had already appeared in Germany, Switzerland and Italy, as had anthologies of sub-Saharan writing in French.[2] In 1969 it was followed by Memmi's anthology of French writers from the Maghreb, the *Anthologie des écrivains français du Maghreb*. That the former sold much better than the latter, he remarked in the foreword of a new and more inclusive anthology published in 1985, said something about the kind of interest in 'francophone' literature, amidst academics and others, that the first volume both answered and encouraged:

> the need for an undertaking of this sort was becoming apparent around the world. Particularly in universities, people were getting interested in these curious literatures which were in French [*francophones*] but came from outside metropolitan France ... Decolonization was on its way in French North Africa, in different ways in each country – more violently in Algeria, more politically in Bourguiba's Tunisia, soon followed by Morocco. It may be regrettable, but only people who fight get the public's attention: so who were these *Maghrébins*? How did they live? What exactly did they want? And who better to speak in their name than their writers, whose numbers had increased to an extraordinary degree? – to speak a language that was not just political or tactical but which cast light on every aspect of their lives... For these and other reasons, it seemed to me that by selecting and introducing the most representative [*les plus représentatifs*] of those writers, I would go some way to meeting that demand.[3]

The writers in the first anthology were chosen, then, on the grounds that they were 'representative' and could be taken to speak for their compatriots; and they were packaged by Memmi for a non-North African (though not solely French) audience, particularly but not exclusively academic, understandably eager to hear the authentic voice of the Maghreb. That such an audience not only existed but also, in a sense, delimited a corpus of writing defined in terms of its representative qualities, is suggested not only by the success of Memmi's volume, but also, I would argue, by the continuing circulation of notions of the 'representative' around North African and other 'francophone' literature, and around other examples of 'minor' or 'postcolonial' literature.[4]

Many of the issues raised by Memmi in his original introduction surface again in the introductions to later anthologies covering other postcolonial literatures. One is the use of the language of the former colonizer, a matter to which I will return a little later. Another is the use of some sort of ethnic criterion to group together writers who are deemed authentic voices: mostly this means 'autochthonous' or native writers, who in the case of Memmi's anthology are distinguished from writers who, though born in North Africa, belong to 'minority' groups (colonial settlers, for instance) and do not really consider themselves North African, and/or are out of touch with the majority of North Africans.[5] We saw in the last chapter, of course, how very unstable such notions of 'nativeness' are in North Africa. What is more, Memmi and his co-editors note disarmingly that certain 'European' writers who were born in the Maghreb have also been included, because they were insistent that they wanted to be.

In each of the anthologies he has edited Memmi has been eloquent and nuanced in his discussion of equivocations of this sort, which need to be understood not only in terms of the sorts of difficulty, not to say impossibility, of ethnic/religious categorization that I discussed earlier, but also precisely in terms of those issues around literary representation and representativity brought into play by such anthologies. Salman Rushdie encounters similar pitfalls in his introduction to the controversial *Vintage Book of Indian Writing 1947–1997*, where he asserts that the 'literary voices' collected together in the volume are 'distinctively Indian' but concedes that 'Bapsi Sidhwa is technically Pakistani' and that Sara Suleri's memoir *Meatless Days* is also 'a visitor from across the Pakistani frontier'. One can see why he thinks that such an anthology 'has no need of Partitions', and many readers will sympathize with his self-conscious defence that 'Literature has little or nothing to do with a writer's home address', but such remarks sit oddly under the rubric of 'Indian writing 1947–1997' (1947 being the date at which India became independent and Pakistan became a separate nation-state). The collection, after all, remains something other than an anthology of writing *about* India selected solely on thematic grounds. It is notable too that Rushdie justifies the decision not to include poetry by stating that 'it was impossible, for reasons of space, to include a representative selection', although the basis on which one might claim the prose to be 'representative' is not clear and certainly not explicit. Comparably, Adewale Maja-Pearce introduces *The Heinemann Book of African Poetry in English* of 1990 by explaining that 'Excellence has been the only criterion in making the selection, which is why some poets have been given more space than others, and why *entire countries have been omitted al-*

together' (my italics); and Achebe and Innes write in their anthology
of African short stories of 1985 that, 'Although the editors were
mindful of the advantages of representing writers of different regions,
sexes and generations in this anthology, their criterion was ultimately
literary merit. And as it turned out their selections went ahead with
gratifying serendipity to meet the other considerations as well! The
subsequent grouping of the stories into broad geographical regions
seemed a handy and practical arrangement. But any other format
might have done just as well.'[6]

What starts to become apparent in reading these various introductions is how consistently there is a certain slippage around the notion
of representation.[7] Discussing this phenomenon (in a different context), Spivak points to the distinction in German between *vertreten*
and *darstellen*, arguing that 'The complicity of *vertreten* and *darstellen* ... can only be appreciated if they are not conflated by a sleight of
word.'[8] (*Vertreten* means 'represent' in senses including that of political representation, and may mean deputize, stand in, etc.; *darstellen*
covers the artistic senses of depiction, portrayal, etc.) The forms that
this conflation may take can be glimpsed in these anthologies. In each
case there seems to be at least a potential tension between the criteria
of literary accomplishment and those of 'representativity', and a
perhaps related uncertainty about the assignation of writers to a
group or a nation of which they are in some sense treated as the
representative. Any writer may write about India, Algeria or anywhere else, 'representing' it in the ordinary literary sense, but only
certain writers are eligible, it would seem, to 'represent' it in the latter
sense, where literary 'representation' becomes linked to notions of
authenticity, typicality, and the ability to speak for others. It is this
knot of concepts that I will begin to unpick in this chapter. My
discussion will centre on two early novels by the Moroccan writer
Driss Chraïbi and their place within the field of 'francophone' literature, a focus that I hope will prove interesting in its own right but also
valuable for the light it casts on wider dynamics through which a
literary text may engage with its own field of reception, and through
which readers and critics may impute different orders of 'representativity' to an author, a text, ('a') literature, and so-called minor or
postcolonial literature in particular.

Representation, minority and the individual

Driss Chraïbi published his first novel, *The Simple Past (Le Passé
simple)*, in October 1954, at a crucial moment in the Moroccan battle

for independence and in North Africa's anti-colonial struggles more generally. The French colonial regime in Morocco under which Chraïbi grew up had been in place only since 1912, when the country became a French 'protectorate' five years after the first French troops had landed in Casablanca. Both the form and duration of French colonization there left it much less profoundly embedded than in Algeria. *The Simple Past* was written by the summer of 1953, the year in which Morocco's sultan was deposed, the French hoping that the change of regime would calm the country's political agitation. Instead it led to renewed militancy, which was further boosted by the declaration of war in Algeria on 1 November 1954 by the Front de Libération Nationale (FLN). Partly in the hope that the fate of Algeria could be kept separate from that of its neighbours, the French government signed the convention of 2 March 1956 abolishing the protectorate and establishing total political independence for Morocco; Tunisia in turn recovered its independence on 20 March.

Partly because of the highly politicized and oppositional political context in which it was published, Chraïbi's novel immediately attracted a certain amount of attention in France. One of the first reviews to appear in the French press, a longish article in the *Bulletin de Paris*, argued that:

> From this novel . . . it seems that the real conflict is not between Morocco and France but between two different generations of Moroccans, or rather between a small minority who have been won over to Western civilization, and the bulk of the population (and their leaders) whose beliefs and traditions are still Islamic. . . . We can only hope that the French read the book . . . and understand the secret appeal that it makes.[9]

Another article, in the right-wing review *Rivarol* (17 February 1955), noted the condemnation by this 'young Moroccan' of the sultan; and another again, having stated categorically that *The Simple Past* was autobiographical, argued that it was 'a story that bore witness most revealingly to a certain frame of mind', concluding:

> As to the three main trends in the Islamic world today – nationalism, the rebirth of Islam, and the desire for social change – it would seem that for most of these people the third of these is far and away the most significant.[10]

In literary-critical terms, of course, such responses seem crude. The reader of *The Simple Past*, as of *Heart of Darkness* and *The Outsider*, must contend with the idiosyncrasies of a first-person narrator. These appear not only on a personal level (the narrator-protagonist Driss, like Marlow and Meursault, is a quirky character, and often an unpleasant one) but also, far more distinctly than in *The Outsider*, on a properly narratorial level. In the case of Camus's story, as we saw earlier, the reader can easily miss the possible a-realism of perspective, and indeed is almost bound to do so. In *The Simple Past*, by contrast, elements are introduced that cannot but disconcert the normal patterns of 'realist' reading. The most notable examples are the fluctuating recurrences of the figure of the 'thin line [*ligne mince*]': these may mark Driss's movement towards an altered state or a personal world of fantasy, but on another level propel the reader lurchingly from the fictional-real to the irreducibly textual and figurative in a way that is consequently impossible to describe adequately here. Something similar happens through the text's self-reflexive gestures of various orders, for example in the fourth chapter, where Driss remarks that he is 'just a character in a novel'.[11] Even if one limited oneself to a realist approach to the fictional world, moreover, it could be argued that treating Driss and his father, the Seigneur, as representatives respectively of progressive Westernized and traditional Islamic culture is tenuous: it was the Seigneur, after all, who got Driss into a French school; the Seigneur is clearly far from being an exemplary Muslim; and Driss himself indicates that his own Westernization has made him into a 'grotesque' figure.[12]

In the heat of the book's initial reception, however, the literary-critical moves that might have brought out such nuances were neglected. The conservative French responses to Chraïbi's text sparked angry reactions among Moroccan militants, but these turned on Chraïbi himself, who even received a death threat from within the Parti Démocrate de l'indépendance (PDI). Initially he appeared unbowed, and willing to accept broadly the interpretative frame into which the novel had been placed. He published a letter in the *Bulletin de Paris* in which he echoed the review article's emphasis on the ambivalent position of Moroccan youth, writing: 'Young people in Morocco are much closer to France than some legitimist or some pacha living shut inside his own limited world – precisely because France has had the honour of educating them.' He then made matters even worse with an article in *Demain*, where he wrote:

> I am not pro-colonial. I am not even anti-colonial. But I am convinced that European colonialism has been necessary and beneficial to the Muslim world. The very excesses of colonialism, combined with Europe's solid values, have served as a catalyst for the *social* rebirth that we are now witnessing.[13]

The PDI's journal *Démocratie* responded by calling Chraïbi an 'assassin of hope'.[14] Apparently shocked by the hostility he was generating, Chraïbi now changed his mind and/or his tactics, writing a conciliatory letter in which he offered a more PDI-friendly reading of the novel and complained about the appropriation of the novel by the French Right. The next number of the journal endorsed his atonement; and a couple of weeks later the affair was effectively sealed by the publication of an interview with the writer Ahmed Sefrioui, who remarked:

> *The Simple Past* was an attempt to translate the emotional turmoil of Moroccans of his generation. But Driss Chraïbi cannot have observed Moroccan life, which is, of course, all poetry. And whatever may have been said, *The Simple Past* is neither Morocco nor Moroccans: it's Driss Chraïbi.[15]

Although various political orientations and various forms of political responsibility had been attributed to Chraïbi and to his novel, what closed the episode was not, then, any recognition on his part of the need for collective solidarity at this point in history, or a politically positive interpretation of the text, and certainly not any consensus on the 'legacy' of colonialism or the contemporary situation in Morocco more generally (as one can tell from Sefrioui's surely ironic remark about 'Moroccan life'). In the course of the *Simple Past* affair Chraïbi discovered, somewhat to his surprise, that he was working in a literary/political situation where, in Yétiv's words, 'the individual gives way to the group of which he becomes the spokesperson and the accredited representative [*le porte-parole et le représentant attitré*].'[16] This process was launched by critics, people who, as Khatibi remarked in his discussion of the *Simple Past* affair, 'are always looking to extrapolate';[17] it was they who offered any such 'accreditation', as one could see in the politicizing vocabulary of the French reviewer who expressed the hope that 'the French' would heed the 'appeal' made to them in and through Chraïbi's novel, or identified the author as the voice of an oppressed minority. Sefrioui's final word worked to block extrapolation, narrowing and destabilizing the grounds of interpretation and refusing the discourse of representativity that had attached to Chraïbi as an individual; and, implicitly, his argument worked on the basis that, in making Chraïbi a spokesperson and his text an act of testimony, his critics had oversimplified and misrepresented the relation between the author and his text and between the literary and the political. In other words, they had confused and conflated different orders of representation.

In this connection, although neither the PDI's frustration with Chraïbi's political equivocations nor the right-wing critics' opportunistic deployment of a pseudo-democratic vocabulary is hard to understand (and although most issues of properly *political* representation fall outside the scope of this book), it is worth noting that, even in narrowly political discourse, confusion may be created by the way that different senses of 'representative' often overlap and run together. Thus 'representative democracy', as Raymond Williams notes, is used variously to mean:

> (i) the periodic election of typical persons, or (ii) the periodic election of persons who will, in general, speak *for* ('on behalf of' or 'in the name of') those who elected them, or (iii) the periodic election of persons who will continually represent (make present) the views of those who elected them.[18]

It is clear, moreover, that, within any such scheme, the representation of 'minorities' is frequently considered an especially vexed issue. The perceived problem, which seems to find a resonance in the *Bulletin de Paris* article, is that in practice minority groups are 'unrepresented' in a democracy, if by 'minority group' one understands a number of people with some significant attribute in common whose worldview and/or interests *as* a group are inevitably consistently ignored or rebuffed by the majority from which, as a group, they differ and sometimes dissent. This suggests that a fundamental double-bind afflicts the minority representative: the same thing that creates the minority group's particular *need* for a representative seemingly also means that it does not qualify automatically for a satisfactory response.

The understanding of democracy in play here has, I believe, a certain currency, but it is somewhat schematic and crude, not least in its implication that the relative disempowerment of a given group may be conceived of primarily as a statistical accident. Among 'minorities', of course, one may count 'the ruling as well as the excluded classes', as Robert Young puts it, and the history of women's political under-representation shows that such a model of democratic power is inadequate, just as the fact that women are sometimes referred to as a minority says something about its tenacity.[19] The phrase 'minority group' may serve, then, as a vague and euphemistic way of describing a section of the population that could be described more precisely as disenfranchised or oppressed, through the effects of a concrete political history.

Insofar as different collective identities are constituted differentially, the socio-historical production of 'minority' groups, as of 'races', needs nonetheless to be discussed also as a matter of representations. Here 'representation' must be understood in a broad sense – not limited, in other words, to representational artefacts – and must take account of people's differing levels of access to and influence upon the means of representation. The degree to which a given group's 'identity' is defined, or embraced, by those 'within' that group varies significantly, as does the extent to which the individual who 'belongs' to a minority group that is constructed as such, and as marginal, within a given social order may dissociate him- or herself from it. It is indeed 'members' of minority groups who are most liable to be *read* as representative, that is, liable to stereotyping, and who find themselves unable to act as individuals to the extent that their every action may be taken as typical of the type to which they find themselves assigned. Conversely, the notional qualifications of the representative of a given minority group are particularly likely to include 'typicality', to return to Williams's remarks. Although such an individual may choose to express the concerns of his or her group, he or she most often cannot choose, in other words, to avoid what Memmi, speaking of the colonized, calls 'the mark of the plural', a phrase he explains thus: 'the colonized is never characterized in an individual manner; he can expect only to be submerged in collective anonymity. (*"They* are such and such . . . *They* are all the same").'[20] At this level of representation, the definition of the group – or, to put it another way, the field of representativity – may expand or contract: thus in the French criticism of *The Simple Past* Chraïbi was taken variously, as we have seen, to speak for Moroccan youth, for Morocco, and, in the case of the most extravagant extrapolation, for most people in the Islamic world.[21]

The way in which the individual may become embroiled in these varied dynamics of representation is central to Chraïbi's second novel, *The Butts* (*Les Boucs*, 1955), where it proves a source of anguish to the novel's writer-protagonist, Waldick, especially in his relations with a group of marginalized Algerian workers, the eponymous 'butts' or *boucs* who, like him, are immigrants in France. Like them, he finds himself treated by others as a generic North African or *Maghrébin*, and often despairs of escaping the constraints this brings, telling himself: 'Drink, I must drink . . . Drink and kill off any hope of redemption and go on being just a Dirty Arab.'[22] The novel suggests how hegemonic representations of this underclass become self-fulfilling, enclosing the men within a social group detached from, and with little investment in, the wider social order. The difficulty of breaking out of this vicious circle is not underestimated by Chraïbi; indeed, as if to acknowledge the ambivalent constraints of literary representation,

The Butts never individuates the immigrant workers whom French society considers habitually as an unindividuated mass. The novel thus represents them only as a group – or, to put it another way, as a group they are represented by/in the novel, but as individuals they remain opaque or do not exist. The text does not offer (a representation of) the 'authentic' voice of this group or of the individuals within it; in Spivak's terms, it refuses to offer the reader 'the ventriloquism of the speaking subaltern' and the falsely reassuring basis for empathy that it might bring.[23]

It is hard not to see in *The Butts* a response to the *Simple Past* affair, and a self-reflexive and fraught engagement with the demands placed upon Chraïbi to represent his fellow North Africans. Waldick wants to help the butts – wants, indeed, to assume a certain solidarity with them and to represent them to the outside world – but also rebels against his social assignation to an ethnic group and against the burden of imputed political responsibilities, remarking at one point, 'I do not see myself as the representative of anyone or anything, except myself.'[24] Moreover, the butts themselves are uncomprehending of Waldick's notion that he might represent them in a book and are generally distrustful of his efforts, thinking of him as 'a Christian' – a use of *Chrétien* that is the counterpart of French colonial uses of 'musulman' ('Muslim') to designate all 'native' peoples in North Africa – and as pretender to the status of prophet.[25] It seems to Waldick that he is trapped within a paradox: that which gives him the capacity to act as a representative for the butts, which is to say his relatively high level of assimilation into French culture, is also that which compromises his 'representativity', distinguishing and distancing him from those for whom he would speak.

The parallels between Chraïbi's situation and Waldick's are readily apparent, not least in that Chraïbi's ability to write these novels was the result, as one of the French reviewers of *The Simple Past* pointed out, of his experience of 'Westernization' or, more specifically, Gallification: Chraïbi's education was acquired as one of a minority of three 'Muslim Moroccans' among the 1000 pupils at the Lycée Lyautey in Casablanca, and he had lived in France since 1946.[26] But between the author and the character there are also significant differences, not least in that Chraïbi did write his novels and did represent the butts, albeit, at least in part, in terms of the 'unrepresentable' – a notion that needs to be considered as a topos of representation. There is more to be said about the political implications of this, but it should be apparent by now that the paradox in which Waldick and Chraïbi may appear to be trapped seems less fraught, and less paradoxical, once different notions of representativity and representation have been untangled, and a distinction made between the roles of the individual and the text. Being (seen as) representative (where representativity = typicality) and *acting* as a representative are very different matters, even if, as I have already noted, it is often expected of the minority representative in particular that s/he 'be' 'typical'.[27]

What is a minority author?

The place of the *writer* in all this bears further discussion, all the same. Under some circumstances – including the circumstances of colonization – writers may indeed be able to raise the profile of, or give imaginary shape to, a particular group, perhaps a group that is denied political representation, and perhaps, but not necessarily, a group to which they 'belong'. Deleuze and Guattari suggest as much in their influential if confused essay 'What is a minor literature?', where they assert that 'national consciousness, uncertain or oppressed, is necessarily routed through literature [*passe nécessairement par la littérature*].'[28] They define a 'minor literature' as the literature of a minority written in a 'major' language; and for them one of the crucial ways of conceptualizing such a minority is in terms of its relation to that language. Their own focus is on the relation of Kafka, a Jew from Prague, to German; they cite Joyce and Beckett as further examples, and they remark at one point: 'How many people today live in a language that is not their own? Or no longer, or not yet, even know their own and know poorly the major language that they are forced to use? This is the problem of immigrants, and especially of their children, the problem of minorities, the problem of a minor literature.'[29]

Minor literature, according to Deleuze and Guattari, has three salient characteristics. First, it is linked with their positively connoted notion of 'deterritorialization', a term whose meaning accrues and shifts across different figures and synonyms offered in the course of the book, including 'a rapid and joyous sliding movement', 'a line of escape', 'disarticulation', and an allusion to Einstein's 'deterritorialization of the representation of the universe'. Prague German is described as 'a deterritorialized language, appropriate for strange and minor uses'.[30] The second characteristic of 'minor literature' is that 'everything in it is political'; and the third, that 'everything takes on a collective value.'[31] The fit between this model and the *Simple Past* affair at first sight appears strikingly neat: the French written by Chraïbi, a Moroccan, would seem to be 'deterritorializing' in their terms, and it certainly turned out that the novel rapidly took on some 'collective value' and threw out political sparks.

It is apparent, however, that in Deleuze's and Guattari's particular version of the representativity of certain authors/texts one sees the sort of slippage between different orders of 'representation' to which Spivak referred. What the *Simple Past* affair makes clear, in fact, is that Deleuze's and Guattari's paradigm, which moves between 'minor literature' and the notion of the literature of a minority in order to attribute 'political' and 'collective' qualities to certain 'sorts' of text, works less well as a model of literary practice than of a certain field of reception. Indeed, it is an instance of the critical practice that helps constitute that field, categorizing certain texts into 'sorts' along partially ethnicized lines, assuming too much, perhaps, about the political importance of literature (their remark that national consciousness *necessarily* exists by means of literature is at best questionable) and reproducing more than theorizing the wider pressure to render the 'minority' individual 'representative'.

The broader context here is formed not only by the sorts of assumption about 'minority' that I have already discussed, but also, clearly, by particular conceptions of the relation of the 'majority' to 'their' language and 'their' literature. In the latter case these conceptions are shaped by the late eighteenth-century notion that each (European) nation possesses a national literature of its own. 'That now common phrase, English literature, is itself part of a crucial development', notes Raymond Williams: 'The sense of "a nation" having "a literature" is a crucial social and cultural, probably also political, development.'[32] I cannot explore the history of this development in any detail here, but would note that it makes itself felt in traditional disciplinary divisions, and that against this conceptual background it has been second nature for literary critics and literary historians to impute to literature as such and to 'each' literature a certain representative quality, even if, and even as, they also seek to pin down and analyse the specifically literary qualities of a given work. Indeed, this dual ambition was prescribed as the fundamental task of the literary historian by one of the founding fathers of modern literary criticism/history in France, Gustave Lanson, who wrote:

> We must thrust simultaneously in two opposite directions, bringing out individuality, expressing its uniqueness, its irreducibility, its irreducible integrity, and at the same time resituating the masterpiece within a series, revealing the man of genius as the product of a social environment and the representative of a group [*le produit d'un milieu et le représentant d'un groupe*].[33]

This Lansonian tradition helps explain why in his anthology, even when incorporating so literarily complex and socio-politically ambivalent work as *The Simple Past*, Memmi could move readily between the literary/aesthetic criteria by which, he explained, his 'representative' writers were primarily selected, the 'documentary' aspects of the texts that were also crucial, and what he termed the 'socio-historical' emphasis of his commentary. 'These new authors are grappling with their country as with their innermost selves', he remarked of the writers in general; 'it's as if in spite of themselves, even their most partial lines of thought give total expression to North Africa.' And he continued: 'henceforth North Africa has its literature.'[34]

In various respects, of course, Lanson's confident cultural nationalism and his associated conception of critical work may now appear anachronistic, but the political and critical circumstances in which 'francophone' literature (to pursue that example) emerged as a body of texts and as a critical category have left questions of 'social environment' at the heart of much criticism in that field, as in the fields of 'commonwealth literature', 'postcolonial literature' and so on, where they are pursued much more vigorously than in most other branches of literary criticism. Indeed, this use of 'francophone', a term that might appear to mean French-speaking, to refer to *writers* of French (from) outside France, but not all of them, is coded in such a way as to imply this distinction of critical practice, and is all about the different ways in which critics attach writers to different ethnic/cultural 'groups'. While authors such as Ionesco or Beckett – and even Camus – have generally been studied on 'French' literature courses without much attention to their non-French origins, then, the North African novel, like other 'postcolonial' texts, has been tied academically to its notional 'place of origin', 'which would appear to constitute', as Charles Bonn puts it, 'both its originality and its limit'.[35] The notion of the 'francophone author' or of the 'postcolonial novelist' thus designates a certain 'author-function', to use the term offered by Foucault in his famous essay 'What is an author?': *particular* aspects of the author's real or imagined biography, in this instance including notably 'race' or national origins, are seen by the reader as pertinent to the text, and as providing a legitimate or even crucial means of making sense of it.[36]

To label a work of fiction or an author 'francophone', then, or 'postcolonial', is already to imply the appropriateness of certain critical and interpretative manoeuvres. This tends to mean that such an author is 'condemned to dialogue with his own country', as Khatibi puts it (which is to say his or her country of 'origin'), adding:

'Let's not forget that if Kateb, Chraïbi, and Dib are accepted by the West it's not as universal representatives [*représentants universels*] but as *Maghrébins*.'[37] Conrad, it may be noted, could be discussed as a converse example from the realm of 'English' literature, his accept-ance into the canon taking place according to dynamics of reception such that his Polish/Ukrainian origins and, more remarkably, the fact that English was his third language, could be seen as largely irrele-vant, and his themes treated as universal. Two possible extremes of critical practice can be glimpsed here – on the one hand the *reduction* of certain texts to their putative cultural context and, on the other, the false transcendence of context through which the critic may embrace a naive conception of literary 'autonomy' or of the universal.

I will have more to say about these issues in the final chapters, but want to turn now to the other key issue raised by Deleuze and Guattari, that of the relation of the writer to the language in which she or he writes. Again, their own remarks on this appear confused: the problem of not mastering the 'major' language where one lives is less often a problem, contrary to what they say, for the children of immigrants than for their parents; and those who 'no longer' know their 'own' language will almost always speak another language instead, and speak it well rather than 'poorly'. Chraïbi's case certainly does not fit this part of their model: when he became an immigrant in France he already spoke and wrote French perfectly, and this placed him in one sort of 'minority' in Morocco and another sort in France – an issue of which, as we have already seen, his first two novels displayed a pained awareness.

The fundamental question here, as one considers the sort of mas-tery of language displayed by Chraïbi in *The Simple Past*, is on what basis French is held not to be 'his' language. Versions of this question emerge persistently in postcolonial literary culture; one of the factors that made Rushdie's anthology of Indian writing controversial was his decision to include only one text originally written in a language other than English. He explained this decision in terms of the editors' criterion of literary quality, but also addressed the criticisms he fore-saw, writing:

> For some, English-language Indian writing will never be more than a post-colonial anomaly, the bastard child of Empire, sired on India by the departing British; its continuing use of the old colonial tongue is seen as a fatal flaw that renders it forever inauthentic.... [Yet] English has become an Indian language. Its colonial origins mean that, like Urdu [Rushdie's mother tongue] and unlike all other Indian languages, it has no regional base; but in all other ways, it has come emphatically

to stay. ... Indian English ... is not 'English' English, to be sure, any more than Irish or American or Caribbean English is. And it is part of the achievement of the writers in this volume to have found literary voices as distinctively Indian, and also as suitable for any and all of the purposes of art, as those other Englishes forged in Ireland, Africa, the West Indies and the United States.

A similar point is made by one of the other anthologists quoted earlier, Adewale Maja-Pearce, who writes: 'English is one of the languages of Africa, at least for the present, because the poets have determined it so, a fact which is readily acknowledged by the African dictators who would silence them'; and Memmi too seemed to have reached a position close to these by the time of his anthology of 1985, persuaded by then that he had been mistaken in his famous prophecy, in *The Colonizer and the Colonized*, concerning the imminent extinction of North African literature in French. Other writers and critics, as Rushdie indicates, take a different view: one of the best-known voices in this regard is that of Ngũgĩ wa Thiong'o, who argues that the continued use of European languages by an African elite perpetuates 'the split between the mind and the body of Africa'.[38] Memmi, comparably, wrote in 1964 that 'the non-coincidence of one's mother tongue and one's cultural language is the source of serious handicaps and even of psychological conflicts.'[39]

In weighing up these different attitudes, it should be borne in mind that as the European imperial powers spread their languages around the globe they also spread their notions concerning the links between national identity, language and literature. The conjoined claims at the level of the universal and of the national made for *French* literature in particular, to return to that example, an entity which may variously include or exclude 'francophone' literature, are closely linked with claims made for the French language itself, imagined in post-Revolutionary France as both a locus of national identity and a universal tool of reason. In 1789, it should be remembered, only about two-fifths of France was French-speaking, and the propagation of French was both a means and an end of political struggle. Reporting on the country's linguistic diversity in 1793 – and recommending that it be eliminated – Abbé Grégoire wrote: 'I cannot repeat too often that it is more important than people realize politically to eradicate this array of crude idioms which prolong reason's infancy and prejudice's dotage.'[40] Louis-Jean Calvet, who cites this report, argues that the linguistic heritage of the Revolutionary period had a profound influence on subsequent conceptions of the French language in three important respects, the first two of which are most pertinent to imperial expansion. First, and most fundamentally, to speak French was thought of as patriotic by those defining the new *patrie* or fatherland – and, one might add, by those later extending it. Secondly, French was conceived of as a (or the) language of culture and progress, defined against inferior 'dialects' such as Breton; and thirdly, relatedly, French became associated with secularism, since the Church, concerned to reach as many people as possible, continued until after the Second World War to publish catechisms in local languages.

The weight of this heritage, and the extent to which it has facilitated or impeded non- or anti-metropolitan political claims, has varied from place to place. The place of French in Québecois nationalism is clearly quite different from its place in Senegalese nationalism, and its place in Algerian nationalism is different again – just as 'nationalism' itself means something different in each case. The historical relation between French, Catholicism and nationalism in Quebec, for example, is clearly a long way from the relation between French, Catholicism and colonialism in Algeria.[41] Comparable issues evidently arise when English serves as a *lingua franca*, having supplanted or supplemented other languages to a greater of lesser degree; again, the implications and resonances of this vary, so that in parts of South India, as Rushdie argues, Hindi may feel more 'colonial' than does English today, while in Scotland a fair number of car-owners choose to have the sticker showing their car's provenance printed with the word *Ecosse* ('Scotland' in French).

Inevitably, the various struggles associated historically with the French language continue to colour the notion of *francophonie*, which is used to refer not just to the ability to speak French, but also to a notional global community of French speakers. The term was coined by Onésime Reclus in a book entitled *France, Algérie et colonies* of 1880, a wide-ranging survey in which he states, almost in passing, that French is 'worthy of its reputation as the liveliest and most civilized language in Europe'.[42] That idea of 'francophonie', clearly consonant with the conceptions of French patriotism and progress of which Calvet speaks, started to be used widely in the 1960s, that is to say in the wake of decolonization, and was promoted by those wanting to strengthen the position of French as a world language and doubtless also, in many cases, to reconsolidate the position of France as a world power. In the eyes of many French speakers, consequently, the promotion of *francophonie* signals a form of cultural imperialism, and works to provide cover for France's neo-colonial economic and political 'interest' in its former colonies. It is for such reasons that Algeria, the country with the largest number of French speakers after France, has refused to associate itself with the francophone movement.[43]

Just as for French critics the very fact that *The Simple Past* was written in French was, then, part of what allowed and encouraged them to read it as a triumph of civilization over superstition, for Moroccan nationalists and anti-imperialists it was part of what made it objectionable. The objection was based not only on the contingent factors making a French-language novel inaccessible to the vast majority of Moroccans, few of whom would have been able to read Chraïbi's novel even if it had been written in Arabic, but also on the perception that French and perhaps also the novel as a literary form were not just historically but *inherently* inappropriate to a description of Moroccan culture or the expression of a Moroccan or North African identity.[44] Conversely, the blurring – in Memmi's commentary, for example – of Morocco(/Algeria/Tunisia) into the North African whole is facilitated by the claims of Arabic as a (would-be) national and supra-national language, and as the language of Islam. One of the most widely quoted North African statements of such a claim is that made by the writer Malek Haddad in a well-known essay of 1961, where he wrote:

> even expressing themselves in French, Algerian writers from an Arabo-Berber background must *translate* thought that is *specifically Algerian*, thought that would have found full expression *if its vehicle had been the Arabic language and Arabic writing*... Our *French vocabulary* corresponds only *approximately* to our *Arabic thought*.[45]

Although it is heartfelt and rhetorically powerful, Haddad's utopian vision of a perfect form of self-expression, in a context where the self is profoundly and fundamentally Algerian and/or Arabic, is not without its ironies and inconsistencies – some of which are apparent when Haddad supports his position by quoting (in French) Albert Memmi, a Tunisian Jew, just after asserting the specifically Algerian quality of his ('our') thought, and not long after discussing in the first person plural the position of 'inconsolable orphans' severed from their mother tongue and bearing 'the indelible mark of Islam'.[46] Above all it is ironic that Haddad on language, like Khatibi on literature, may embrace too uncritically a view that could be seen as markedly European, and even French, both in overestimating the inherent weight, so to speak, of Frenchness in French, and in its assumptions about the ways in which any language may encapsulate and express a 'national identity', or indeed what it is means for a language to be one's (or one's country's) 'own'.[47]

The same issue arises when Fanon writes, in his chapter on 'The black man and language' in *Black Skin, White Masks*, that 'To speak means to be in a position to use a certain syntax, to grasp the morphology of this or that language, but it means above all to assume a culture, to bear the weight of a civilization', or, when Deleuze and Guattari remark: 'What can be said in one language cannot be said in another.'[48] Certainly there is a sense in which such claims are true, but they risk sliding towards an untenably deterministic model of language's relation to consciousness. It is worth recalling that Fanon makes this remark, in a book that is highly critical of and in many ways distant from French culture, in French; and that what is lost as his remark is translated into English appears, for most purposes, much less important than what is successfully captured. Moreover, the way in which a writer such as Chraïbi may, in Deleuze's and Guattari's terms, 'deterritorialize' the language, feeding in the influence of other languages and renewing the language through the work of reconnotation, shows that the values borne in a particular language are not all so deeply anchored as to be forever invisible and immutable.

My main argument here – and it is a point to which I will return in the next chapter – is that those drawbacks to the use of a former colonial language that seem inherent, rather than contingently uncomfortable as a result of colonial history, must actually be apprehended historically, both in terms of the continuous evolution of the language – not least through its role in colonial and postcolonial encounters – and, as I indicated earlier, in terms of the history of the *idea* of language's relation to (national) culture, identity, politics and so on. This has ramifications for the conceptual coherence of any notion of French (or English) literature: today any narrow association of French with Frenchness or with France appears far from inevitable, which suggests that the 'French' part of 'French literature' – or, by analogy, the English part of English literature – should be defined only in terms of the shared use of a particular language. I would argue, then, that a notion such as 'francophone literature', freighted as it is with confused assumptions about 'representativity', French, literature and national identity, is redundant. My purpose in saying this is not, however, to suggest that the contextualizing framework usually associated with 'francophone' or 'postcolonial' literature, or the search for a certain cultural specificity, be abandoned, or to dismiss the emotional and political aspects of what one might call linguistic belonging. Rather, it is to suggest that, if one takes a sceptical, historicizing view of any 'national' body of literature, or a body of literature in a given language, the particular significance of 'sharing' the language and even the *extent* to which 'it' is shared, both across time (between Chaucer and Woolf, say) and across the globe, come to seem far from clear, a matter of diverse overlapping histories rather than something that can be captured at the level of a general 'identity'.

Although Rushdie's remarks about 'Englishes forged in Ireland, Africa, the West Indies and the United States' imply something similar to this, it is striking that the argument he makes for his choice of texts and his authors' use of English is made from within the logic of authenticity: as noted earlier, he writes that 'it is part of the achievement' of the writers in his volume to have found literary 'voices' that are 'distinctively Indian', as well as 'suitable for any and all of the purposes of art'. The case of *The Simple Past*, to which, by way of a conclusion to this chapter, I want to turn one last time, suggests that artistic exigencies (or artistic pluralism) and the impulse towards the expression of cultural identity do not always coincide so smoothly.

The uneasy relation of Chraïbi's text to these twin dynamics is not just a matter of the events surrounding its publication but once again is prefigured within it. For example, the search for representative representatives of a culture – especially by outsiders – is sharply parodied through an anecdote told by Driss, which goes:

> 'This morning, on my way here, I met an American from the Military Police. He stopped his Jeep. "You French?" he asked. "No" I answered. "Arab dressed as a Frenchman". "Um, so where are the Arabs dressed as Arabs who speak Arabic and..." I gestured towards the old Muslim cemetery. "Over there".'[49]

In its political context, of course, that last image of the irreversible hybridity of Moroccan identity, and of the effective obliteration of pre-colonial 'Arab' culture, must have looked to Chraïbi's nationalist critics like a shaky form of self-justification on the part of an author who generalized too hastily (or, at least, permitted hasty generalizations) from his personal distance on an Arab/Muslim culture which, though altered through the French colonial encounter, was by no means dead and buried. Any assessment of the text's supposed irresponsibility is complicated, however, by the sense that Driss's anecdote must also be considered in relation to his context of literary reception, of which it may serve as a parody. Something of that context is captured elsewhere in the same episode, part of a particularly rich passage reproducing Driss's school essay on the theme of *liberté, égalité, fraternité*, where we read his caricatural list of the characteristics of '"a good novel of the old school"': the list begins with 'Morocco, a country of the future, sun, couscous, wogs, a darky on a donkey with Mrs darky behind, belly dancing, souks...' and spirals off deliriously into the general exoticism of 'coconut trees, banana trees, poisoned darts, Indians, Pluto, Tarzan, Captain Cook...'.[50] In this and many other ways the novel seemingly tries to make readers aware of their expectations, and to frustrate the search for a reliable and authentic Moroccan 'voice', taking its distance from early francophone literature of North Africa – what Khatibi terms 'the ethnographic and folkloric novel'[51] – and from a certain tradition of French travel writing whose exoticizing tendencies it shared.

This is *not* to say that the novel becomes wholly non-referential, or that it does not engage with Morocco as a real historical context as well as the object or product of a certain history of representations, or indeed that the novel's 'voice' is not distinctly Moroccan in important respects. But on these points, too, the novel seems to be a step ahead of its critics. Driss writes (or Chraïbi writes through Driss):

> I am well aware, Esteemed Examiners, that a pupil's exam paper must be anonymous, free from any signature, name, or anything else that might identify its author. I am also well aware, however, that when one looks at a painting one can see the painter. For some time now, in other words, my personality will have been apparent to you: I am an Arab.[52]

One is reminded of Memmi's (later) remark on his anthologized authors, who included Chraïbi, 'it's as if in spite of themselves, even their most partial lines of thought give total expression to North Africa.'[53] The complexities of a novel such as Chraïbi's make such a remark appear not exactly wrong, but a little flat-footed or tendentious; among the 'purposes of art', it would seem, and among Chraïbi's achievements, may be the disruption of those dynamics of representativity that identify writing with a person, a 'voice' or a place.

5

Writing and Voice: Women, Nationalism and the Literary Self

Invited to speak at Berkeley in 1995, Assia Djebar delivered a paper on Camus's *The First Man*. One of the notes that Camus had written to himself on the character who is his 'double', she remarked, reads: 'it was the Algerian in him that they disliked.' For her, she continued, things are rather different:

> I smile at that Algerian, welcomed as I am from so far away in a prestigious university because I'm a writer, because I'm a woman and because I'm Algerian. And I in turn note, as a counterpoint to Camus, 'it is the Algerian in me that they recognize.' 'That they recognize?' Let's be more precise: 'What they hope for from me is Woman Algeria.'[1]

Djebar published her first novel during the Algerian war, in 1957, and by 1967 had published three more. Looking back on this period she recalls that she began writing impulsively, 'doubtless too young, during the Algerian war – the other one, which happened when I was twenty – and what is more wrote not nationalist essays, not lyrical or polemical declarations of faith (which was the sort of testimony I was expected to produce), but novels, which seemed gratuitous.' Partly, it seems, because of the weight of expectations confronting her – she refers to the 'Zhdanovist' attacks, still continuing in the late 1970s, that she suffered in relation to her early work – she published nothing for over a decade, until *Women of Algiers in their Apartment* appeared (in the original French) in 1980.[2]

Djebar, it is apparent, is keenly aware of the academic, political and intellectual frameworks within which her work is received. The shift in

the field of reception or *horizon d'attente* such that her own 'Algerianness' has become such a positive quality for much of her audience – and
such that Camus's 'Algerianness' (and its putative repression) has
become a more conspicuous aspect of his work – has taken place in
the broad historical context and the narrower intellectual context of
which postcolonial studies forms a part. Her published work from
1980 could be considered what one critic, Gafaïti, labels 'an exemplary
expression' of the literature of postcoloniality, literature that Donadey,
in her discussion of 'women writing between worlds', characterizes in
terms of 'a to-and-fro movement *between the oppositional and the
complicit*'.[3] As Chraïbi was well aware, to be seen as 'exemplary' or
representative in this way is a mixed blessing, and one to which Djebar,
as we will see, responds with a certain mobility and equivocation.
Accordingly, what this chapter will try to elucidate are not only the
themes, forms and sources of inspiration that make Gafaïti's description of Djebar's writing apt – including notably her representation of
gender politics in the context of post-independence Algeria, her use of
Delacroix's 'orientalist' imagery, her relation to the French language,
and her practice of autobiography or 'self-writing' – but also, as with
Chraïbi, the sense in which that writing may be positioned, and may
position itself, in an ambivalent relation to a certain literary/critical
field, driving towards a notional literary space where the very language
of position and opposition starts to lose its force.

Women, nationalism and the bathhouse of language

Djebar's awareness of and discomfort with the demands of 'representativity' placed upon her began, clearly, long before her talk at Berkeley. She introduced the stories of *Women of Algiers* with a preface or
'Overture', in which she wrote, in an allusion to the ten-year 'silence'
from which she was emerging:

> For at least ten years now – as a result, no doubt, of my own silence, in
> fits and starts, as an Arab woman – I have been aware of the extent to
> which speaking in this area has become (except for the spokesperson or
> the 'specialist') some sort of transgression.
>   Don't claim to 'speak for', or worse 'speak on', barely speak along-
> side, and if possible right against them: this is the first gesture of
> solidarity to make if you're one of the few Arab women who obtain
> or acquire freedom of movement, of body and of mind.[4]

It is made apparent both that in this collection she will be especially
concerned with the representation of women, and that she is alert to

the risks of misrepresenting the 'underrepresented' or 'silent', and of seeing the trick of literary ventriloquism as a substitute for political voice. As her later remarks about the expectations of her audience at Berkeley remind us, this refusal, or problematization, of her own representativity touches both her 'Algerianness' and her 'femininity'; and she is wary of what in her collected essays *Ces voix qui m'assiègent* (a title whose significance I will discuss later, and that I will render for now simply as *Voices*) she alludes to as 'a certain sort of criticism which, as soon as it gets near the feminine domain, makes do with sociological or biographical commentary, thus recreating in its own way a pseudo-literary harem.' It is for such reasons that in the final article of *Voices* she instructs herself: 'you will not say "we", you will not hide yourself, a singular woman, behind "Woman"; you will never, neither at the beginning nor at the end, be a "spokesperson".'[5]

In this respect Djebar's stance may resemble Chraïbi's, but there are significant differences between them. The disappointments that Chraïbi seemed to fear concerning the political compromises of the post-independence period have been felt by Djebar – all the more keenly because of her own involvement in the fight for liberation, no doubt – and she goes much further than Chraïbi in the depth of her engagement with colonial history, viewed with a certain hindsight and considerable erudition.[6] Chraïbi was perhaps naïve about the impact of expressing dissent when he did, in a context where, as Fanon analysed it, the struggle against the colonial power served to unite the colonized people and to lend nationalist rhetoric credibility and urgency. By 1980, nearly two decades after independence, the situation had changed. This is not to deny that a country such as Algeria continued to experience neo-imperialist economic pressures, but to argue merely that at some point it surely becomes legitimate, as Djebar seemingly feels, both to measure nationalist rhetoric and the mythologizing of the nationalist fight by standards more nuanced than what passed for political expediency in the mid-1950s, and to raise the question of gender politics as a pressing issue in its own right.

Women of Algiers offers elements of an assessment, or reassessment, of the legacy of the anti-colonial and post-independence years from a feminist perspective. Certain women characters' recollections of wartime experiences are a reminder that women as well as men were involved in the war, and suffered torture, for example, as did men.[7] Indeed, during the war French public opinion was swayed against colonialism by reports of the torture of Algerian women by the French, and the 'Postface', 'Forbidden gaze, severed sound', alludes to the cases of women such as Djamila Boupacha and Djamila Bouhired, whose brutal treatment was publicized in France by Simone de Beauvoir among others.[8] The fate of Leila in the first story, 'Women of Algiers in their apartment', resonates against this history: a victim of torture and a drug addict, she is conscious of her former rhetorical worth for nationalist propaganda, and of the fact that, now, she seems to attract no particular kudos or even sympathy as a war veteran. It is against this same historical backdrop that the startling opening sequence of 'Women of Algiers' should be seen: in a book about Algeria, the first sentence – 'A young woman's head, blind-folded, the neck thrown backward, her hair pulled back . . .' – is likely to make the reader think of the French military's torture of Algerian combatants. It turns out, however, that we are inside the dream of one of the protagonists, a surgeon called Ali, that the figure is his wife Sarah, on whom the story centres, and that what is being described is a nightmarish conflation of torture and operation.[9] At this point, then, the story is already playing on the reader's expectations, making it apparent both that it will engage with the colonial legacy, and that it will do so in unconventional ways, literarily and politically.

It soon emerges, through figures such as Leila, that a central theme of Djebar's collection is the cultural isolation or marginalization of women in Algeria, and their encounters with various social, historical and psychological constraints. Djebar focuses especially on forms of communication among women and those that are particular to women; Sarah in 'Women of Algiers' could be articulating Djebar's own ambitions when she says:

'For Arab women I see only one way to unblock everything: talk, talk without stopping, about yesterday and today, talk among ourselves, in all the women's quarters, the traditional ones and the ones in the housing projects.'[10]

Present in that particular conversation, it should be noted, and one of the main characters in the story, is a non-Arab woman, Anne, who is visiting from France and is a close friend of Sarah's: so Sarah's invoca-tion of an ethnic category is not meant, it would seem, to exclude Anne from the sort of conversation among women that this is, and that it proposes. All the same, even though the closeness of the two friends throws into relief the poverty of communication between Sarah and Ali, Djebar's portrait does not idealize relations between these women, or ignore the ways in which colonial history and issues of ethnic affiliation thread in and out of their consciousness and so through their relationship. There are moments when Anne's naïvety appears to be an impediment to intimacy: in the hammam, for example, she asks Sarah about her scar, not realizing that it is the result of the torture she suffered at the hands of the French. Later, when she accompanies the masseuse to the hospital, she asks Sarah to find out the masseuse's name; the latter understands the question, and says to Anne: 'Explain to her that in our country all *fatmas* are named Fatma', making it clear that past and continuing condescension from the former colonizers can still be bitterly felt.[11] Nonetheless, Anne stays with the masseuse in the hospital; and though other patients assume that she is her daughter-in-law, and that her son will soon turn up – assume, in other words, that their relationship follows a traditional familial pattern, and moreover that their female relationship is mediated by, and subordinate to, their relationship to a man – in this instance, clearly, they are wrong.

All in all, between the various women depicted in the collection one sees divisions as well as forms of solidarity. Women too live with distinctions of social hierarchy – the masseuse, for instance, is exploited by, and feels exploited by, her female boss – as well as distinctions inherited from, or recast by, colonialism, including not just ethnic distinctions but also those between the young and the old. All the women in 'Day of Ramadhan', for example, have been marked by the violence of the war, but their reactions vary greatly. One of the young women, Nadjia, quickly grows tired of 'the interminable polite formulas' at a social gathering, and protests: ' "No!" she snorted, "All that nattering, eating cakes, gorging oneself before morning, is that why we've suffered bloodshed and mourning? No, I won't have it ... I ... ," and her voice filled with tears, "I thought, you see, that all this would change, that something else would happen, that ... ".'[12] The younger women apparently feel torn between their frustration that their freedom remains circumscribed, and their guilt about the relative independence that distances them from their 'foremothers' [*aïeules*]. The generation gap cannot, then, be understood simply as a gap between tradition and modernity (or indeed 'postcoloniality') as such, but rather is linked to the different ways in which different generations make sense of the present through their understanding of the past and of the future that it may or may not resemble. The 'postcolonial' society in which these women find themselves is 'post-traditional' in Giddens's sense: traditions persist, but participation in them is coming to appear optional, and their capacity to organize experience meaningfully, or to authorize automatically certain forms of behaviour, is no longer universally accepted.[13]

One could view it as an example of both cultural continuity and discontinuity, then, that different women in the stories fulfil a role as guardians of tradition – itself a conventional representation of North African women – in both positive and negative respects. Sarah's work, a project assembling documentation on, and recording, 'hawfis', a form of poetry sung by women (as the reader is informed in an endnote), could be considered one version of a new/traditional relation to tradition; another appears when an eminent patient of Ali's dies on the operating table, ravaged by cirrhosis – and implicitly by alcohol, which is forbidden by Islam – and Ali suggests to the man's sons that they tell their 'devout wives' that he died of cancer.[14] Women may play their part, it would seem, in sustaining real and represented divisions between the male and female worlds, and allowing the malleability, in practice, of (gendered) religious strictures. One might compare the moment in 'Nostalgia of the horde' where an elderly woman tells the story of how she was injured by her violent husband, but was encouraged by her female in-laws – who were cruel to her when she first arrived in their household – to keep this a secret. At one startling moment she recalls how he threw a stone at her face, and remarks: 'The stone cut open my forehead just above my eye (the Prophet, may he be praised, protected me!) and my husband went back to praying imperturbably.'[15] This notion of providence seems curiously and troublingly flexible and intermittent, but the fictional text draws no explicit moral from the incident. Prior to and beyond any possible questioning of Islam or tradition as such, the story uses the literary space to re-present religion and tradition, and women's relationship to them, as the fields of *interpretation* that they always are.

The same holds true of Djebar's treatment of the war of independence, or more precisely the history of (gendered) representations to which it has given rise, representations that at moments likewise appear unchallengeable and unchangeable. This issue starts to come into focus when, in the first 'Interlude', she describes how the wife of the *hazab* (who reads the Qu'ran in the mosque), having worked hard all through the war to support her imprisoned husband, returns at the earliest opportunity to the work of reproduction in order to provide him with the son for which he yearns. When Djebar writes: 'She had picked up the regular rhythm of giving birth "at the dawn of the era of independence" (many far nobler tales still begin with this oratorical expression . . .)', her inverted commas, the adverb 'still' and the adjective 'oratorical' suggest an ironic distance from a superannuated nationalist discourse that is becoming ossified and sanctified, and seem to call into question the gendering of both the division of nationalist labour and the notion of 'nobility'.[16]

Though *Women of Algiers* is concerned above all with women, the stories suggest that young men too in the post-independence era suffer under the weight of a certain gendered notion of nationalist heroism.

Complaining disappointedly about his father Ali's role in the war, Nazim asks:

> 'What's he ever told me about his five years in the resistance? ... The way he opened the official ball at the Kremlin, just before the sixties (there were five of them, the first "student-*fellaghas*" to get to the Soviet Union thanks to the resistance network and the "brother nations") ... And as for life in the resistance, one single miserable detail: holed up in some caves, they used to kill their lice in winter! A comrade from that glorious period even added, in front of me, one day when he was more or less sozzled: "We killed so many of them and we became such experts at it that when we crushed them under our nails it really sounded just like a machine-gun!".'[17]

The bathos of the last sentence points to a gulf between heroic rhetoric and the sometimes banal history to which it was applied, and the varied forms of alienation it may foster. The theme is explored again in 'The dead speak', where even Hassan, a 'real' hero, seems to have been left cold, perhaps traumatized, in the aftermath of the war: we read, for example: 'Recently, Hassan has been measuring time. Others are already summing it up: "seven years," as they say in the classic conformist histories: "the Seven Years' War", "the Hundred Years' War." Here the formula is set: "The War of Liberation." A liberation of the scenery and of other people, but ...'.[18] In spite of this, when he is called upon to make rousing speeches he does so. The reader, it seems, is encouraged to take a certain distance from this final scene, when the floating narratorial voice, italicized in the text, remarks:

> A burial of no importance, admittedly, but the poor cousin's melancholy does not dissipate, the sharecropper in the procession is still lost in his daydream, while the eyes of all those who might bear witness are trained on the grandson alone. And in his heart, an arid expanse. Worse than being consigned to oblivion.
>   Still the dead speak. The old woman's voice murmurs alongside Aïcha ... How much of this is noticed by the man towards whom Hadda's last hopes were turned? Nothing.[19]

Just after this, the final paragraph, evoking the different (more traditional and more local) work of memory carried out by the women, and the rhetorical uses that the living make of the dead, reads:

> For a long time he [Hassan] spoke about the dead, all those dead buried beneath the underbrush, dead in battle, massacred, 'all the dead who would continue to live' he said. His speech was received with such

prolonged enthusiasm that the women's ululation ascended in languor-
ous spirals from the esplanade above the harbour where the meeting
was being held to the cemetery, where Aïcha had come by herself to pay
her respects. It was the seventh day after Yemma's death. By her side,
her little boy – already five years old – was contemplating the panorama of the city over the wall, a view made iridescent by the shifting
coloured dots of the meeting.[20]

As the young boy's attention wanders and is captured by Hassan,
whose behaviour he consequently echoes in not mourning at his
mother's grave, the reader is left with a multivalent image of national
unity, in the immediate wake of the colonial era, as at once a reality
and a fantasy projected onto a diverse social fabric.

To the extent that any sense of national unity is a fantasy of this
order, or is 'imagined', in Benedict Anderson's well-known phrase, to
describe it in such terms is not necessarily to criticize it, at least not in
the sense of comparing it unfavourably with the standards of other
nations.[21] Djebar's fiction makes space for criticism, though, and for
the different history of representations of which it would be a part, in
that it gives a sense of the cultural diversity that the image of unity
may disguise. Gender, as we have seen, is one crucial part of that
diversity. Another, particularly for the writer, is linguistic. 'My country', she comments, in the subsection of *Voices* entitled 'Francophonie?', 'under a genuine cultural dictatorship, has been plagued by a
pseudo-identitarian monolingualism.' She points out that Apuleius
could be viewed as the first Algerian writer, and that, although he
wrote in Latin, he was known for his prowess in Greek, and would
have spoken Punic or Libyan as his mother tongue. Against this historical background, Arabic monolingualism appears 'entirely theoretical',
whereas multilingualism, with different languages serving as the language of power at different points in history, appears to have been a
constant facet of North African culture.[22] At a more general level it
might be added that, although in many countries linguistic 'unity'
appears often to be thought of as a vital element of national unity, to
have a variety of distinct languages within given national borders is
probably the norm: French may be the *lingua franca* and main language of modern France, to take only that example, but other
languages are still spoken as a mother tongue by significant sections
of the population (including recent immigrants, but also Breton
speakers, say), as they always have been. Such linguistic diversity
figures repeatedly as a theme in Djebar's fiction: in 'Women of
Algiers', for instance, there is a scene where, just after being spoken
to by a Berber woman whom he cannot understand, Ali's son Nazim

writes a note in Arabic addressed to his father, knowing that he will not be able read it. Ali has not managed, we are told, to 'retrain himself in the national language' (he speaks Arabic, but is not literate in it), yet clearly it is not really his fault that his literacy is in French – and the fact that Nazim, who *is* literate in Arabic, cannot communicate at all with one of his compatriots reminds us that the idea of Arabic as a 'national language' is less straightforward, as an actuality or as a programme, than it may appear.[23]

Clearly all of this could be seen as a justification for Djebar's own use of French, as could the much earlier story 'There is no exile', written in Tunis in 1959. In that story a character called Hafça, an Algerian exile who works as a French teacher, delivers an emotional speech about her love of her motherland, and later quietly promotes the benefits of learning a foreign language. The story is narrated by a young woman who knows only Arabic, and who comments on her own attitude to language (with a perhaps implausible degree of self-criticism): 'I never felt any need to shake up my ideas.'[24] Not only does her attitude to French and to education generally appear somewhat backward, then, but through its narrative structure the story implicitly makes a claim for the ability of the writer to think him/herself into the position of someone else, irrespective of mother tongue or choice of language of expression (and so implicitly makes an argument, to return to an issue raised in my previous chapter, against any overly deterministic model of language to consciousness).

This is not to say, however, that Djebar presents herself as being 'at home' in French. Like Haddad, she has the sense that she is engaged in a kind of translation; but, unlike Haddad, she does not believe that Arabic or any other language would be the perfect and natural medium of expression. In the 'Overture' of *Women of Algiers*, she writes: 'I could say: "stories translated from...", but from which language? From Arabic? From a popular Arabic, or a feminine Arabic; in other words from an underground Arabic.'[25] These remarks indicate her particular take on the notion of a 'national' language, or of a sort of natural linguistic belonging, inflecting it, through her allusion to 'feminine Arabic', not only in terms of Arabic's geographical diversity but also in terms of gender. On this point her post-1970s attitude to Arabic, French and language in general was almost certainly influenced, directly or indirectly, by work on women's language and writing by feminist theorists such as Cixous and Irigaray, from whose perspective she would not be 'at home' in any existing language.[26] She was in any case certainly influenced, as she herself explains, by her experiences on a film project (comparable, it may be noted, to Sarah's work in 'Women of Algiers') documenting elements of women's *oral* culture vehicled by languages – colloquial Arabic and Berber – that are normally unwritten.

Accordingly, the French in which Djebar writes bears the trace of the other languages with which she is familiar, Arabic and Berber; and the literary forms with which she works are influenced by and in some sense seek to capture and convey elements of that non-literate, non-literary tradition. On a certain linguistic level this means tapping into a more general pattern of the mixing or *métissage* between different languages that is, notwithstanding the efforts of the Académie Française, inevitable; on another, it concerns Djebar's more personal efforts to work French into a distinctive idiom of her own. In this she fits Ngũgĩ wa Thiong'o's general observation that 'Nearly all African writers have returned to African languages. What they write in whatever language derives its stamina, stature, identity from African languages' – one concrete manifestation of which is her use of words derived from Arabic.[27] Some of these are already effectively part of French as a result of longstanding contacts between the cultures: 'oued' for example, a temporary stream or river, has, according to the *Robert* dictionary, been in use since the eleventh century, and 'henné' (hennah) since the sixteenth century. Others, with other distant roots, are a reminder that the earlier North African cultures evoked by the words were themselves already 'hybrid': 'odalisque', for example, comes from Turkish, and 'narguilé' from Persian, while the synonym 'hookah' used more frequently in English, or appearing as 'houka' in French, comes from Arabic via Hindi and Urdu. More recently, other Arabic words appeared in French as the language expanded with the empire: 'casbah', it seems, entered French in 1830, as the French entered the casbah in Algiers; and others again – such as 'haoufis/hawfis' and 'hazab' – are introduced by Djebar where no French equivalent exists, either to be explained, within the story or in a footnote, or left unglossed, accessible to readers who know Arabic but representing moments of cultural opacity to those who do not. The cultural baggage of certain (other) French words, meanwhile, emerges in a new light when they appear in Djebar's text; 'faire carême' (to fast or to observe Lent) in the story 'Day of Ramadhan' refers to fasting not in Lent but in Ramadhan; 'Dieu' (God) and 'Allah' are both used – perhaps because neither, in a sense, can translate the Arabic *allah* perfectly – and the term 'maquis', which most often refers to Frenchmen fighting the German occupation in the Second World War, is applied here to Algerians fighting the French occupation of Algeria.

At one point Djebar describes French as having functioned for her as a kind of veil, remembering how in 1982 she suddenly thought to herself: 'Until now I have used the French language as a *veil*. A veil on me as an individual, a veil on my body as a woman; I could almost say a veil on my own voice.'[28] The image captures something of the non-transparency of her literary style, which helps mark her writing's distance from political rhetoric and which complicates and fore-grounds the complexity of its own claims as a form of cultural 'representation'. On another level, the image of the veil also functions reflexively as part of her work of reconnoting French: she describes it too as 'A veil not of dissimulation or of masking, but of suggestion and ambiguity' and reworks the image in another, beautiful passage, which reads:

> a childhood memory, a scene that all those who lived in the Maghreb when they were young, boys or girls, could relive from their childhood routine: when I went out, as a very small girl, with my mother, or an aunt, or some other relative, there was always a moment, in the hall, when the veiled woman, before facing the street, slowly prepared to unfold her veil.
>
> When you unfold the veil and put it on – and in my memory it is always a veil of white watered silk – these few moments of preparing, protecting oneself, of handling the material, are essential: for each woman has her own particular way of putting on a veil.... A way of wrapping it around her hips, folding it at shoulder level, drawing the ends in beneath her chin; of these rapid, assured gestures, every child is aware....
>
> Every child believed, like me, that her mother had the noblest, most elegant way of wearing the veil! And in the street, the men must have recognized my mother – probably because, in that small city, they recognized me...But as a young girl, I was completely sure that if people recognized my mother, even in her veil, it was obviously because she had the most beautiful eyes and the most beautiful ankles (because of course all that could be seen of her was the eyes, above the other small veil that rested on her nose; and one could just about make out her ankles). Or sometimes, more subtly, I thought at the time, if people recognized her, it was because in some sense she had expressed herself in the way the veil was draped, her inimitable way of wrapping herself in the silk.
>
> There are a thousand ways to wear a veil.[29]

This image serves to challenge and recast those commonplace conceptions of the veil that take it merely to signal Muslim women's lack of agency and constrained or disguised identity; it also, of course, says something about Djebar's perception of her own relationship to French, about her own real, if limited room for manoeuvre within a given cultural context and a particular tradition, and about the possibilities of expressing agency and individuality in the cultural forms available to her. 'The first thing about veiled women', she remarks in a footnote in *Women of Algiers*, 'is that they are free to move around';[30] writing (in French), comparably, has allowed her a certain freedom.

Brilliant and innovative though Djebar's use of the imagery of the veil often is, it is marked by the sort of ambivalence to which I alluded at the start of this chapter, not least in that there are points in her writing where its associations are more conventional. For any postcolonial critic anxious about her work's reception, moreover, her decision to associate herself, a North African woman from an Islamic background, with even a 'reconnoted' veil must appear to dally dangerously with stereotypes – as indeed must the decision to give to the work that relaunched her writing career the title *Women of Algiers in their Apartment*, and to adorn the cover with the Delacroix painting from which the title was drawn. Of course, something of its *thematic* attraction quickly becomes apparent: for Djebar, the painting foregrounds the relationship of the women to one another, to their own bodies and to the room in which they are enclosed, and one can see parallels between Djebar's work and that of Delacroix – for example, when she describes the women's meeting within the hammam, another 'female' space, and 'paints in' details of their physical appearance, including intimate details of their naked bodies. But for some critics, precisely such parallels are alarming. Marnia Lazreg, for one, remarks disapprovingly that 'She somehow considers the painting an expression of the lived reality of a group of women who had been corralled in one room to satisfy the curiosity of a French painter. Eager to provide historical evidence of women's "oppression" [a term Lazreg considers over-simple], she failed to see in the painting the product of the collusion of two men, a defeated native and a colonial artist.'[31]

From the latter perspective, Delacroix's painting is a highpoint – or lowpoint – of colonial triumphalism and masculine Orientalist fantasy. How such 'discourses' were prolonged and widely disseminated in the early twentieth century, especially as a visual tradition, has been analysed by Malek Alloula in his book *The Colonial Harem*, which offers a powerful polemical interpretation of the colonial postcards depicting North African women that appeared under the rubric 'Scènes et types'. Indeed, he compares one in particular to Delacroix's famous painting. 'The exotic postcard', he argues, 'is the vulgar expression of colonial euphoria just as much as Orientalist painting was, in its beginnings, the Romantic expression of the same euphoria'; and he concludes: 'Summarily, and in its customarily brutal idiom, the colonial postcard says this: these women, who were reputedly invisible or hidden, and, until now, beyond sight, are henceforth public.' Thus these images become a symbol of dispossession and the emblem of the colonizers' victory over the masculine society that held prohibitions on women in place.[32] Haddour pursues this argument, writing that: 'Unconsciously, unveiling her [the Algerian woman] meant breaking the "kernel of resistance" of the indigenous society, opening the inside store of tradition for European colonization. Delacroix's *Femmes d'Alger*, Camus's *The Outsider*, the "exotic" photographs studied by Alloula in *The Colonial Harem* are all representations of this colonial fantasy inscribed within a libidinous colonialism.'[33]

To the extent that Delacroix's picture must be interpreted, then, as an influential part of this tradition of representations and its imaginative/imaginary consolidation of the imperial project – on which the French had just embarked in Algeria when he painted it in 1832 – it seems a curious choice for the cover of Djebar's book. To critics such as Lazreg, it appears to offer literary 'scènes et types' that prolong that tradition still further. Such reflections cast a different light on some of those linguistic 'imports' I discussed earlier: if words such as 'odalisque' and 'narguilé' or 'houka' still sound 'foreign' after being used for so long in French, that may be because these notions are, as Alloula argues, a mainstay of certain European fantasies, those words studding 'mainstream' French with the alluringly and unassimilably foreign and exotic, the rivets of the Orientalist imagination.

How, then, can Djebar's use of Delacroix be justified? Although the context is very different, we are close, from a theoretical point of view, to issues raised in chapter 2 about Conrad's use of racist and imperialist discourse. Once again questions arise about the writer's responsibilities in relation to both the history of representations on which he or she draws and his or her own context of reception; and once again the sort of textual evidence that I will discuss here cannot give a fully convincing answer to the charge that the writing falls into complicity with a certain imperialist or neo-imperialist rhetoric, though it is a crucial sort of evidence to consider if one is to approach colonial history through fiction (or vice-versa) at all.

As we have already seen, Djebar's writing repeatedly alludes to, draws on, and positions itself in relation to, and within, colonial history, but is also unmistakably engaged in an international, post-independence context where colonialism and/or its 'legacy' need not, in her view, always be her prime concern (and a context of reception where a complex and equivocal prefiguration of such issues may attract literary-critical prestige).[34] The use of Delacroix is first a provocative means of asserting the validity of a certain focus on

gender and of recasting the relationship of her material to the framework of colonial and anti-colonial ideologies, even if those ideologies,
as we have seen, are shown nonetheless to impact on gender relations
in the post-independence era. Although it would be easy, then, and in
some contexts legitimate to apprehend Delacroix's position solely in
terms of stark 'colonial' oppositions – between colonizer and colonized, between 'indigenous' and 'foreign' culture – Djebar's gesture
may suggest that this 'colonial' framework, whether given a pro-
colonial or anti-/post-colonial inflection, can obscure or belittle the
importance of gender oppositions, and contribute to the continued
cultural marginalization of women in North African society.

Rather than dismissing the painting as just one example of the
Orientalist obsession with the harem, and of the colonialist's voyeur-
istic gaze, Djebar, as Lazreg notes, treats it as a form of testimony:

> That particular gaze had long been believed to be a stolen one because
> it was the stranger's, from outside the harem and the city.
>   In the last few decades – as each nationalism triumphs from place to
> place – it has become apparent that within the Orient, when it has been
> left to its own devices, the image of woman is not perceived differently,
> be it by the father, the husband, or, more uneasily, the brother or the
> son.[35]

Such remarks are uncomfortable not only, of course, in relation to the
historical context of Delacroix's work (Lazreg's point, one Djebar
clearly seeks to forestall here) but also in relation to the neo-imperialist
discourse wherein the status of women becomes a justification for
a prior condescension towards, and distrust of, 'Islam' and/or the
'Arab world', grasped at too high a level of generality in terms of
both ideology and culture.[36] Women's status across the whole varied
range of Islamic cultures is not a topic I can take on here, though it is a
pressing one in view of the widespread tendency to generalize wildly
about 'Islam' and treat Islamic history as if its historical 'development' were arrested (an attitude sometimes supported by half-baked
allusions to the current 'middle ages' of the Muslim calendar). Against
this backdrop it may indeed appear irresponsible to use the shorthand
of 'the Orient' or to posit a continuity for Arab women between the
harems of the past and the contemporary HLM (*habitation à loyer
modéré*, which was translated above as 'housing projects') – albeit
through the ambivalent gesture, in that quotation as in the subdiv-
isions of *Women of Algiers*, of linking (and separating) 'Today' and
'Yesterday'. It is against this backdrop too that Djebar's use of imagery of 'the veil' runs the risk of pandering to stereotypes: too often

many different sorts of scarf, headdress and so on are treated uncritically as manifestations of a single – and, for the opponents of 'veiling', monolithically oppressive – religious phenomenon, 'the veil', when from an Islamic perspective it is possible, and from a secular perspective necessary, to historicize and differentiate such varied habits and practices of dress – rather than 'explain' them in terms of a putatively timeless and self-explanatory religious 'fundament'.[37]

In considering Djebar's use of veil imagery in this light, I would argue that the ambivalent association of veiling in her work with self-expression and freedom as well as silence, anonymity and constraint should be seen as a form of engagement with these very issues – issues around the tradition of representations with which she is involved, and the relation between art and broader patterns of perception. In a sense, we are back in the territory of the 'representation of representations' discussed in chapter 2. Those remarks of Djebar's on Delacroix do not immediately concern the status of women, but rather draw attention to a certain 'gaze', and to the way that the 'image' of woman is, at a second remove, 'perceived', an image with its own history that is somewhat independent from the fluctuating and variegated historical reality to which it is applied. The 'freedom' afforded her by her writing is itself constrained and even, in a sense, tainted: running through much of her work is the pained sense that her personal and literary freedom has been bought at terrible historical cost. She puts this starkly when she remarks: 'I felt, finally, to how great an extent the French language that I write is based on the death of my brothers and sisters, plunging its roots into the corpses of those defeated in the conquest.'[38] It seems to me that her incorporation of Delacroix into her work could be felt to capture the same tension. If, on the one hand, her use of his title appears to claim for her writing a role in conveying a certain feminine reality, on the other hand, it also emblematizes something of her complex relationship not just to French history but also, specifically, to the French history of representations of Algeria and Algerian women. By writing in French she could be said to enter 'the French tradition', yet this too is highly ambivalent: in doing so, she helps redefine and expand that tradition, problematizing its 'Frenchness' both through her range of reference and by creating her own distinctive folds within the language; but she also encounters new constrictions and undergoes a different sort of depersonalization.[39] The reader, correspondingly, may gain certain insights, but may also be drawn into a certain voyeurism.

Whatever the parallels and continuities between Delacroix's and Djebar's work, there are also, of course, significant differences between his painting and her writing, not least in their relation to their respective subjects and audiences. On Djebar's interpretation Delacroix's women appear, in their silent confinement, 'absent to themselves, to their bodies, to their sensuality, to their happiness'.[40] The female characters in Djebar's text, by contrast, are able to speak, to act and indeed to problematize the terms of their own 'representation'. 'Their' agency falls within the space of fiction, but the leeway of interpretation is real, and Djebar acts upon it in the same moment that she depicts it.[41] To speak of 'voyeurism', then, may be to underplay the textual complexity of her *Women of Algiers*. At the same time, though, it may be to overplay the coercive powers of the visual, and of the visual tradition; it should be remembered, after all, not only that Djebar is responding to Delacroix's paintings but also, as her Postface indicates, that she is inspired by the whole series of canvases where Picasso reworked Delacroix at the time of the Algerian war. The title *Women of Algiers in their Apartment* comes to her not simply from Delacroix, in other words, but from, and via, Picasso too. So although it is true that Delacroix's paintings – made possible, like her own writing, by the French colonization of Algeria – contain stock elements of exoticism (a water pipe, slippers, jewellery, and the Black slave about whom Djebar, to some critics' consternation, has little to say), the terms in which Djebar describes them imply not only (as does Alloula) that even a stereotype may have some connection with the truth, or that the history of representations of North African women is in some sense her topic, but also that non-exoticist perspectives on such representations will always be possible.

Djebar's own perspective, according to which the whole scene in the harem is bathed in 'the light of a hothouse or an aquarium', opens Delacroix's paintings to a certain self-reflexive 'reading'.[42] That light makes the women both present and distant, and one might surmise from her description that it is palpably heightened so as to suggest not only, at the level of figuration, that the women are cultivated and contained like so many exotic specimens, but also, at the level of representation as such, that the paintings' own authority as 'testimony' is rendered indeterminate by the artifice that makes it possible to see the women in this light, and to 'see' the women at all. One might compare her recollection that when she wanted, as part of the cinematic project alluded to earlier, to film certain Berber women, she had to respect – but also in some sense to overcome – their resistance to having their image captured and exported; about this experience Djebar writes: 'I had to work with that constraint, and I can say that in a certain way I sought to respect it, to make a blank space [*ce vide*] become fiction.'[43] The remark could be taken, I think, to sum up Djebar's conception of fiction's work, calling into being imaginarily a reality or a history of which her fictions provide an imperfect representation, and, as I suggested earlier, (re-)opening a field of interpretation.

These claims, I should add, do not convert into speculations on the likely responses of Delacroix's and Djebar's audiences, or on Delacroix's personal attitude towards his subject: indeed, in a footnote Djebar remarks: 'The innovative talent of the painter Delacroix contrasts with the traditionalism of Delacroix the man.'[44] But Djebar's use of Delacroix serves to show that, as cultural artefacts, Delacroix's paintings are not reducible to the context from which they emerged and in relation to which they may be understood. Beyond that it appears evocative of the enabling constraints of any tradition of representations, endlessly, though not limitlessly, malleable and interpretable, and of the 'French' tradition, for her, in particular. Some of the same constraints that make the tradition an imperfect means of 'self'-expression (again, in general and for Djebar in particular) and a less than reliable historical record also serve partially to release the individual work from the circumstances of its production; the aesthetic conventions through which artists (or writers or viewers) approach a given historical reality also distance them from it.[45] So although one can interpret Delacroix's painting in terms of his personally retrograde views on women and his place in colonial history, and can treat it as a distinctly masculine and colonial work, it would be misleading to suggest that in discussing such factors one has arrived at the sole 'truth' of the painting, or even of its genesis. Rather, the significance of these factors is again precisely a matter of interpretation. Without having access to the real women and within certain conventions of representation, both Picasso and Djebar found it possible to formulate new interpretations of the historical material, and, in response to their work, their audience may do so too.

Fiction/autobiography: the literary self

Djebar's *Fantasia: An Algerian Cavalcade* is a somewhat different sort of text from *Women of Algiers*, at once more historical and more personal, and is often discussed by its author and critics as a work of autobiography. The cover of the original French edition is stamped with the word 'roman' (novel), but the decision to apply this label was apparently made not by Djebar but by publishers nervous about how the public would respond to a work of uncertain generic affiliation;

indeed, Djebar recalls that she had trouble finding anyone willing to publish it at all. Looking back on her decision to branch out in a new direction, she later remarked: 'I was not content, after the critical success of *Women of Algiers*, to keep singing the same old song: "how miserable to be a North African woman, a Muslim woman, a victim"!'[46] Her ironic tone may imply a certain critical distance from her earlier work, and certainly betokens a renewed wariness concerning the (largely non-Algerian) cultural context within which it was (favourably) received. What interests me here is the sort of response to this by now familiar problem that *Fantasia* may represent, especially in its involvement with autobiography as a genre.

Fantasia intercuts scenes from Djebar's own life and Algeria's past, and from both oral and written history. Revisiting colonial-era documents and placing them in a new context, Djebar pieces together scenes from the colonial encounter, underscoring its violence and, still more explicitly this time, the stake of representations within it. Djebar's literary reworking of these mainly French documents gives them a new emotional weight: in the remarkable chapter entitled 'Women, children, oxen dying in caves', for example, she gives a moving account of how 1500 members of the Ouled Riah tribe were slaughtered by the French army; soldiers lit fires billowing heat and smoke into the caves where the Ouled Riah had taken refuge, and they died there, crushed by their panicking animals or asphyxiated. In reconstructing this story, Djebar draws on a variety of sources, including a letter by an anonymous soldier, an eyewitness account published by a Spanish officer, and the official report by Colonel Pélissier. Although Pélissier's account of the action caused an outcry back in Paris, not everyone disapproved; another army man, Lieutenant-Colonel Canrobert, remarked: 'Pélissier made only one mistake: as he had a talent for writing, and was aware of this, he gave in his report an eloquent and realistic – much too realistic – description of the Arabs' suffering…'[47] 'Words can travel', remarks Djebar, who goes on: 'Yes, I am moved by an impulse that nags me like an earache: the impulse to thank Pélissier for his report which unleashed a political storm in Paris, but which allows me to reach out today to our own dead and weave a pattern of French words around them.'[48]

Djebar's surprising gesture of 'incongruous gratitude' towards Pélissier seems analogous to her earlier use of Delacroix, and makes it all the more apparent that she does not wish her appropriation of colonial representations to be read as an exculpation of colonialism and its agents. For most of her readers, historical material such as the story of the Ouled Riah is likely to be straightforwardly informative,

while the autobiographical material, or the presentation of her material as autobiographical, allows her to explore how, in ways for which
she cannot be held responsible, she as an individual and a writer is the
product of colonial history, and a beneficiary as well as a victim of its
legacy. Tied to an individual case, the narrative arguably has even
more minimal and uncertain claims of representativity than those that
are usually associated with (the notion of) fiction.[49]

Yet autobiography as a genre is not necessarily any less controversial than is fiction for a writer such as Djebar. In this connection
various critics have discussed North African cultural constraints on
speaking in the first person; Jean Déjeux, for instance, draws on
Mohammed Kacimi's recollections of a childhood 'in the religious
atmosphere of the *zaouïa*', where the mothers used to say: '"Only the
devil says 'I', only the devil eats alone, only the devil sleeps alone."'[50]
The taboo, Déjeux suggests, is especially strong for women: 'The
feminine "I" is doubly unconventional, since traditionally the
woman, consigned to the domestic space, is not expected to go public,
in masculine society, through an affirmation of personal autonomy.'[51]
According to Fatima Mernissi, it is this notion of personal autonomy
that runs counter to much North African and/or Islamic culture,
especially for a woman: 'Individualism, the person's claim to have
legitimate interests, views and opinions different from those of the
group, is an alien concept and fatal to heavily collectivist
Islam.... The woman, identified in the Muslim order as the embodi-
ment of uncontrolled desire and undisciplined passions, is precisely
the symbol of heavily suppressed individualistic trends.'[52] All the
same, however keenly such prohibitions may be felt in some quarters,
it should be pointed out that the cultural history through which they
are justified is, as ever, open to different interpretations. Again, then,
to talk of 'Islam' in these terms may already be over-general, although, insofar as what Déjeux describes is not really a taboo on a
pronoun but some sort of injunction against self-centredness, one is
dealing with a broad cultural phenomenon that would probably
stretch across not just the whole Islamic world but more or less all
other societies.

A related misgiving about North African autobiography is the
notion that the form or genre as such is itself alien and inappropriate.
Georges Gusdorf, for one, once argued that autobiography is an
inherently 'Western' (and imperialist) form, stating that 'it would
seem that autobiography is not to be found outside of our cultural
area; one would say that it expresses a concern peculiar to Western
man, a concern that has been of good use in his systematic conquest of
the universe and that he has communicated it to men of other cul-

tures; but those men will thereby have been annexed by a sort of intellectual colonizing to a mentality that was not their own.'[53] Such an argument appears over-simple, however, and somewhat ahistorical, when confronted with Djebar's writing, which attempts to complicate monadic versions of North Africa's cultural/linguistic history and to suggest that as a writer she has a place within a tradition that might stretch back not only to Apuleius' fiction but also to the *Confessions* of Augustine, who lived near present-day Annaba. Both writers, it may be noted, are also alluded to by Memmi in his 1964 anthology, where he refers to them as 'Latin-speaking North African writers'.[54] From such a perspective it is apparent that Algeria's and North Africa's cultural traditions are internally discontinuous and heterogeneous, that the fantasmatic boundaries of what Gusdorf speaks of as 'our' cultural area are unstable, and that his gesture of self-criticism is in effect double-edged, paradoxically ethnocentric in its denunciation of ethnocentrism.

The point on which I want to insist most strongly, though, is that it cannot be assumed that *'saying "I"'* and/or individualism are to be associated automatically with the practice of autobiography.[55] *Fantasia* unfixes any such association not only because the referent of the first-person pronoun is frequently unclear, and is evidently not always Djebar, but more importantly in that its textual treatment of selfhood appears only obliquely 'self-expressive' and does not support an understanding of the individual as self-centred, as autonomous, or as by definition a potential agent of imperialism.[56] Even if approaching *Fantasia* as 'autobiographical', the reader is unlikely to feel after reading it that she or he is in firm possession of many biographical facts, or indeed that Djebar 'has' a stable prelinguistic self or individual identity that the text secondarily captures. In this respect, in fact, 'autobiography' as a term may be misleading, or may serve to describe a mode of reading more than of writing.

An account of how the text 'resists' a conventional 'autobiographical' mode of reading can be offered on at least two levels, in terms of two different concepts of 'voice' (a term associated by Djebar with the notion of veiling, as we saw earlier). The idea of 'voice' that is widely used in relation to fiction appears highly pertinent to autobiography, and perhaps especially so (for reasons linked to the demands of representativity placed upon 'minority' writers) for women writers from former colonies. As Celia Britton notes,

> at the intersection of postcolonial and feminist theory, a substantial body of critical texts now exists on literary representations of the subjectivity of postcolonial women. These representations may be

fictional or autobiographical, and in any case the difference between
the two genres is minimized... The fact that both the authors and the
protagonists of these novels are female in itself encourages critics
to assume some kind of autobiographical continuity between the
two – what Carole Boyce Davies and Elaine Savory Fido in their
introduction to *Out of the Kumbla* call 'a doubled female voice of
woman-poet-author and woman-speaking-subject'.

   This specifically female *voice* is in fact a central concept of this
critical discourse; the concern is with (de)colonized women as silenced
subjects finding a voice, being 'authorized' to 'speak'. The theorization
of subjectivity in autobiography is underpinned by the notion of
'coming to voice', as Sidonie Smith and Julia Watson point out in
their introduction to *Women, Autobiography, Theory*.[57]

Britton goes on to suggest that 'the theoretical move from the human-
ist full subject to the postpoststructuralist subject... is paralleled on
the level of postcolonial fiction by a move from a modernist lack of
self to a postmodernist plurality of self', and argues that the latter
does not always escape an over-simple model of expressivity and of
ultimately unified selfhood. Against this she champions a Lacanian
model wherein, 'unlike the "coming to voice" model, the subject is
never in conscious possession of his/her voice.'[58]

   Britton's model lends itself well to Djebar's autobiographical
writing, implying that, while it may, then, be an example of how
women may 'write themselves into history', in Smith's and Watson's
phrase (and show that they are already a part of that history, though a
neglected one),[59] the self that Djebar expresses or writes exists only in
dialectic with history. History, so to speak, writes itself into and
constitutes the self. The 'voice' embodied in the text is correspondingly composite and fluctuating, to a degree that distances it from any
cohesive *sense* of self or identity, the latter emerging as a kind of
fiction. 'An identity', as Derrida puts it, 'is never given, received, or
attained, only the interminable and indefinitely fantasmatic process of
identification endures.'[60] Reading and writing (of fiction, history, or
for that matter theory) become part of the process through which
identity or the sense of self is constantly sought and 'found'.

   Here this first point about the compositeness and fictionality of
identity splits into a second, and precisely here the distinction between fiction and autobiography starts to dissolve, raising doubts
about any interpretation of the text that makes it testify to what the
self (including even the non-identical Lacanian self) actually is. The
experience that *Fantasia* offers is less that of any conventionally
'unreliable' narrative 'voice' or of any such testimony than of a certain
kind of restless and at times impenetrable textual work. As such it is

distinctly a matter of writing rather than 'speech', a 'postcolonial' literary supplement to the colonial historiography on which it draws. The self of the autobiographical text, arrested on the page, is captured as a work of fiction in the sense of being something constituted not only, from one direction, through the mobilities of identification and of history but also, from the other, through the framework of literary genre. For the reader, it should be noticed, biographical accuracy thus becomes indeterminable, but in a way that means it is unlikely to appear the most important aspect of the work: in practice it may not greatly matter, then, if Djebar's autobiography is about the author-figure to whom the pen-name points as much as the individual whom it veils. Especially in view of Djebar's own soft-spot for wordplay, perhaps it is not too preposterous to hear an echo of her pen-name in the title *Ces voix qui m'*assiè*gent*: so to put it another way, although from one perspective Djebar's 'autobiography' – like her collection of essays – records and is woven from the multiplicity of voices that 'besiege' and 'woo' her, including colonial voices, nationalist rhetor-icians and Zhdanovist critics, from another it is her texts, cross-shot with historical threads, that constitute 'Assia Djebar' as a literary identity and as their own object of literary description.[61]

If, then, Djebar's work corresponds to Sheringham's eloquent de-scription of 'the sense of a disparity between the self as a historical phenomenon, perceptible in a life history, and the self as something outside and perhaps at odds with history', and if this 'recurrent theme' in autobiography points to 'a picture of autobiography as a passage through and a constant negotiation with different forms of otherness', a crucial part of that process, for reader and writer alike, could be said to consist in the encounter with the otherness of literary form.[62] In this connection it is illuminating to realize that the title *Ces voix qui m'assiègent* is inspired by Beckett's *The Unnamable*, which provides the epigraph for the subsection of Djebar's book on 'The writing of autobiography'. That epigraph reads:

> This voice that speaks...It issues from me, it fills me, it clamours against my walls, it is not mine, I can't stop it, I can't prevent it, from tearing me, racking me, assailing me [*m'assiéger*]. It is not mine, I have none, I have no voice and must speak, that is all I know, it's round that I must revolve, of that I must speak, with this voice that is not mine, but can only be mine, since there is no one but me.[63]

The quotation is resonant on various levels in relation to Djebar's work, not least in that it recalls the specificity of Beckett's own relationship to colonial history, and his decision to write in two languages, one of which was for him, as an English-speaking Irish-man, both his mother tongue and an imperial language. The gesture of disowning his own voice, perhaps reminiscent of Djebar's sense of 'translating' into French, may be seen at once as specific to that context and as a more general point about language, and it is a gesture echoed almost verbatim by Derrida (a French-speaking Algerian Jew) in *Monolingualism of the Other* when he writes: 'This language, the only one which I am thus destined to speak as long as speaking is a possibility for me . . . never will this language be mine.'[64] But that gesture is also, of course, a distinctly literary one, and the 'voice' that *emerges* in this way, in Beckett as in Djebar, to the extent that it is irreducibly literary, is in a crucial sense not a voice at all.

At issue here is a particular conception of literature as the 'grounds of the groundless [or place of the non-place, *lieu du non-lieu*]', whose 'oracles', Djebar notes, were Kafka, Beckett and Blanchot. Indeed it owes a great deal to Blanchot in particular, who is not only named but also echoed several times in this passage: in the same paragraph Djebar talks of 'the writing of disaster', and that phrase *lieu du non-lieu* (one I will discuss further in the Conclusion) is distinctly Blan-chotian.[65] The 'narrative voice' for Blanchot is distinct from an authorial or narratorial one, and is described as 'a neutral voice that speaks the work from that placeless place [*ce lieu sans lieu*] where the work is silent.'[66] Correspondingly, when Blanchot himself turns his attention to Beckett's *The Unnamable*, he writes:

> Who then is speaking here? Is it 'the author'? But to whom can such a term refer since anyhow he who writes is no longer Beckett but the urge that sweeps him out of himself, turns him into a nameless being, the Unnamable, a being without being [*un être sans être*] who can neither live nor die, stop nor start, . . . the vacant site [*le lieu vide*] where speaks the redundancy of idle words under the ill-fitting cloak of a porous, agonising I?[67]

This '*lieu vide*' is reminiscent of the 'blank space' or '*vide*' into and from which Djebar's fiction projects itself, while the notion of the 'neutral' may be linked to that Barthesian concept of *écriture blanche* that was discussed in chapter 3. By this point, clearly, we are dealing with concepts of literature and 'voice' that are at some distance from those notions of national literature, authenticity and identity con-sidered in the last chapter. Djebar's 'literary' autobiography, I am suggesting, is in many ways far closer to the concerns of the subcanon to which she herself alludes, the one that includes Kafka, Beckett, Blanchot, Mallarmé, and even Derrida. It seeks to resist those readers who would make her 'speak' for a particular place, or even for her self, and in so doing dissolves at once towards history and towards fiction. Therein lies its particularity, but that movement of dissolution may also be, in ways that the Conclusion will now explore, exemplary of the literary as such.

6

Conclusion:
Literature and the Work
of Criticism

In an essay on postcolonialism, postmodernism and poststructural-ism, Stephen Slemon writes that, in postcolonial criticism, the question of representation 'necessarily bifurcates under a dual agenda: which is to continue the resistance to (neo)colonialism through a deconstructive reading of its rhetoric *and* to retrieve and reinscribe those post-colonial social traditions that in literature issue forth on a thematic level, and within a realist problematic, as principles of cultural identity and survival.' For him, postcolonial criticism is thus 'radically fractured and contradictory'.[1]

As I suggested in the Introduction, I have to some extent followed this 'dual agenda', seeking to explore the idea, especially in the chapters on *Heart of Darkness* and *The Outsider*, that different varieties of 'realism' from the colonial era may be involved with and lend support to colonial discourse. The way that history mediates the relation of the realistic to the real means that what may appear the merely descriptive turns out to contain an ideological thrust, as was seen in my discussions of Marlow's/Conrad's (non-)description of Africans and Meursault's/Camus's (non-)description of Arabs. On the other side of Slemon's fracture was my discussion of texts by two North Africans, where I broached various themes of 'cultural identity', among them the status of 'minorities', women's relation to nationalism and post-independence culture, the complexities of the colonial 'legacy' (including its linguistic mark), and the weight of social tradition in the post-independence era.

At the same time, however, I have tried to question the basis on which the perceived and real dualism of the colonizer/colonized has tended to translate into divergent or even, as Slemon suggests, contradictory approaches among literary critics, and to uncover other fractures in critical practice and its objects. With *Heart of Darkness*, for example, I tried to show how the text engaged with a series of discursive contexts, internally and externally – literary, generic, ideological, historical – out of which it emerged and in relation to and through which it would have been read when first published. In this way I wanted to show that what was at stake in any particular instance of colonial 'rhetoric' needs to be reconstructed before it can be 'deconstructed' or criticized. The past, to coin a phrase, is another country, and one risks anachronism, a sort of ethnocentricity of time, if one takes colonial 'discourse' or rhetoric out of history, views 'it' as monolithic, or assumes that a single smooth path leads from colonialism to neocolonialism.

My argument about *Heart of Darkness* showed the pitfalls, for literary critics who speculate on the ideological work of fiction, of making assumptions that are unwarranted historically. I returned to this theme in my discussion of *The Outsider* and the notion of identification, examining that concept first, again, on a historical level, then on a more theoretical plane where, as I implied in that chapter, perhaps the most fundamental fracture in the mind of many critics is the one dividing them from those other readers who are assumed to submit passively to fiction and history alike. Of course, many of the conventions of reception, along with many other conventions and assumptions of one's time, are assimilated unconsciously, and the particular mixture of historical connectedness and disconnectedness in all the texts I have discussed was doubtless the result of forces that exceeded the bounds of the author's or readers' consciousness. There is a reasonable basis, then, for critics' anxieties about how conservative facets of the history of representations or of consciousness renew themselves, irrespective of authors' intentions. As I emphasized in connection with Djebar's *Women of Algiers*, however, in counterbalance rather than contradiction to such anxieties, Djebar's experiences as a writer and a reader show not only that conventions of reception shift (partly under pressure from fiction itself), but also that they afford any reader room to read creatively and critically.

The examples of Djebar's and Chraïbi's work showed too what may be oversimplified or lost if one allows one part of the critical agenda to apply to 'colonial' works and another part to the 'postcolonial'. For one thing, the chronology and nature of the shift from 'colonial' to 'postcolonial' literature are evidently fuzzy; it would be difficult to find a text that moved more disorientatingly than *The Simple Past* between what Donadey called 'the oppositional and the complicit', a movement that, it will be remembered, she identified as a characteristic of 'postcolonial' fiction – yet Chraïbi's novel was 'postcolonial' in this sense both *avant la lettre* and before Moroccan independence. But, as I emphasized in chapter 4, what is more important, for both its relation to history and, so to speak, its resistance to it, is that its slipperiness is not just ideological but also distinctly literary, in a way that may indeed make it difficult for the postcolonial critic not to be drawn into compromise or contradiction. Some time before postcolonial criticism emerged as such, novels such as Chraïbi's were already using specifically literary strategies at once to address and to frustrate those readers/critics who would approach his work as naïve realism and seek to recuperate from it certain social and political themes.

In this Conclusion I want to think some more about how the 'specifically literary' might work in such respects, how it might be defined, and what its implications are for the work of criticism, with whose history it is entwined. The first thing to notice about the example of *The Simple Past* is that its uncertain 'realism' puts it in an uneasy relation to either strand of the critical agenda as described by Slemon, in such a way as to raise doubts about his account of the 'realist problematic'. That account draws on Bhabha, who argues that 'realism manifestly den[ies its] own material and historical construction' and that, when an '"image"' in colonial literature is 'measured against the "essential" or "original" in order to establish its degree of *representativeness*, the correctness of the image[, t]he text is not seen as *productive* of meaning but essentially reflective or expressive.'[2] But, as I argued in my discussion of identification, to imply, as does Bhabha, that 'realist' literature propagates an illusion to which (other) people fall prey is an unjustifiable, if commonplace, critical simplification, whose tendentiousness can be seen in his anthropomorphic attribution of agency to 'realism', and in his use of the bug-words 'essential' and 'essentially'. I suggested earlier that the ways in which we as readers imagine a literary representation to 'be' real are inextricable from our fundamental awareness that in crucial respects it is not; at the same time, however, it inevitably connects with reality in various ways, and indeed may represent it more or less correctly.

'Measuring' a text (and here I, like Bhabha, am talking primarily about fiction) against (one's sense of) reality, and in that sense testing its representativity, need not imply a naïve understanding of reference, and is in any case an integral and basic part of interpretation. From this perspective the 'suspension of the referent' which Slemon sees as marking poststructuralism's break with the 'realist problematic' would instead appear to be consonant with that problematic and with the constitution of the literary as such. As Derrida puts it (in terms that I hope will become clearer in the course of this chapter), 'There is no literature without a *suspended* relation to meaning and reference. *Suspended* means *suspense*, but also *dependence*, condition, conditionality.'[3] This notion of suspension should be distinguished, then, from any concept of literary fiction that makes it appear wholly non-'referential', that *opposes* semiosis to mimesis, or that dwells exclusively on its 'unreality'. 'Literature' is often understood not only as designating books of an imaginative or creative kind, but also more specifically as applying to imaginative or creative subject matter, an understanding that has a theoretical counterpart of sorts in those strains of poststructuralist thought that treat the reader's sense of referentiality as a form of naïvety. Yet as Thomas Pavel points out, 'Beyond particular objects [individuals, actions . . .], writers of fiction do not invent very much, since properties and abstract notions found in fiction are virtually always part of the actual world.'[4] The way a certain racial/racist discourse traverses *The Outsider* is an example of this, and Camus's text could be said at moments merely to re-present habitual representations of racial difference that exist only through and in their representations. Not only the notion of *autonomy* but also notions such as *identification* and even *realism* or *reference*, in their conception of the separation of the text and the world, may thus suggest too self-contained a model both of the self and of fiction. To repeat my earlier example, they may thus disguise the ways in which discourse on the 'Arabe' may effectively be *identical* across the fictional and non-fictional worlds, and may be entwined through the reader's and the author's psyche as much as through the narrative.

If readers are carried beyond the textual bounds of the fictional world it is firstly, then, because texts are themselves worldly, in the sense that they are already involved with and constituted through extra-literary discourse. Secondly it is because, as Pavel puts it, 'works of fiction, just like historical studies, are *inferential projects* that entice the reader to link particular events narrated about particular objects to properties and abstract notions at various levels of generality.'[5] For such reasons, treating literary texts as 'representative' of *something* is probably inevitable, and is certainly an element of how they are usually read. It is partly in this sense that the specificity of literature can be defined by Derrida as a paradoxical non-specificity: in his words, 'literature . . . always is, it says, it does something else, something other than itself, and it itself moreover is only that, something other than itself.'[6]

These remarks may be compared with an argument about reception made by Rabinowitz, who comments with reference to *Heart of*

Darkness that critics tend to follow what he calls 'the Rule of Abstract Displacement':

> The first step involves an act of substitution: according to this rule, good literature is always treated as if it were about something else.... This substitution is linked, however, to a second step, an act of generalization. As Holland puts it, traditional interpretive practice assumes that 'literary meaning is a statement of what in the literary work is of sufficient generality to be "worth something to everybody"' – often in the form of a 'universal proposition'.[7]

In certain respects, I am suggesting, it may in fact be unavoidable that, as Iser puts it, 'Whatever realities are transposed into the text, they turn into signs for something else.'[8] For the reader this may mean minimally the inevitable play of association; for the critic, it mostly means offering a relatively sustained interpretation that goes beyond mere summary and reiteration of plot. The interpretations that emerge from this process are clearly highly varied, however, politically and in many other ways, and need not lead in the direction of 'traditional interpretive practice'. Nor, as I hope my own interpretation of *Heart of Darkness* demonstrated, need they lead away from the 'specific', itself a relative term (every generalization is specific at some level); so, contrary to what Rabinowitz suggests, the interpretative move 'away' from the specific, and in a sense from the text, need not be considered inherently problematic from a political point of view.

All the same, the 'politics of displacement' become an issue as one considers historical variations in what has qualified as *significant* (in) criticism and what has passed for appropriate professional comment on a literary text. The notion that literature delivers up 'universal propositions', to take Holland's phrase, has been under attack for some time from various sorts of critic. Postcolonial theorists are among those to have argued repeatedly that a certain notion of universal values, for example as vehicled in Christian doctrine, served as a justification for imperial expansion, and that particular values that appear or are treated as universal turn out to be culturally and historically specific. I do not think that these are grounds on which to criticize the notion of the 'universal' as such, contrary to what many postcolonial critics believe – a topic I will pursue further in the Afterword; they are, however, strong grounds on which to question the notion that literature is a repository of 'timeless' values, or to explore links between literary criticism, canon-formation (to which issue I have been able to give only limited attention), the notion of national literature as at once specific to a national 'identity' and universal in its scope, and imperialism.

Said's critique of the 'ethos suggesting universality and humanism' that has (or had?) surrounded *The Outsider* is an example of the kind of criticism that arises from these premises, but, in hesitating over the way that certain 'facts of imperial actuality' are 'plainly given' in the text, Said appears unsure, as I noted in chapter 3, how far the author, or indeed the text itself, should be held responsible for its interpretative fate – a question that arises whether one is more preoccupied with the ideological complicity into which fiction may fall or the criticism it may offer, and whether or not one makes space for any unconscious (or not fully conscious) facets of writing and reading. It is striking in this regard to compare the reception of Camus's novel, where the dominant critical response, at least until recently, took no account of its colonial context, with that of *The Simple Past*, a text not so distant historically or in its geographical 'origins' and setting, but one for which, as I noted earlier, the dominant critical response was radically different – and different not only in that its colonial context was paramount, but also, relatedly, in that the question of the author's responsibilities in regard to his own field of reception arose so quickly and so violently. What has become apparent by this point is that, in thinking about what the literary text is, what its impact has been, and what its 'responsibilities' might be, the critic must take account of the history of criticism itself.

Before thinking about the implications this may have for the work of criticism, I want to say a little more about the problems of defining literature as such. Although certain uses of language, for example, may in themselves seem characteristically literary, such as the exorbitancy of language that could be said to distinguish *Heart of Darkness* or *Fantasia* from speech, say, or from political discourse, it is evident that speech and political discourse may also be exorbitant, and that other literary authors favour linguistic simplicity and/or the rhythms of spoken language. In the end the difference between the literary and the non-literary, or the fictional and non-fictional, is not reliably marked in the language of a given text, either stylistically or in terms of its semantic composition (in the sense that the 'fictional world' is not necessarily unreal).[9] Any attempt to pin successful 'literariness' or fictionality to enumerable textual characteristics is thus likely to prove inadequate to the range of texts to which it might be expected to apply, as indeed is quickly apparent when discussing the sort of writing that has forced postcolonial critics to rethink the relations between literature, literacy, canonicity and oral culture, or to reconsider the legitimation of particular forms of a given language as standard – or as literary.

Here one is dealing not with vagueness but with a quite particular form of indeterminacy. As Derrida argues, 'there is no text which is literary *in itself.*' Consequently, 'even if a phenomenon called "literature" appeared historically in Europe, at such and such a date, this does not mean that one can identify the literary object in a rigorous way. It doesn't mean that there is an essence of literature. It even means the opposite. . . . Literarity is not a natural essence, an intrinsic property of the text. It is the correlative of an intentional relation to the text.'[10] Derrida's characterization of literature in these terms is to a significant degree inspired by Blanchot, to whose notion of voice and of the literary Djebar too, as we have seen, owes an acknowledged debt; it also draws on (and problematizes) a phenomenological vocabulary that I do not intend to deploy or discuss here.[11] But, to use a somewhat different vocabulary, what the literary *is* could be said to exist in dialectic between particular forms of writing and reading. Emerging and changing historically, it at once derives from and makes possible particular works of literature *and also of criticism*, which have treated it variously as a repository of timeless values or a dangerously seductive version of imperialist discourse. Something about its historical constitution, as Derrida suggests, has made literature as such simultaneously accessible and resistant to *all* sorts of interpretation/appropriation, and so resistant to interpretative closure. It is on such grounds that Derrida embarks on a critique of 'the very possibility of thematic criticism';[12] and, discussing 'literature' as a development distinct from *belles-lettres*, he argues that it has become linked with conventions (which might include the writer's/ reader's 'suspension of the referent') and institutions that 'guarantee it in principle the right to say anything [*le droit de tout dire*]'. In this way, he goes on, 'literature links its destiny to a certain non-censorship, to the space of democratic freedom', adding:

> But this authorization to say anything constitutes the author, paradoxically, as an author who is responsible to no one, not even to himself, for what, for example, the people or the characters in his works say and do, nor consequently for what he is supposed to have written him (or her-) self. . . . This authorization to say everything (which goes hand in hand, however, with democracy as the apparent hyper-responsibilization of the 'subject') recognizes a right of absolute non-response, where there can be no question of responding, of being able or obliged to respond. . . . Something of literature has begun if it becomes impossible to decide whether, when I speak of something, I am speaking of some thing (of the thing itself, this one, for its own sake) or whether I am

giving an example, an example of something or an example of the fact that I can speak of something, of my way of speaking about something, of the possibility, in general, of speaking of something, in general, or there again of writing this word, and so on. For example, what if I say 'I', if I write in the first person or if I write an 'autobiographical' text, as they say. No-one can seriously contradict me if I affirm (or imply, through an ellipsis, without making it a theme) that I am not writing an 'autobiographical' text but a text *on* autobiography of which this text is an example. No-one can seriously contradict me if I say (or imply, etc.) that I am not writing about myself but about my 'self', about one self among others or about the self in general, offering an example: I am merely an example or I am exemplary.[13]

These remarks seem particularly suggestive in relation to the blurring of the fiction/autobiography distinction in Djebar's writing, with its inbuilt consideration of what about it is exemplary and what not, but more broadly they cast light, I think, on what one might call the *mode* of all the literary texts on which I have focused, or the mode in which I and other critics have focused on them as literature. As I suggested in connection with *Heart of Darkness*, an analysis along the lines that Derrida sketches out ('it's not racism, it's *about* racism', etc.) is by definition possible for *any* literary text; but it works best, and becomes relatively convincing, in the case of a text that is 'highly' literary in Derrida's or Blanchot's sense (or that corresponds to Genette's understanding of modernism). To put it another way, it is precisely because it consists of complex narrative layerings and is bathed in semantic uncertainty – precisely, then, because of a certain indeterminacy – that *Heart of Darkness* seems a successful and preeminently literary text (thereby positioning Conrad, as I suggested in chapter 2, as a 'man of letters' in the literary field), and that it makes Achebe's charge seem not wrong, perhaps, but misplaced. Likewise such characteristics are integral to its attraction for those critics who have returned to and reinterpreted it time and again. *The Inheritors*, by contrast, though *more* 'fictional' in the sense that its world is unreal and impossible, and also (as we saw earlier) more unequivocally metaphorical, is less literary, in that it is more one-dimensional, more of a *roman à clef* whose interest died with the context to which it was tied. So the fact that the putative timelessness of literature is, in crucial respects, a myth, has not prevented it from shaping what constitutes the literary and affecting its relation to time and to history – and not necessarily or only in negative ways: Morel's *Red Rubber*, a non-literary text that made determinate claims about the Congo Free State, was far more important politically in its day than was Conrad's story, but few people read it now, and few, for that matter, read *The*

Inheritors. Among those who do, moreover, a good proportion must have come to those texts, and come to know anything at all of the Congo's colonial history, via *Heart of Darkness*.

The characterization of the literary given by Derrida also implies, of course, that 'literariness' cannot *force* people to react to the text 'literarily' in his sense, and that literariness cannot travel outside the conventions and institutions to which he alludes. In the context in which *The Simple Past* was published, for example, it is clear that the 'right of absolute non-response' was not definitively won. Even within those countries where conventions and institutions have made legal or official condemnation of literature relatively unlikely, it should be added, the 'right' of literature to 'say anything' is, as Derrida notes, far from universally recognized. Evidently, the currency of any notion of literary/authorial 'autonomy', or of any model of the capabilities and responsibilities of 'literature', is culturally and historically limited. The *Satanic Verses* affair provides another striking illustration of this fact; as with *The Simple Past*, the novel's qualities as a sophisticated and stimulating piece of fiction were effectively imperceptible, and/or irrelevant, to those approaching it within a certain political framework and/or outside a certain literary culture which, though international and cosmopolitan, remains far from global. As Richard Webster notes, for many people around the world, Rushdie's conception of the work of fiction – a conception suggested in his remark, in response to the burning of his book in Bradford, that for him literature fills a 'God-shaped hole' – would be baffling.[14]

Although much of the debate about *The Satanic Verses* or *The Simple Past* actually had little to do with the texts, providing a conduit for political and ideological contests whose motives and goals lay elsewhere, both texts were genuinely provocative (at least within a certain context) in the sense that they contained elements of social and cultural critique, broached controversial themes, and used language that many readers might find vulgar or aggressive. It is evidently more because of than in spite of this that such writing appeals to many critics, in a way that says something further about current conceptions of literature and of critics' own role. 'The purpose of literature, we have come to believe', writes Stanley Fish (where 'we' must refer primarily to critics), 'is to problematize, to disturb the settled surface of commonly held truths. John Beverley is only one of the more recent theorists to proclaim that we "tend to think of literature as a sanctioned space for the expression of social dissidence".'[15] The conquest of such a space is almost bound, I think, to seem valuable to the literary critic, and its dimensions, consistency and security can be tested (and the space thus in some sense conquered) only through testing its limits. Literature that does this – including not just Chraïbi's work but also Djebar's, viewed in its own slightly different context or contexts – evidently achieves something of its effect through a sort of parasitism on the taboos that it makes a display of transgressing, such that it not only exercises a certain freedom but reminds you, so to speak, that it is doing so. In the face of the expectation that he as a writer should act as a spokesperson, then, or of the 'mark of the plural' described by Memmi, Chraïbi's evasiveness must appear at least understandable to the critic, while in relation to the demands of representativity characteristic of its literary/critical context the riotous prose of *The Simple Past* itself is likely to seem admirably complex and resilient.

From this perspective, the vexedness of *The Simple Past*'s reception could be seen to offer a perverse vindication of Chraïbi's choices. I want to argue in conclusion, however, that to accept this is to accept that, while it may, then, be tempting to see the novel, taken as a whole, as subversive or progressive in terms of 'literary politics', that subversiveness is fundamentally politically indeterminate, or 'political' only in the (important) sense that it is specific to and constitutive of that a-responsible space of representation described by Derrida.[16] Another way of putting this, as Derrida's allusion to censorship suggests, is in terms of the emergence of a specifically literary freedom of expression, a notion that echoes through various passages in his work: his phrase about literature's right to 'say everything' nods to the Marquis de Sade, with whom the phrase is closely associated, particularly, of course, in relation to censorship and censorious reading practices; following Blanchot, he remarks that 'narratorial voice' (as distinct from 'narrative voice') '(cor)responds to a form of policing, to its force, to law and order'; and he insists that the writer 'must sometimes demand a certain irresponsibility, at least as regards ideological powers, of a Zhdanovian type for example, which try to call him back to extremely determinate responsibilities before socio-political or ideological bodies.'[17] The latter comments were made partly, it should be noted, to explain why he signed a petition in defence of Rushdie in the face of the death sentence pronounced on him from Iran (despite his misgivings about the the petition's phrasing concerning literature's 'critical function'); and in the present context, the reference to Zhdanovism recalls Djebar's tangles with, and resistance to, what she called 'Zhdanovist' critics.[18] All of this suggests that, when Djebar speaks of literature as the *lieu du non-lieu* (which I translated in chapter 5 as the 'grounds of the groundless' or 'place of the placeless'), the legal resonance is crucial: if juridically a *non-lieu* is declared it means that there are no grounds on which a prosecution may take place. The literary is being defined here as the notional 'space' in relation to which any such prosecution, any attack on the author's freedom, would appear illegitimate.[19]

To promote freedom of literary expression, or the broader freedom of expression of which it is a part, one need not believe that every use of it is 'responsible' or positive, in whatever terms (indeed, logically, one need not even believe that *on balance* this will be the case), and those promoting it need not pretend otherwise. Such freedom must be imagined to exist in some sense prior to and distinct from the uses made of it – something hinted at provocatively by Chraïbi in *The Butts* through his three subtitles, 'Copyright', 'Imprimatur' and 'Nihil obstat'; the phrases all pertain to the right to publish one's ideas, but have no precise relation to the sections' contents. In sanctioning a space for 'social dissidence', to look at it another way, one is potentially also sanctioning a space for social conformism and conservatism. It should be recognized, moreover, that dissidence and conformism alike are contextual and historical; we have seen how Chraïbi's *The Simple Past* and Djebar's *Women of Algiers*, for example, or at least certain aspects of those texts, have appeared conservative in some contexts, although – and as – they are dissident in others. Colonial history is one such context, literary history another, and literary-critical history another again (though all, as we have seen, are linked); and it is worth noting that, while on one level, or in some contexts, a novel such as *The Satanic Verses* may indeed 'disturb the settled surface of commonly held truths', in so doing it meets quite comfortably the expectations of those critics who have come to valorize exactly this sort of thing in literature.

To some extent, of course, my discussions of Chraïbi and Djebar have followed that familiar critical line, valorizing their own particular forms of dissidence. Against the sense that their resistance to appropriations and final judgements is the culmination of a certain sort of literary 'development', however, that their writing is (in certain respects) subversive, and that they work both from and towards a certain idea of artistic 'autonomy', I have tried to balance a sense of the limits and conventions, contextual and textual, within which they have operated. In particular I have tried to emphasize the inherent openness of their texts to history and indeed judgement, their particular political equivocations, and their inevitable dependence on norms of interpretation that link the fictional to the real.[20]

All of these issues are pertinent to *Heart of Darkness* too, to which I will now turn one last time, in order to recap and make some concluding remarks about two different aspects of the postcolonial literary-critical work that this book has tried to explore both in theory and in practice. I remarked earlier, in connection with Conrad's text, that if one's ultimate concerns are political, then a certain focus on the literary may seem only trivially legitimate. But when a critic writes impatiently that 'The "message" of *Heart of Darkness* is that Western civilization is at base as barbarous as African society – a viewpoint which disturbs imperialist assumptions to the precise degree that it reinforces them', the inverted commas around 'message' signal that the relation between the world, the text and the reader is being oversimplified – and that the critic knows it.[21] One of the aims of this book has been to show that a censorious gesture of this sort neglects forms of literary/critical attention that are worth sustaining, and that the gesture's apparent political incisiveness is undercut by its disregard for the detail of the text's historicity and literarity.

As far as textual historicity is concerned I have tried to explore different ways in which all writing, as I argued earlier in this Conclusion, is 'worldly', for good and for bad. The first aspect of postcolonial criticism on which I have wanted to insist consists in fleshing out and assessing that worldliness, which means, most obviously, recovering those colonial and post-independence contexts and ideologies that the texts bring into play. As we have seen, qualities such as reflexivity, polysemy, 'modernism', 'realism', 'unrealism', or 'fictionality' do not place writing outside the historical and ideological problematics raised in this way. The work of narrative fiction, I have argued, can never be *wholly* or 'purely' literary; it 'always is, it says, it does something else', to repeat Derrida's phrase. So if racist discourse, say, can be found within the text, then in a sense, as I reiterated earlier in this Conclusion, it is simply present – and in some sense active – as well as 'represented'. By the same token, it is apprehended through modes of cognition that orient the reader in relation not just to the fictional world but also to the world more widely. The critic wanting to assess the ideological work that a given piece of fiction has performed must recognize, however, that literature can frame ideological and historical material in different ways, and that particular readers' responses will have varied historically. Among the contexts and modes of cognition with which the reader is involved, in other words, and of which he or she must have some degree of awareness, are the historical conventions of reading and literature as such.

The second strand of criticism on which I have focused consists in that form of attention through which 'literature as such' comes to light. At least as far as narrative fiction is concerned, 'readings' in that particular critical mode are not really instances of reading in its usual sense at all; normally when one reads fiction, as I have suggested already, the urge to settle on a meaning, to find a significant level of coherence, and to find ways of (re-)connecting the text to the real, is probably irresistible. A certain sort of 'criticism', however, makes any 'reading' in this ordinary sense seem incomplete, finding in the text ambiguities and richnesses to which any one interpretation appears inadequate. Its peculiarly detailed scrutiny (taking account of how the narrative is 'framed', and so on) thus comes to seem necessary to do *justice* to a text such as Conrad's, perceiving – and creating – 'layers of insulation' (to repeat Achebe's phrase) between the author/reader and the moral universe of the story, and between the text and the critic (or censor).

If this second strand of criticism serves to counter the sort of pointed ideological attack made by Achebe, then, it does so not really by contradicting or blunting it, but by deflecting it, or by undermining the basis on which *any* such conclusive judgement may be made. Responding to Achebe in his essay ' "A bloody racist": about Achebe's view of Conrad', and trying to avoid any reductive notion of an ideological 'message', Cedric Watts argues that 'the moral value of literary works may lie in their dialectical rather than their exemplary force: in the vigour of their challenges to moral presuppositions rather than in their commendation of any readily-paraphrasable and accept-able moral position.' He soon concedes that even this model may be tendentious, however, and concludes:

> it appears that the originality of mind that makes an admirable literary work is often linked to a subversive attitude to cultural prejudices and presuppositions. However, we should be aware of sentimentalizing such subversiveness by assuming that it is necessarily 'liberal' or 'pro-gressive'. As the available mishmash of cultural prejudices and presup-positions includes both the liberal and the illiberal, so the work may as readily subvert the former by its illiberality of outlook as the latter by its liberality.[22]

A text would seem to qualify as 'subversive' in this sense only if it is not reliably distinguishable from the thing it could be said to subvert, and if it may fail to confront reactionary myths, or may even be taken to support them. There must be the possibility, in other words, that, in its peculiar freedom, such a literary text is actually not subversive at all.

Consequently, while in its own terms that deft argument from Robert Hampson that *Heart of Darkness* 'offers a representation of representations of Africa' seems to me incontrovertible, I do not believe that it provides any real support for his conclusion that 'far from purveying "comforting myths" (as Achebe alleges) the narrative strategies of both Conrad and Marlow work to subvert many of the "comforting myths" accepted by the implied reader.'[23] On one level, the problem is that offering 'a representation of representations of Africa' is not actually incompatible with offering the reader 'a representation of Africa', which it cannot avoid doing simultaneously. Secondly, the same facets of the text making it unclear that Marlow or indeed the text is actually racist or imperialist, and making it a simplification to categorize 'him' or it in this way, also make it unclear that he or it is actually offering a critique of racism or imperialism. Finally, the problem, as we have already seen, is that to discuss meaningfully the racism, sexism or subversiveness of a text leads necessarily (if not always explicitly) to speculations on reading and reception, whose dynamics can only be grasped historically. Readers' responses cannot be extrapolated solely from texts; consequently, to consider the subversiveness or indeed conservatism of the literary text *as such* or in itself may not mean a great deal.

My argument is that what emerges from critical 'readings' in the mode of literary indeterminacy is *not*, finally, a more accurate or nuanced view of a text's ideological 'message' or orientation. Rather, criticism of that sort problematizes the identification of any such orientation, as it both nourishes and feeds off the notional indeterminacy that Derrida describes as the beginning of literature (as, in its own way, does Derrida's theory). Consequently, such criticism ultimately is not and cannot be grounded in any specific political agenda, serving instead what is, in a sense, a highly theoretical notion of what literature is (albeit one that in some societies has acquired a certain historical weight). It may be tempting to try to articulate what a work of literature *does* when it 'achieves' this indeterminacy, so to speak; Taussig's description of *Heart of Darkness* is one such attempt, as is Watts's essay, and the issue is central to the subcanon of writing, with Blanchot as its most persistent champion, that I discussed in the last chapter. Literature may be what Derrida has in mind when he says, 'there are perhaps forms of thought that think more than does that thought called philosophy' – a remark that is remindful of Djebar's comment (which formed my epigraph) on 'Fiction as a way of "thinking"'.[24] But Derrida's 'perhaps' is crucial: if truly one is dealing with a thought that is irreducible to theory or philosophy, any attempt to theorize it or frame it philosophically will either betray it or will itself gravitate towards the literary, moving into that space where its meaning too becomes indeterminate. A certain sort of attention to the literary text and a certain sort of literary theory alike, then, do not advance any specific political programme but work from and in the interests of that abstract meta-freedom which, to repeat Derrida's phrase, 'constitutes the author, paradoxically, as an author who is responsible to no one' and allows him or her 'to say everything he wants to or everything he can, while remaining shielded, safe from all censorship', and safe, in a sense, from all criticism.[25]

In the end it would seem, then, that there is no direct contradiction between the two different aspects of criticism I have discussed. Rather, their objects and their ends are different, and they operate on different levels. Because the 'mishmash of cultural prejudices and presuppositions' within a text such as *Heart of Darkness* is not only concrete and determinable but still has ideological potency and relevance, the pressure towards political position-taking is hard to resist. Critics should be wary, though, of spending time 'preaching to the already converted', as Conrad put it; and in any case, anyone can take a position on the political issues without making the detour via literature. For the postcolonial critic wishing to grasp the text historically and understand the work it does (or did), giving due weight to the historical complexities of reception and remaining alert to that indeterminacy that marks literature as such may seem frustratingly pernickety and at times apolitical tasks. At least in these two areas, though, the work of criticism has a distinctive contribution to make.

7

Afterword:
Theory and Relativism
(Fanon's Position)

Towards the end of the Conclusion I suggested that a certain sort of theory, as exemplified by Blanchot's or Derrida's writings on literature, itself drifts towards the literary. The passages in Djebar, too, that one might label 'theoretical', such as the 'Overture' in *Women of Algiers*, are at times oblique or lyrical and include autobiographical and historical elements; conversely, although the essays in *Voices* can be seen to offer theoretical leverage on, and provide a context for, Djebar's 'literary' works, on another level, as I implied earlier, they can be considered one element among others in an ongoing project of writing, whose goals need to be understood not just in terms of representation but, as Djebar herself says, as a form of provocation and of action.[1]

At times, then, the distinction between theory and literature appears frail. One reason for this is that the language of theory necessarily draws on and overlaps with 'everyday' language, as does the language of literature, and so the two overlap with one another.[2] Theorists, like anyone else, take on board a certain amount of cultural baggage through the language and common frames of reference available to them. Freud, who turned repeatedly to literary texts in developing his theories, is a notable example: in 'The unconscious', for instance, he writes that:

> Among the derivatives of the *Ucs.* instinctual impulses, of the sort we have described, there are some which unite in themselves characters of an opposite kind. On the one hand, they are highly organized, free from self-contradiction, have made use of every acquisition of the system *Cs.*

and would hardly be distinguished in our judgement from the forma-
tions of that system. On the other hand they are unconscious and are
incapable of becoming conscious. Thus *qualitatively* they belong to the
system *Pcs.*, but *factually* to the *Ucs.* Their origin is what decides their
fate. We may compare them with individuals of mixed race who, taken
all round, resemble white men, but who betray their coloured descent
by some striking feature or other, and on that account are excluded
from society and enjoy none of the privileges of white people.[3]

I do not propose to discuss the specific implications of Freud's startling comparison here, but it is powerfully indicative, I think, of how
theorists may become tacitly involved in ideological debates far wider
than those with which they are explicitly concerned, and how racist/
imperialist ideology has worked its way into many different discourses. Freud, to take one further example, also wrote famously
that 'the sexual life of adult women is a "dark continent" for psychology.'[4] The phrase has often been borrowed and reworked, but it is
not usually recognized that 'dark continent' is in English in the
original German text and that Freud must have taken it from Stanley,
not so long after Conrad had echoed it in *Heart of Darkness*. To a
significant degree these very different figures, working in the context
of an international European and imperial culture, breathed the same
air.

Clearly theory, like literature, may be situated (or 'positioned') and
interpreted historically and culturally. Numerous critics have ap-
proached Freud in this way, revealing elements of ethnocentricity in
a theory that strives towards the universal. The conclusions drawn
from such critical moves vary, of course: some critics wish to dismiss
Freud on these grounds, whereas others seek only to limit the applic-
ability of his theory – to turn-of-the-century Vienna, say, or to
Europe. Or, to take a different example, some critics have attempted
to historicize the French 'high' theory on which many postcolonial
theorists have drawn. This may mean arguing, as does Robert Young,
that 'the French critique of humanism was conducted from the first as
a part of a political critique of colonialism', or it may lead to the
conclusion that structuralist and poststructuralist critiques of the
subject, identity, agency and so on, whose academic ascendancy
coincided with the crumbling of the French empire, need to be understood as a late, peculiarly academic twist in those colonial discourses
that consistently undermined any theoretical basis on which colonized
peoples might build their political claims.[5]

Postcolonial theory itself, not least insofar as it is associated with
psychoanalysis and poststructuralism, is sometimes accused of being a

distinctly European/Northern phenomenon – another unwelcome empire whose would-be global reach is illegitimate, and a mode of thought that is inappropriate to many of its culturally distant objects. It will be evident by this point that I do not agree with the charge if it is stated at this level of generality; for one thing, as I indicated in the Introduction, I do not believe that much is worth saying about 'postcolonial theory' in general, although the charge of disavowed ethnocentricity sticks, in my view, to some of the work that falls under that rubric. One may also argue, as Robert Young has shown in *Postcolonialism*, that much of that theory stems from anti-colonial activism and thinking in former colonies and 'developing' countries, and that its geographical credentials, so to speak, are therefore sound.

The issue that will concern me here, however, is the basis on which a properly 'theoretical' defence of any theory might be elaborated; to which end, I will argue, it is necessary to protect at once a certain notion of the universal (a notion that is frequently dismissed within postcolonial studies) and certain distinctions between the literary and the theoretical. I propose to pursue this issue through a discussion of the work of Frantz Fanon, a key figure in postcolonial studies whose own perspective on relativism and universals is often misunderstood. To see how he arrived at that perspective, and how, relatedly, he comes to fulfil an exemplary 'author-function' as a postcolonial theorist, it will be necessary, as with Djebar, to make some gestures 'positioning' him biographically; but my argument will be that at a certain point, as with Djebar, the pertinence of such information, and with it a certain ethnicized author-figure, must dissolve.

* * * * *

When 'universalism' and universals are criticized within postcolonial studies, it is usually in terms of 'the link between the universal and the Eurocentric, and in particular the link between universality and the canon of texts that represents English literature', as Ashcroft, Griffiths and Tiffin put it in *Key Concepts in Post-Colonial Studies*. The criticism is often directed, then, as we have already seen, at the notion of literary 'timelessness', the choice of (European/'timeless') texts constituting a certain traditional canon, and the purportedly universal worth of that canon.[6] Contrary to what is suggested in the tendentious 'definition' of universalism/universality offered in *Key Concepts in Post-Colonial Studies*, however, the historical uses to which pseudo-universal values – or indeed universal values – have been put by colonialism do not necessarily discredit the very notion of the universal. The attempt to dismiss that notion *theoretically* and in general indeed places one in an impossible position, and is quite rightly given short shrift by many philosophers and theorists: Peter Hallward, for instance, writes:

> As Appiah very sensibly points out, it is characteristic of those (he is referring to Chinweizu, but we might include Bhabha as well) who 'pose as anti-universalists [that they] use the term "universalism" as if it meant "pseudo-universalism"; and the fact is that their complaint is not with universalism at all. What they truly object to – and who would not – is Eurocentric hegemony *posing* as universalism'. The performative contradiction involved in a principled condemnation of *all* universals is too obvious to warrant analysis.[7]

This 'performative contradiction' stems, I think, from the assumption that, if one is a relativist (and a historicist) at all, all universals appear suspect. Yet some commonplace forms of relativism entail no such suspicion: to accept that varied ways of greeting someone – by shaking hands, rubbing noses or kissing – are all legitimate in their own cultural contexts, and that outside those contexts none is inherently preferable to any other, is to espouse a form of relativism that could be called broadly 'cultural' and is easily defensible, but which extends only so far. It is not difficult, after all, to think of more provocative examples (concerning the legal parity of men and women, for example) where the bounds of what can be justified in terms of cultural specificity or 'tradition' are much more difficult to define and defend.

Two points need to be emphasized straight away. The first is that no *action* follows automatically if and when it transpires that one set of cultural and political values is on some conceptual level genuinely incompatible with another, which is to say that, from within one set of values, the other *cannot* be recognized as valid. There is always a decision to be made about whether and how to react to such an incompatibility, in a complex context where different values (and rights) around issues such as equality, toleration and political autonomy may not be fully commensurable. Secondly, there are clearly different *orders* of relativism. In a useful taxonomy Hollis and Lukes name five, of which I will give just a brief summary here. The 'cultural' relativism that underpins equanimity in the face of nose-rubbing, hand-shaking etc. is so mild a form, it should be noted, as scarcely to register even at the bottom of their conceptual hierarchy, in which they distinguish between (i) moral relativism, which is to say the notion that morals hold only in relation to the cultures from which they develop and within which they are upheld; (ii) conceptual relativism, which means the notion that some concepts hold only in relation to their own delimitable context; (iii) perceptual relativism, whose thesis, they write, 'is evoked by the suggestive but elusive formula that different communities or groups of scientists "live in different worlds".' This, they argue, breaks down into two interlinked ideas: 'One is that what we perceive cannot be explained by the nature of the object perceived....The other is the specific diagnosis that language in some sense determines or constitutes what is perceived'; (iv) relativism of truth, which is the next step from the relativizing of perception to language or to paradigms; and finally (v) 'relativism of reason', meaning that 'what counts as a reason, or as a good reason, for holding beliefs' is held to be relative.[8]

Even from this brief summary it is clear, I think, that when we are told in *Key Concepts in Post-Colonial Studies* that 'the apparently culture-free discourse of mathematics, whose universal truths appear indisputable, is actually a very culturally determined mode of imperialist discourse', the statement runs together different sorts of claim.[9] There are doubtless numerous ways in which mathematics, in its evolution, institutional supports, uses and status, can be historicized, and its different value relative to different cultures weighed up. Yet even where those cultures are (or were) themselves broadly imperialist, it is not necessarily the case that mathematical 'discourse' or *any* particular discourse within them is itself imperialist too. The point is not only that imperialist societies have also produced anti-imperialist discourse, but also that at a certain crucial level some discourses simply have no relation to imperialism. The correctness of a calculation, for example, is judged by standards that in themselves bear no relation to history and in that sense are indeed universal (though whether 'truth' is the most appropriate term in this instance is another question).

Would Fanon, an anti-colonialist who is frequently perceived as a radical relativist, be able to agree with this sort of defence of a certain universalism? I will argue that he would, but the question is difficult to answer, not least because his work's at times markedly anti-universal strain is linked in complex ways with his own sense of his position in history, and also because the different kinds of claim that he makes in this connection seem explicable in part as a response to, and observation of the proprieties of, different discursive contexts. Fanon's texts could be categorized in different genres (journalistic, theoretical, scientific, etc.) and in places they could even be termed 'literary' in the same way as much of the literature that I have discussed, in that their uneven and disconcerting rhetoric, or their elaborate use of extended metaphor, makes it difficult to reduce them to a single 'message'. In places, nevertheless, his statements appear sufficiently categorical – or sufficiently *theoretical* – for the reader to feel that on various topics, including that of his and his texts' own 'situatedness', the signals he gives are contradictory.

It is remarkable that, unlike most nationalist leaders, Fanon did not come from the nation of which he became a spokesperson. He was born and grew up in Martinique, and trained as a doctor in France, before moving to work in Algeria and then becoming a prominent spokesperson for the FLN and for anti-colonialism more widely. His writing draws repeatedly on personal experience, to which it remains in a close, if equivocal, relation. In the introduction to his first major work, *Black Skin, White Masks* (*Peau noire masques blancs*, 1952), for instance, he writes: 'As I am from the Antilles, my observations and conclusions are valid only for the Antilles'; but he goes on to state, towards the end: 'The dense weight of History does not determine a single one of my actions. ‖ I am my own foundation.'[10] In the realm of his writing, at least, he seems to have transcended his background, in the sense that his publications found such wide resonance and in that he was apparently sufficiently unconstrained by his ethnic identity to identify completely with the 'Algerian people' (which comes to mean, in his usage, those people who throw themselves behind the Algerian fight for independence). Not only did he feel able to use a figure such as 'North African blood' in his articles originally published under the cover of anonymity in *El Moudjahid*,[11] but he also used the first person plural 'nous', 'we', to refer to Algerians in signed texts. And, strikingly, he never used that pronoun unequivocally to mean West Indians, even in an article such as 'West Indians and Africans' of 1955, where he argued that the different histories of the West Indians and the Africans gave them different perspectives on race and colonialism.[12]

Sometimes in Fanon's work it seems he believes that beyond any such ethnic perspectives and affiliations, the anti-colonial war should be fought in the name of universal human values: thus in *Studies in a Dying Colonialism*, for instance, he writes:

> the death of colonialism is at once the death of the colonized and the death of the colonizer.
>
> The new relationship does not mean the replacement of one barbarism by another, and it does not mean one way of crushing men replaced by another. What we Algerians want is to discover the man behind the colonizer...
>
> We want an Algeria that is open to all, in which every kind of genius may grow.[13]

Repeatedly, however, he also expresses his suspicion of supposedly universal values (such as *liberté*, *égalité* and *fraternité*, whose universalism Chraïbi too, it will be remembered, called into question) which seem to have coexisted all too easily with particular forms of exploitation and degradation. The would-be universal category of Man in particular comes under attack in this connection; he admonishes a departing Frenchman, for instance, with being 'Concerned for Man but markedly unconcerned for the Arab'.[14] The same idea is expressed more generally near the end of *The Wretched of the Earth* when he writes:

> Let us leave Europe, the Europe that talks endlessly of man while slaughtering every man in its path, in every corner of the world. . . . In this Europe they never stopped talking of man, and never stopped proclaiming that their sole concern was mankind, but we know now with what suffering humanity has paid for every one of their triumphs of the mind.[15]

At times, then, it seems that the problem is that the French are not true to their own principles, which in themselves are apparently held to merit the status of universality – he writes, for example, that 'Europeans who practise torture demean their people and are traitors to their history';[16] but at other times, his position appears more profoundly relativistic. Elsewhere in *The Wretched of the Earth*, for instance, he remarks,

> The problem of truth must also be considered. Among the people, in every age, truth resides only in the national cause. No absolute truth and no discourse on the purity of the soul can undermine this position. . . . Truth is that which protects the indigenous people and ruins foreigners. In the colonial context there is no such thing as truthful conduct. And good is quite simply that which is evil for *them*.[17]

Or later on, 'The colonized find that objectivity is always directed against them.'[18] Similarly in his article about the radio he writes,

> The oppressor's truth, previously rejected as an absolute lie, was eventually countered with other truth in action. The occupier's lie thereby gained in truth, as it was now a lie in danger, put on the defensive. It is the very defences of the occupier – his reactions and resistances – that underscored the effectiveness of national action and made it participate in a world of truth. The Algerian's reaction was no longer one of pained and desperate refusal. *Because avowedly unsettled, the occupier's lie became a positive aspect of the new truth of the Nation.*[19]

One way of discussing these two distinct strains within Fanon's writing, which is at times anti-universal and at times pro-universal (and anti-pseudo-universal), would be to relativize/historicize them in terms of his personal history and the changes of opinion that his experience produced. Another would be to treat his varied claims as a writer's rhetorical and/or strategic gestures, and to consider their efficacy in mobilizing opinion, generating solidarity, etc. Another again, of course, would be to attempt to adjudicate between the theoretical claims that they advance, implicitly or explicitly.

The inter-relation and the *distinctness* of these three approaches become clearer, I think, when one contemplates changes in Fanon's perspective on scientific objectivity, as narrated, perhaps surprisingly, in certain of his scientific papers. Notable in this context is his paper 'Occupational therapy in a Muslim men's department' of 1954, in which he and his co-author recount his attempts to introduce occupational therapy into the hospital. Under his care were 165 'European' women and 220 'Muslim men'. In both sections his ideas met with initial resistance from staff and patients alike, but quite quickly thereafter in the European women's section a whole social life was built up centring on the activities that Fanon had introduced – group meetings, cinema evenings, the production of a hospital newspaper and so on. The same programme of events completely failed to take root in the Algerian men's section. Reflecting on this, Fanon soon acknowledges his naïvety in ever having thought that the same activities would work in both sections, and reveals that, out of the 220 male patients, only five were literate in Arabic, and only two could read and write French – which makes the poor circulation of the newspaper in the men's section relatively easy to explain.

On the basis of this experience, Fanon came to realize that:

> unthinkingly, the psychiatrist adopts the politics of assimilation ... The onus to make an effort is upon the 'native', who has every reason to try to resemble the type of man suggested to him. Assimilation in this instance does not imply any reciprocity between different perspectives. One whole culture must make way for another....
>
> Thus a revolutionary attitude was vital, whereby one moved from a position where the supremacy of Western culture appeared obvious, to a position of cultural relativism.[20]

When Fanon was appointed to his job in Blida, he and his employers must have been confident that his French training equipped him to deal with mental problems in Algeria, and presumably anywhere. In important but not all respects, experiences such as his misjudgment over the hospital newspaper changed his mind. Abruptly he gained a heightened sense of his own situation and its contingencies; and the boundaries between psychiatry and politics started to blur. Leaving his job in 1956, he wrote in his letter of resignation:

> Madness is one of the means man has of losing his freedom. And from the crossroads at which I find myself, I can say that I have witnessed with horror the extent of alienation [/madness] in this country.
>
> If psychiatry is the medical technique that aims to enable man no longer to be a stranger to his environment, it is my duty to declare that the Arab, permanently alienated in his own country, lives in a state of absolute depersonalization....
>
> The present social structure in Algeria frustrates any attempt to return the individual to his rightful place.[21]

Fanon's use of political vocabulary (particularly 'liberté') to describe the process of psychiatric therapy is striking here, and his comments not only indicate that he recognizes limits to what can be done within the psychiatric framework, but also imply that the fundamental conceptual categories of psychiatry – even, as it were, *within* that framework – are problematic in a context such as his.[22]

Further evidence of this crisis regarding his most basic concepts, and a sense of how it manifested itself within his work, is provided by a case history recounted at the end of *The Wretched of the Earth*. It concerns a French policeman who came to Fanon because he was unable to sleep at night, as he constantly heard the screams of Algerians whom he had tortured. He wanted Fanon to put an end to this. The situation was no doubt already difficult enough ethically for Fanon, but became impossible when the policeman happened to bump into an Algerian militant who was in the hospital because he had fallen into a state of profound depression after being tortured by that same policeman. The encounter led to a suicide attempt by the Algerian, and the staff placated him by lying to him about the incident, telling him that it had been a delusion and that policemen were not allowed on the premises. The policeman, for his part, was thrown into a state of anxious depression, and shortly afterwards was sent home on medical grounds.

The case gives a dramatic sense of what was intolerable about Fanon's situation, how such an experience disrupted his professional ethics of objectivity and disinterestedness and compromised truthfulness, and how his conception of dualisms as fundamental as health/sickness or sanity/insanity faltered. But radical though the jolt was to his values and his sense of his own social role, it must be recognized that the relativism for which he calls in the 'Occupational therapy' article is specifically – and only – a cultural relativism ('a revolutionary attitude was vital, whereby one moved from a position where the supremacy of Western culture appeared obvious, to a position of cultural relativism'). Fanon's reaction to the initial failure of that project was to inform himself much more thoroughly about Algerian social conventions, and to introduce types of activity compatible with the male patients' culture – the chance to go to a café, occasional visits from story-tellers drawing on oral tradition, and so on. Although, in other words, he moved beyond his initial French socio-centrism, at a certain level his methodological assumptions and the theory behind them stayed intact; so even though his turn to cultural relativism was a radical move, and represented a profound shift of attitude, the implicit and semi-explicit political criticisms in the article remain within a certain scientific discourse that is, on one level, oblivious to context and, on another, appropriate to the psychiatric journal in which the paper was published.[23] Notwithstanding the anecdotal elements of this case history, his use of 'nous' in such medical writing betokens a distinctly scientific 'author-function' (to use Foucault's terminology once more); unlike the political 'nous', that scientific 'nous' is not generally a locus of identity, signalling a 'position' as scientist/observer that anyone duly qualified might adopt.[24] And even when, in the wake of incidents such as the one involving the torture victim, Fanon felt that his position as a psychiatrist was untenable, he would have had no reason to disown an article of that sort.

Fanon's perspective on the relativism or otherwise of scientific discourse is perhaps at its clearest in his essay 'Medicine and colonialism', in *Studies in a Dying Colonialism*, which describes the way in which 'Western' medicine was viewed by Algerians. That article provides a kind of counterpart to the 'Occupational therapy' piece, discussing medicine from a political perspective rather than vice-versa. It is tempting here to read the text against the grain of its own claims to generality, and to find in it the reflection of Fanon's own situation: one can perhaps hear his frustration when he notes that 'The statistics on improved sanitation are generally interpreted by North Africans not as a sign of progress in the fight against disease, but as fresh proof of the occupier's strengthening grip on the country', or when he complains: 'North Africans are genuinely mentally restricted, in that their situation makes it difficult for them to be objective and to separate the wheat from the chaff.'[25] Something of the anti-science attitude to which he is alluding – and its specificity to a certain point in anti-colonial history – is captured in Djebar's 'Nostalgia of the horde' when the old woman tells with equanimity the story of how one of her husband's brothers died, unattended by a doctor, after an accident in a stagecoach. When she is challenged on this, she replies haughtily: 'In those days ... if you said "doctor and hospital," it meant a French doctor and a French hospital.'[26] The association was doubtless at once substantial – in that doctors sometimes collaborated with torturers and could not be trusted to carry out their work with proper impartiality – and symbolic; and, a little further on in the article, Fanon acknowledges that 'The idea of a depoliticized science, of science placed in the service of man, is often a nonsense in the colonies.'[27] For Fanon, the situation was one in which the apolitical became politicized, for good and for bad, and in which politics came to seem more important than medicine.

Fanon's politicization in relation to (and of) his *scientific* work took place, then, as ground he had thought solid suddenly shifted beneath him, and activities that previously had seemed neutral to him took on a political hue. The point at which he started to work political critique into his scientific work was the point at which he started to think that every discourse and every activity had to be 'situated' in its social and political context if one wanted to understand fully the purposes it came, in practice, to serve. Yet this particular form of relativism did not prevent Fanon from believing in objectivity, as is clear, paradoxically, from his statement: 'Truth, objectively expressed, is constantly vitiated by the lie of the colonial situation.'[28] Objectivity as such is not at stake here; the statement itself is supposed to be treated as objective, presumably, and on an epistemological level, correspondingly, the position from which he himself is speaking/ writing, and who he is, is of no relevance. Ultimately for Fanon the factors making 'depoliticized science' a nonsense in the context of colonialism were, precisely, contextual, which is to say that these factors were contingent and political, with no inherent relation to science (or medicine) as such.[29]

Under colonialism, in Fanon's eyes, there was a disjuncture between what the colonized were and what they needed to become, and the transition could be achieved only politically. When he says that 'De-colonization really means the creation of new men', the notions of creation and novelty are radically enough conceived to indicate that, for him, within the colonial situation, the decolonized world for which he was fighting was unimaginable.[30] This helps explain why he was critical of *négritude*, considering the very idea of the *nègre* or negro and indeed of a pan-African culture flawed in its dependence on racialized European thought that trapped it within the colonists' conceptual dualisms where the 'European' term of the dualism was always privileged over the other. It meant accepting African culture via its European mediations, in other words, and embracing negative aspects of that culture along with the positive aspects that it sought to rehabilitate and revalorize.[31] The rupture that was necessary to get out of this framework could not, according to Fanon, be produced by an act of individual will or autonomously from within the artistic or cultural sphere. Fanon's 'new man' was to be created through the dialectic between revolutionary consciousness and revolutionary acts.[32] All of this helps explain the 'literary' aspect of Fanon's theorizing, its ambivalences and stylistic quirks: he writes self-reflexively in *The Wretched of the Earth* of the powers of a certain style of 'broken' writing favoured by 'colonized intellectuals who decide to give expression to this phase of consciousness which is in the process of becoming liberated' and which he sees as creating moments of explosive potential.[33] Perhaps, then, beyond questions of objectivity, the highest goal of Fanon's *political* texts was to be inspirational; he used language not only to frame propositions about the world but – like many 'literary' writers – to provoke his readers, and accordingly those propositions repeatedly signal the fact that the situation from which they were uttered made them contingent and unstable.

All writing, scientific/theoretical, 'literary' or otherwise, demands interpretation; it may (as was discussed in relation to 'racial' and genetic science) be put to political purposes or prompt political actions in various ways, in accordance with or contrary to its author's intentions; its sphere of application, which is to say the area in which its claims are correct and verifiable, may be smaller than its author expects or believes; and even scientific writing may at times be secretly shaped by personal/cultural values of the sort that it usually purports to exclude. There are good reasons, then, to pay attention to issues of positioning and to be mindful of the permeability of all sorts of discourse, and indeed of consciousness, to historically embedded cultural values of the sort that now stand out so starkly in some of Freud's writing. It is doubtless for such reasons that, as I indicated in the Introduction, many theorists today, and perhaps especially postcolonial theorists and/or those who are concerned with the constitution of 'identity', frequently feel obliged to say something about the position from which they themselves speak, identifying themselves by ethnicity, gender, professional status, etc. To the extent that the values in question are so deeply psychologically/historically entrenched as to be second nature, however, and to appear inherent in the world itself, no attempt to describe one's own position is going to take one any closer to objectivity. After all, if my perspective is genuinely specific to my situation not in the trivial, contingent sense that it is shaped by the things I happen to have read, but in the sense that my situation limits *as* thinking *all* of my thinking, structurally and in advance, then it is impossible for me to be truly aware of that specificity (or its limits), whatever gestures of awareness I may make. (This argument is close, incidentally, to the one made in chapter 4 about a deterministic model of language's relation to consciousness.) The attempt to find determinate *theoretical* support for the conviction that *all* thought is relativizable in such terms leads one back into that 'performative contradiction' mentioned earlier.

As was apparent from my quotations from Freud, cultural and historical distance makes it easier to perceive how certain values may be tacitly circulated and recirculated by theoretical and other discourses alike, and to historicize texts accordingly. As we have seen, the techniques of historicization can be applied to Fanon, as can certain of those literary-critical techniques that find and promote literary-textual indeterminacy: even Fanon's statements on universals can indeed thus be relativized, in that, as I noted earlier, one can read them as the trace of his own peculiar situation, or recuperate them as a rhetorical strategy (his 'identification' with the Algerian cause, for example, might be discussed in these terms, and his 'voice' considered in a sense a fictional one), or cite the very plurality of voices and perspectives within his work as a sign that there is no objective truth, and that he has no illusions about this. But, to the extent that one reads Fanon's work (or indeed Freud's) as *theory*, the procedures through which one makes sense of it and the criteria against which one measures it must not be relativizable at the level of truth.

As I suggested in the Introduction, 'situating' a piece of theoretical or critical writing, locating the historical and cultural 'position' from which it emerged, may give the theorist clues as to where its theoretical weaknesses – and strengths – may lie. But if there is confusion around the notion of positioning or situation, it is partly because it is tempting to slip illegitimately between an account that is merely genetic and one that claims to offer some critical or epistemological leverage. Success in the attempt to situate someone's thought, in other words, is inherently on a limited scale. To propose that Fanon thinks such-and-such a thing *because* he is from Martinique, for example, may make a legitimate starting point or even conclusion for certain types of discourse, of which biography would be one; but within a discourse that engages with his theory as such, any such proposition, even if it is true, is neither here nor there.

Notes

Quotations from French-language texts are given in English. In most cases published translations are available and I refer to these, though I sometimes adapt their wording. The notes provide the original French in instances where there are particular problems of translation and for quotations from primary texts by Chraïbi, Djebar and Fanon in chapters 4, 5 and 7 respectively.

Introduction:
Postcolonial Criticism and the Work of Fiction

1 The epigraph from Conrad is taken from p. 83 of the Penguin edition, that from Djebar from pp. 233–4 of the original (my translation): 'La fiction comme moyen de "penser", un lieu, un territoire, un continent: ce n'est pas, vous vous en doutez, écrire une pure "fantaisie", j'allais dire une *fantasia*. || C'est plutôt retrouver, grâce à une construction imaginaire (que ce soit une intrigue, des situations entrecroisées, des dialogues hasardeux ou banals), grâce à une *fiction* donc, c'est habiter, peupler ou repeupler un lieu, une ville, à partir à la fois des fantômes de ce lieu, mais aussi de vos propres obsessions...'

2 Achebe's paper has been reprinted several times. When it appeared in *Hopes and Impediments*, Achebe had replaced 'bloody' with 'thorough-going'. References are to the latter edition, which is the most accessible: see 'An image of Africa', 8.

3 Certain themes and questions arise for the first time in the discussion of *Heart of Darkness* that resurface and are reworked across the book as a whole, whose overall shape is intended to reflect both a conceptual and a chronological progression. Although each chapter is nonetheless fairly self-contained, readers interested in one particular figure, text or issue should consult the index accordingly.

4   See Young, *Postcolonialism*, 25.
5   Achebe was born in 1930; Nigeria achieved independence in 1960. His best-known work is his first novel, *Things Fall Apart*, published in 1958. Djebar was born in Algeria in 1936.
6   The latter issue is central to Huggan's *The Postcolonial Exotic*. I came across this book too late to be able to discuss it further, but Huggan's chapters on 'African literature', 'Staged marginalities' and 'Ethnic autobiography and the cult of authenticity' address many of the questions raised by my chapters 4 and 5.
7   McClintock, 'The angel of progress', 255.
8   Moore-Gilbert, *Postcolonial Theory: Contexts, Practices, Politics*, is a good example.
9   Said, *Culture and Imperialism*, 8. For an introduction to the history of the notions of imperialism, colonialism, neocolonialism and postcolonialism, see Young, *Postcolonialism*, 15–69, and *passim*.
10 Williams and Chrisman, *Colonial Discourse and Post-Colonial Theory*, 2.
11 Williams, *Keywords*, 159–60.
12 For such criticisms and others, see, for instance, Ahmad, *In Theory*, and Parry's influential 'Problems in current theories of colonial discourse' and 'Resistance theory/theorizing resistance'.
13 For a historical overview of the anti-colonial thought on which postcolonial studies draw, see Young, *Postcolonialism*.

Chapter 1
Colonialism and Colonial Discourse

1   See Ndaywel è Nziem, *Histoire générale du Congo*, 273. The most accessible English-language history of Belgian imperialism in the Congo is Hochschild's *King Leopold's Ghost*.
2   See Levering Lewis, *The Race to Fashoda*, 35, and Hochschild, *King Leopold's Ghost*, 44–5.
3   Hochschild, *King Leopold's Ghost*, 45.
4   The general act is reproduced as an appendix in Berriedale Keith, *The Belgian Congo and the Berlin Act*.
5   See Hampson, 'Introduction', xvii–xviii; xxi.
6   Morris, *News from Nowhere*, 98. Incidentally, in the light of the ravages wrought by diseases carried by colonizers, the phrase 'the germs of empires' in *Heart of Darkness* (17) may be double-edged.
7   The figure is for sales in English, and is given by Boehmer, *Colonial and Postcolonial Literature*, 31.
8   Conrad, 'Geography', 235–6.
9   Cited by Hochschild, *King Leopold's Ghost*, 147. The friend in question was the critic Edward Garnett.
10 Cited by Morel, *Red Rubber*, 77.

11 Naval Staff Intelligence Dept, *A Manual of Belgian Congo*, 263.
12 Hochschild, *King Leopold's Ghost*, 91, 170–1. In French the inscription reads: 'Le chemin de fer les libéra du portage' (see cover).
13 13 million is Ndaywel è Nziem's figure for 1880–1908. *Histoire générale du Congo*, 344.
14 Hochschild, *King Leopold's Ghost*, 280.
15 Shankar, 'The origins and ends of postcolonial studies', 146.
16 Ascherson, *The King Incorporated*, 11.
17 Hochschild, *King Leopold's Ghost*, 168.
18 Cited by Ndaywel è Nziem, *Histoire générale du Congo*, 335.
19 Yacono, *Histoire de la colonisation française*, 99 ('Il ne manquait que 587 députés').
20 See Conrad, 'An outpost of progress', 255n. One might compare the rhetoric on 'material interests' of Leopold's contemporary, the British politician Joseph Chamberlain, which is analysed by Benita Parry in relation to Conrad's *Nostromo* in the following terms: 'In his frequent pronouncements on imperialist themes, Joseph Chamberlain, a vigorous exponent of Britain's expansion, reiterated precisely this phrase as a synonym for the acquisition of territory, overseas commercial enterprise, returns on investment in the colonies, the garnering of natural and mineral wealth in imperial possessions, and the exploitation of the empire's labour resources. Here the incongruity is located not within the term, but in the misalliance between mercenary ambition and economic gain, and the boast that these constituted devotion to "national duty", "high ideals", "dreams", "high sentiment", "imagination", "mission", "responsibility", and "honour".' Parry, 'Narrating imperialism', 239. Parry refers to Chamberlain, *Foreign and Colonial Speeches*, 78, 101, 195.
21 See Ndaywel è Nziem, *Histoire générale du Congo*, 237, 287–93, and Hochschild, *King Leopold's Ghost*, 28.
22 *Heart of Darkness*, 83–4. This is the passage from which my first epigraph in the Introduction was drawn.
23 Referred to by Ndaywel è Nziem, *Histoire générale du Congo*, 348.
24 A useful brief survey of uses of the term by Foucault and others is given by Hawthorn, *A Concise Glossary of Contemporary Literary Theory*, 54–8. The term is used in different ways at different points in Foucault's work; see, for instance, *The Order of Things, The Archaeology of Knowledge,* and *The History of Sexuality.*
25 Said, *Orientalism*, 273.
26 Prendergast, *The Triangle of Representation*, chapter 6; see also, for discussion of the notion of discourse in Said, Foucault and related contexts, Young, *Postcolonialism*, 383–410.
27 Peter Hallward is quite right, I think, to stress, in counterbalance to writers who are intrigued by the general 'ambivalence' of the colonial relationship and its patterns of mutual influence, that that relationship was primarily divisive and exploitative: as he puts it, 'Surely we don't

need a *postcolonial* theorist to tell us that colonialism installed an "ambivalent and symbiotic relationship between coloniser and colonised" [Gandhi, *Postcolonial Theory*, 11], if we recognize from the beginning that *all* human relations are to some degree ambivalent and symbiotic, that every subject is constitutively related to others.... What is remarkable is that postcolonial theory should so often have argued that the colonial relationship is especially "ambivalent and symbiotic," rather than minimally or trivially so' (*Absolutely Postcolonial*, xiv–xv).

28 The phrase describes Marlow's boat in *Heart of Darkness*, 28. The best-known image of the *Roi des Belges* appears in Sherry, *Conrad's Western World*.

Chapter 2
Racism, Realism and the Question of Historical Context

1   Watts, '"A bloody racist": about Achebe's view of Conrad', 408.
2   Genette, 'Vraisemblance et motivation', 85.
3   Ibid., 94.
4   Ibid., 97.
5   Prendergast, *The Order of Mimesis*, 68.
6   Genette, 'Vraisemblance et motivation', 96n.
7   Heath, 'Realism, modernism and "language-consciousness"', 110.
8   Genette, 'Vraisemblance et motivation', 77.
9   See Hampson, '*Heart of Darkness* and "The speech that cannot be silenced"', 203, 213.
10 Ibid., 210.
11 Genette, 'Vraisemblance et motivation', 86.
12 Achebe, 'An image of Africa', 7.
13 Ibid., 12, 2.
14 Hampson, '*Heart of Darkness* and "The speech that cannot be silenced"', 204.
15 Conrad, *Heart of Darkness*, 134, n.64.
16 Miller, *Blank Darkness*, 180; cf. *Heart of Darkness* 35, 63–4, 108.
17 See Bhabha, 'Signs taken for wonders', and 'Of mimicry and man', in *The Location of Culture*. 'Hybridization' is now often used somewhat banally by critics to describe states of cultural mixity; Bhabha's notion is more complex, but to my mind unconvincing in its assumptions about the subversiveness of the processes of mimicry etc. that he describes. For further discussion of this notion, see Huggan, 'Decolonizing the map', 126, and Young, *Colonial Desire*, 1–28.
18 A comparable reversal is effected in the quotation – notable for its place of publication and for its date – used as an epigraph by Annie Coombes in *Reinventing Africa*, ii: 'One cannot reside for any time in England or in any part of Europe without discovering the strange but significant

fact that in African matters, and as to the destiny of this race, Europe is a veritable "Dark Continent", having much to learn, much suffering to undergo, and much suffering to inflict upon others, before the lesson will be acquired' (John Payne Jackson, *Lagos Weekly Record*, 23 October 1897).

19 Hampson, 'Conrad and the idea of empire', 65–6.

20 Bristow, *Empire Boys*, 160.

21 Parry, *Conrad and Imperialism*, 34, 35.

22 Cf. *Heart of Darkness*, 15, 18, 106, 110, 114, 119.

23 For further discussion of the gender politics of *Heart of Darkness*, see Jones, *Conrad and Women*; London, 'Reading race and gender in Conrad's dark continent'; Mongia, 'Empire, narrative and the feminine'; Nadelhaft, *Joseph Conrad*; J. Smith, '"Too beautiful altogether"'; and Straus, ' The exclusion of the Intended'. These critics establish telling parallels and points of contact between feminist and postcolonial concerns, which I cannot pursue further here; I return to the topic of gender in chapter 5.

24 Hampson, 'Conrad and the idea of empire', 71.

25 Ibid., 68–71.

26 Austin, 'Joseph Conrad tells what women don't know about men', 4, 20. Stanley, letter to James Osgood.

27 Achebe, 'An image of Africa', 8.

28 Ibid., xi, 8.

29 See Hochschild, *King Leopold's Ghost*, 102–9. Williams died in August 1891.

30 See Brantlinger, *Rule of Darkness*; Sherry, *Conrad's Western World*, 95–118. Hodister and various other possible models for Kurtz are discussed by Watt, *Conrad in the Nineteenth Century*, 141–5.

31 See Lemarchand, *Political Awakening in the Belgian Congo*, 34, and Cookey, *Britain and the Congo Question*, 39–41.

32 On Dilke and his concept of 'Greater Britain', see Young, *Postcolonialism*, 35–41.

33 Cited by Firchow, *Envisioning Africa*, 97.

34 See Lindqvist, '*Exterminate all the Brutes*', 24, and Cookey, *Britain and the Congo Question*, 41–2.

35 Conrad, 'An outpost of progress', 11.

36 See Porter, *Critics of Empire*, 260.

37 At least one critic sees Stanley's account of his Emin Pasha expedition as a specific intertext of *Heart of Darkness*. See Youngs, *Travellers in Africa*.

38 Lindqvist, '*Exterminate all the Brutes*', 29, 44.

39 Firchow quibbles with this, but thinks that Conrad did read Glave's story. See *Envisioning Africa*, 129–30.

40 Quoted in Sherry, *Conrad: The Critical Heritage*, 132–3.

41 In *The Athenaeum*, 20 December 1902, 824; in Sherry, *Critical Heritage*, 139. Ivory was the other major product associated with the CFS.

Economically its relative significance diminished because of the rubber boom.

42   Watts, *Conrad's 'Heart of Darkness'*, 60; Conrad, *Heart of Darkness* 132, n45; Parry, private communication; Ledger, 'In darkest England', 223; Hawkins, 'Conrad's critique of imperialism', 291–2. Hawkins further explains: 'Leopold was unusual among colonial rulers in that he had nothing to sell' – and so no incentive to impose a unified money economy and develop the market. He goes on: 'The absence of a stable standard currency had the further consequence of hampering private traders by obliging them to rely on barter and a number of purely local, highly unstable currencies. In 1890 at least seven different currencies were in use in the Congo, including on part of the upper river brass wires from eighteen to fifty-two centimetres long (called *mitakos*). In 1887 the state issued its own currency, consisting of gold, silver, and copper coins, but by 1893 only three hundred thousand francs had been put in circulation and these were restricted to the lower river. || Conrad was well aware of the confused currency situation' (p. 291).

43   See Cellard, 'Le Vicaire et la rabouilleuse', 144 – a discussion of the representation of sex in Balzac.

44   Miller, *Blank Darkness*, 174.

45   See Vidan, 'Conrad in his "Blackwood's" context'.

46   Genette, 'Vraisemblance et motivation', 77 (discussed above); Nadel-haft, *Joseph Conrad*, 45; McDonald, *British Literary Culture and Publishing Practice*, 67.

47   See Watt, *Conrad in the Nineteenth Century*, 141ff; Watts, *Conrad's 'Heart of Darkness'*, 65–7; Hawkins, 'The issue of racism' and 'Conrad's critique of imperialism', 288–91.

48   Ford Madox Ford, *Joseph Conrad: A Personal Remembrance* (Duckworth, 1924), 133–4; cited by Knowles and Moore, *Oxford Reader's Companion to Conrad*, 197.

49   Conrad and Hueffer, *The Inheritors*, 44–6.

50   Ibid., 33.

51   Publications – some sponsored by Leopold's government – contesting the imputed atrocities continued to appear long after the annexation. One example is the bilingual work (compiled by one Owen Letcher) entitled *Congo Belge*, whose subchapters included 'All homage to the pioneers', 'Service to the natives' and 'Progress – always progress'. This last incorporates the memorable statement 'There are no politics in the Congo Belge' (p. 9).

52   In Carabine, *Joseph Conrad: Critical Assessments*, I: 294–5, and II: 296–7. One might compare Conrad's remark to Richard Curle: 'Didn't it ever occur to you, my dear Curle, that I knew what I was doing in leaving the facts of my life and even of my tales in the background? ... You seem to believe in literalness and explicitness, in facts and also in expression. Yet nothing is more clear than the utter insignificance of explicit statement and also its power to call attention away from things

that matter in the region of art.' Watts, *Conrad's 'Heart of Darkness'*, 50; cited from R. Curle (ed.), *Conrad to a Friend* (London: Sampson Low, Marston & Co., 1928), 142.

53   Taussig, *Shamanism, Colonialism and the Wild Man*, 10–11. Cf. the discussion of *Heart of Darkness* by another anthropologist, James Clifford, in *The Predicament of Culture*.

54   Achebe, 'An image of Africa', 7.

55   Much light is cast on this issue by Porter's *Critics of Empire*. Porter notes that 'The more Afrocentric attitude was only to appear prominently in discussions after the turn of the century' (p. 33). He also remarks, in relation to Morris's arguments against imperialism, 'Among English socialists Morris was the first to relate imperialism so closely to over-production. But the idea was not his. He was only repeating the common view of the imperialists themselves. . . . It was one of the main *justifications* for imperialism, not a criticism of it' (pp. 44, 47).

56   For some interesting reflections on the East India Company as 'the first great transnational company before the fact', see Spivak, *A Critique of Postcolonial Reason*, 164, 220–1. Cf. also Marx's comment in 'Future results of British rule in India', 'The profound hypocrisy and inherent barbarism of bourgeois civilization lies unveiled before our eyes, turning from its home, where it assumes respectable forms, to the colonies, where it goes naked' (cited by Hampson, *'Heart of Darkness* and "The speech that cannot be silenced"', 205).

57   Ndaywel è Nziem, *Histoire générale du Congo*, 311. The fullest account of the impact of Morel's campaign, and of the change of régime, is given by Marchal in his ground-breaking work *E. D. Morel contre Léopold II*.

58   One striking example of free-trade rhetoric comes in the letter (dated January 1907) to Morel from John Holt, whose Liverpool company was one of those suffering financially from the Belgian monopoly: 'The beneficent daughter of liberty & industry! The giver of human happiness! The creator of wealth! The supporter of social existence! Blessed commerce the friend of the slave the deliverer of the oppressed . . . . Hail God's means of blessing mankind with comfort and joy & hope in this mortal life!' (cited by Porter, *Critics of Empire*, 249).

59   Watts, *Conrad's 'Heart of Darkness'*, 50.

60   Ndaywel è Nziem, *Histoire générale du Congo*, 299–304; 286.

61   Morel, *King Leopold's Rule in Africa*, x.

62   Twain, mimicking Leopold's voice (and drawing attention to the importance of photographic evidence within the debates) wrote: 'The kodak has been a sore calamity for us. The most powerful enemy that has confronted us, indeed. In the early years we had no trouble in getting the press to "expose" the tales of the mutilations as slanders, lies, inventions of busy-body American missionaries and exasperated foreigners . . . Yes, all things went harmoniously and pleasantly in those good days, and I was looked up to as the benefactor of a down-trodden and

friendless people. Then all of a sudden came the crash! That is to say, the incorruptible *kodak* – and all the harmony went to hell!' (Twain, *King Leopold's Soliloquy*, 37–8). As Reilly notes (*Shadowtime*, 170), the status of the Congo debate as 'one of the great public topics of the year' in the wake of the Casement report is registered in *Ulysses* in the form of an indignant pub conversation (Joyce, *Ulysses*, 274).

63 Morel, *King Leopold's Rule in Africa*, 351–2.

64 Brantlinger, *Rule of Darkness*, 258.

65 Andersen et al., 'Introduction', v/xix.

66 Cunninghame Graham had struck up an approving correspondence and a friendship with Conrad after reading 'An outpost of progress', feeling on the strength of that story that he recognized in Conrad 'a soulmate in the criticism of imperialism and hatred of hypocrisy'. Conrad's letter continues: 'I am being stupid. Honour, justice, compassion and freedom are ideas that have no converts. There are only people, without knowing, understanding or feeling, who intoxicate themselves with words, repeat words, shout them out, imagining they believe them without believing in anything else but profit, personal advantage and their own satisfaction.' Cited by Lindqvist, '*Exterminate all the Brutes*', 83.

67 White, *Joseph Conrad and the Adventure Tradition*, 173.

68 *Manchester Guardian* 10 December 1902, 3; in Sherry, *Conrad: The Critical Heritage*, 135.

69 Deurbergue, 'Notice et notes', 1263.

70 I return to the issue of critics' speculations on (other) readers' reactions in the next chapter. Here one might compare Bette London's argument that Marlow's audience (and beyond them, the text's readers) are feminized, in that they are outside the adventure and are excluded from knowledge and truth – though not, of course, as fully excluded as the Intended. See London, 'Reading race and gender in Conrad's dark continent'.

71 Hampson, '*Heart of Darkness* and "The speech that cannot be silenced"', 211. The first critical examination of the text's biographical and historical background was, according to Knowles and Moore, Jean-Aubry's *Joseph Conrad in the Congo* (1925–6); Sherry's magisterial *Conrad's Western World*, published in 1971, also predates Achebe's lecture, and helped promote historicizing approaches to the text.

72 Said, *Culture and Imperialism*, 32.

73 Cited by Watt, *Conrad in the Nineteenth Century*, 148.

74 Conrad to Blackwood, 31 December 1898; in Sherry, *Conrad: The Critical Heritage*, 129.

75 The letter is quoted in full in Said, *Joseph Conrad and the Fiction of Autobiography*, 201–3. Conrad's remark that he starts from 'definite images' may lend support to Lindqvist's account of the immediate historical origins of *Heart of Darkness*.

Chapter 3
'Race', Reading and Identification

1 Said, *Culture and Imperialism*, 208, 219; Barthes, *Writing Degree Zero*, 64/56.
2 In addition to Said's work see, for instance, Apter, *Continental Drift*; Bouguerra, *Le Dit et le non-dit*; Davis, *Ethical Issues in Twentieth-Century French Fiction*; Djemaï, *Camus à Oran*; Dunwoodie, *Writing French Algeria*; Erickson, 'Albert Camus and North Africa'; Haddour, *Colonial Myths* (which traces Barthes's notion of 'writing degree to zero' back to Camus: see 42); Hughes, *Camus: Le Premier homme*; King, *Camus's 'L'Étranger'*; O'Brien, *Camus*; and Smets, *Albert Camus*.
3 In this chapter, references to Camus's *The Outsider/L'Etranger* are given in the main text, with the page number from the English edition first.
4 Some of Barthes's work, notably in *Mythologies*, does engage with the issue of colonialism. For an interesting treatment of Barthes's relationship with French colonialism, see Knight, *Barthes and Utopia*.
5 Said, *Culture and Imperialism*, 208.
6 Said is similarly equivocal about whether or not he is criticizing Camus as an individual (or, to put it another way, whether he uses 'Camus' to mean a person or a body of work). He criticizes O'Brien for letting Camus 'off the hook' (*Culture and Imperialism*, 209), for instance, but states later that his intention is not to 'blame' Camus (p. 212).
7 O'Brien, *Camus*, 21; Sartre, '"Aminadab" or the fantastic considered as a language', 65, 67/133, 136.
8 Said, *Culture and Imperialism*, 219.
9 I return to the notion of the 'universal' in the Afterword.
10 See Yacono, *Histoire de la colonisation française*, 67. Yacono gives the population of Algeria just before World War II as 7,235,000, of whom 946,000 were European.
11 Derrida, *Monolingualism*, 16/35.
12 Camus, *The First Man*, 55/70. 'Algérien' was generally used only in reference to settlers. Cf. Jacques's mother's remark: 'The French are good people' (57/73). For Henri (Jacques the protagonist's father, who went off to fight for France in the First World War and was killed there), France was, Jacques notes, 'a strange land' (21/31); and Jacques's mother never went there and had never seen her husband's grave. The war meant nothing to her: as Jacques explains in a remark that builds to a somewhat exaggerated climax, 'she had never heard of Austria-Hungary nor of Serbia, Russia – like England – was a difficult name, she did not know what an archduke was, and she could never have articulated the four syllables of Sarajevo' (54/68–9). Similarly, there is a passage (112–13/136–7) where Jacques discusses the exotic, almost mythical quality of the stories in his schoolbooks about children wearing woolly scarves and carrying firewood in the snow.

13   Camus, *The First Man*, 24/35.
14   Ibid., 45/60. On such notions of the Mediterranean, see Dunwoodie, *Writing French Algeria*, chapter 5, and Haddour, *Colonial Myths*, chapters 1 and 2. In an essay, comparably, Camus commented: 'Russia or America have the means to rule and to unify the world in the image of their society. I find this repugnant, as a Frenchman and even more as a Mediterranean' (Camus, *Actuelles* (1950), 133).
15   Camus, *The First Man*, 108/132.
16   Ibid., 115/140.
17   Derrida, *Monolingualism*, 42/73 ('La *métropole*, la Ville-Capitale-Mère-Patrie, la cité de la langue maternelle, voilà un lieu qui figurait, sans l'être, un pays lointain, proche mais lointain, non pas étranger, ce serait trop simple, mais étrange, fantastique et fantomal').
18   Camus, essay of 1945 in *Actuelles III*, 94–5. In another article reproduced in the same collection he remarks: 'There has never yet been an Algerian nation. The Jews, the Turks, the Greeks, the Italians, the Berbers would have just as much right to claim the direction of that putative nation [*nation virtuelle*]. At present the Arabs alone do not make up the whole of Algeria. The size and seniority of the French settlement [*l'importance et l'ancienneté du peuplement français*], in particular, are enough to create a problem that cannot be compared with anything in history. The Algerian French are likewise, and in the strongest meaning of the word, natives [*des indigènes*]' (202). *Actuelles III* consists entirely of essays on Algeria; a selection appears in English in Camus, *Resistance, Rebellion and Death*, 79–110 (incl. last quotation, 104). If Camus speaks against 'colonialism', this seems to be because Algeria is not, in his view, a 'colony' in the sense that Morocco and Tunisia, say, were (*Actuelles* III, 126, 202) – and because 'colonist' for him designates a particular social class.
19   Bourdieu, *Sociologie de l'Algérie* ([1958]), 112. '*Francaoui*' is the Arabic word for French; the term 'pied noir', whose precise etymology is uncertain, generally designates a French person born in colonial Algeria.
20   Sartre, 'Camus's *The Outsider*', 24, 26, 40/102, 120.
21   Fanon, *The Wretched of the Earth*, 242/356–7. 'Pithiatism' is a somewhat archaic term meaning a type of hysteria or hysterical symptom that may be cured through suggestion.
22   Ibid., 239–40/353–6.
23   Ibid., 246n/362n.
24   Historically, English usage has pushed the confusion still further, permitting reference to both Othello and Muslims in India as 'Moors'. For a discussion of Othello as 'Moor', see Bate, 'Othello and the other'.
25   Stéphane Gsell, quoted by Servier, *Les Berbères*, 13. Naturally I run into similar descriptive problems throughout this chapter; the reference of terms such as 'native Algerians' and 'White' is no more stable or satisfactory, but I have tried to avoid an undue proliferation of inverted commas.

26 See the entry on 'Race' in Ashcroft et al., *Key Concepts in Post-Colonial Studies*.

27 Cavalli-Sforza et al., *The History and Geography of Human Genes*, 19–20.

28 On this point, see Young, *Colonial Desire: Hybridity in Theory, Culture and Race*, *passim*.

29 A statement released a few years ago by a coalition of seventeen different groups with misgivings about genetic research stated: 'In the long history of human destruction that has accompanied western colonization, we have come to realize that the agenda of non-indigenous forces has been to appropriate and manipulate the natural order for the purposes of profit, power and control' (cited by Ochert, 'In Everyman's footsteps', 17). I return to the issue of the political framework of scientific knowledge in relation to Fanon in the Afterword.

30 Cited by Ochert, 'In Everyman's footsteps', 17.

31 This is certainly the response of the narrator of Julian Barnes's *Flaubert's Parrot*: see chapter 6, 'Emma Bovary's eyes'.

32 For a different interpretation of the role of indifference in this scene, see Davis, *Ethical Issues in Twentieth-Century French Fiction*, 71.

33 A further point about Meursault's identity as a *pied noir* arises from these first words, incidentally. O'Brien notes (*Camus*, 87n) that 'Anne Durand, a French-Algerian contemporary of Camus's, writes as follows about the opening words of *The Outsider*: "But we Algerians are pulled up by the first words: 'Today mother [*maman*] died...' Among us *maman* is used as a vocative, never otherwise... The Meursault in question is a stranger to us."'

34 Fitch, 'Narrateur et narration dans *L'Étranger*', chapter 4.

35 For a different argument concerning the self-reflexive elements of the trial scene, see Fitch, *The Narcissitic Text*, chapter 4.

36 There is a comparable moment when Meursault is invited to admire the defence's performance (161/101). Meursault notes, 'I heard them [the lawyer's colleagues] say: "Magnificent, old chap." One of them even called on me to bear witness to his achievement: "Don't you think?", he said to me [*L'un d'eux m'a même pris à témoin: "Hein?" m'a-t-il dit*]'. Thus Meursault is treated as a third party, and turned into a 'witness', in the context of his own trial.

37 J. M. A. Paroutaud, *Confluences*, 13 (October 1942), cited by Bagot, *L'Etranger*, 81.

38 O'Brien, *Camus*, 22–3.

39 Barthes, *Writing Degree Zero*, 67/57 ('Si l'écriture est vraiment neutre, si le langage, au lieu d'être un acte encombrant et indomptable, parvient à l'état d'une équation pure, n'ayant pas plus d'épaisseur qu'une algèbre en face du creux de l'homme, alors la Littérature est vaincue, la problématique humaine est découverte et livrée sans couleur, l'écrivain est sans retour un honnête homme').

40 For a discussion of this matter in relation to Barthes's reading of Sade, see Harrison, *Circles of Censorship*, 183–98; and, in relation to film, see Bordwell, *Making Meaning*, 135 and *passim*.

41 Barthes, *Writing Degree Zero*, 65/57 ('Malheureusement rien n'est plus infidèle qu'une écriture blanche; les automatismes s'élaborent à l'endroit même où se trouvait d'abord une liberté, un réseau de formes durcies serre de plus en plus la fraîcheur première du discours, une écriture renaît à la place d'un langage indéfini').

42 Willmott, *Pleasures, Objects and Advantages of Literature* ([1851]), 19–20; 56. I hope to pursue this topic in greater historical depth in later research. An excellent account of the notion of character as applied to film, which raises many issues pertinent to fiction and to the concept of identification, is Murray Smith's *Engaging Characters: Fiction, Emotion and the Cinema*.

43 Žižek, *Everything You Always Wanted to Know*, 224–5.

44 Steiner, *Language and Silence*, 81–2.

45 See Laplanche and Pontalis, *The Language of Psychoanalysis*, 'Identification'.

46 Grant, 'Characterhysterics', 146. This article provides a useful summary of Freudian notions of 'identification'. One might also compare Borch-Jacobsen's argument in *The Freudian Subject* (277–8) concerning Freud's relation to the 'social', and especially his point: 'That "identification" is never anything but another name for "suggestion"'. It should be noted in passing that 'mass psychology' is probably a better translation of the German than is the *Standard Edition*'s less politically charged 'group psychology'.

47 Connerton, 'Freud and the crowd', 194. Freud, of course, had reason to feel threatened not only by left-wing revolutionaries but also by anti-Semitic mobs; this too has implications, which I cannot explore here, for the relation between his theory and the historical context in which it emerged.

48 Freud, *Standard Edition*, XVIII, 88; 78; 80.

49 hooks, *Reel to real*, 2, 3. Cf. Kael's remarks on Pontecorvo's *The Battle of Algiers*: 'people's senses are so overwhelmed by the surging inevitability of the action that they are prepared to support what in another context – such as newsprint – they would reject. It's practically rape of the doubting intelligence' ('The Current Cinema', 238). My thanks to Emily Tomlinson for this reference.

50 It should be noted that on this precise point there are also significant differences between the texts cited. For one thing, Steiner's 'we' is sometimes more uncomfortably specific to the critic (making greater rather than lesser 'literacy' a risk); while Žižek's notion of fantasy may be such that his 'we' is conceived of as genuinely inclusive at certain points.

51 An argument close to this is made in relation to comics by Martin Barker, who concludes that the term 'identification' should be abandoned as

unscientific and reactionary. 'Identification', he argues, 'is not properly a concept, but a focal point where a number of social and political concerns have come together' ('The vicissitudes of identification', 97, 103).

52   Prendergast makes this point in relation to Barthes's essay 'The reality effect' in *The Order of Mimesis*, 70. Recent film criticism has pursued the argument against 'illusionism' in some depth, and to my mind convincingly: see in particular (in chronological order) Allen, *Projecting Illusion*; Carroll, *Theorizing the Moving Image*; Allen and Smith, *Film Theory and Philosophy*; and Carroll, *A Philosophy of Mass Art*.

Chapter 4
Representation, Representativity and 'Minor' Literature

1   '*Nice, very nice, this song*', Jock kept saying. '*Is it folklore?*' 'Folklore yourself', said Tarik (pp. 79/130).

2   See Memmi, *Anthologie des écrivains maghrébins d'expression française*, 11.

3   Memmi, *Ecrivains francophones du Maghreb*, 7-8.

4   To give another example, Mostefa Lacheraf, interviewed by the famous Parisian journal *Les Temps modernes* in October 1963, responded to the question 'Which among the writers you have mentioned are the most representative, the most authentic?' by saying: 'the most representative, in my view, are first Kateb Yacine, then...Feraoun and Mammeri. Without a doubt they are the ones who instinctively, or thanks to experiences in their youth, have the best knowledge of the country or their native area and are more or less familiar with the Algerian people' (reproduced in Khatibi, *Le Roman maghrébin*, 134-5). Similarly, Germaine Brée uses the term to characterize a particular list of writers as 'highly individual and yet "representative"' in the preface to an early critical work on North African literature (cited by Yétiv, *Le Thème de l'aliénation dans le roman maghrébin*, 8).

5   Memmi, *Anthologie des écrivains maghrébins d'expression française*, 9-14.

6   Rushdie, 'Introduction', xii-xv; , Maja-Pearce, Introduction to *The Heinemann Book of African Poetry in English*, xiii; Achebe and Innes, Introduction to *African Short Stories*, x.

7   For a summary of some of the term's key senses, see the title essay of Prendergast's *The Triangle of Representation*.

8   Spivak, *A Critique of Postcolonial Reason*, 260. Her remarks are made in criticism of Deleuze and Foucault. This section of the book provides a slightly revised version of the issues raised in her well-known essay 'Can the subaltern speak?' Her use of the term 'subaltern' derives from the work of Gramsci, who used it to describe groups under the hegemony of the ruling classes; more immediately, Spivak used it initially in response

to the work of the Subaltern Studies Group, historians including Ranajit Guha and Partha Chatterjee who worked on subaltern groups in South Asia.

9 Anon., 'La Révolte d'un jeune homme ou le Maroc mis à nu', 9–10.

10 Simiot, 'Espoirs et tourments de la jeunesse marocaine', 472.

11 Chraïbi, *The Simple Past*, 202.

12 Ibid., 18. For a discussion of such issues see, for instance, Bounfour, 'L'autobiographie maghrébine et sa lecture'.

13 Chraibi, letter in *Bulletin de Paris*, 4 March 1955, 3; *Demain* (29 November–5 December 1956), 20, cited by Seidenfaden, *Ein kritischer Mittler*, 70. The *Chambers* dictionary defines a legitimist as 'one who believes in the right of royal succession according to the principle of heredity and primogeniture', and pasha as 'a Turkish title (abolished 1934) given to governors and high military and naval officers'.

14 *Démocratie*, 2 (14 January 1957), 10; cited by Seidenfaden, *Ein kritischer Mittler*, 71.

15 *Démocratie*, 5 (4 February 1957), 10; cited by Seidenfaden, *Ein kritischer Mittler*, 74–5. Seidenfaden's book gives a more detailed account of the '*Passé simple* affair' than I have (68–75), as does Kadra-Hadjadji, *Contestation et révolte*, 54–63.

16 Yétiv, *Le Thème de l'aliénation*, 45.

17 Khatibi, *Le Roman maghrébin*, 80.

18 Williams, *Keywords*, 268.

19 Young, *Colonial Desire*, 58. Young draws attention to the older sense of the term 'minority' as an elite.

20 Memmi, *The Colonizer and the Colonized*, 151/106.

21 The particular use of 'Islam' in the reviews derived in part, of course, from the specific (and slightly different) difficulties of religious/national categorization presented to French colonial discourse by Algeria.

22 Chraïbi, *The Butts*, 106/162 ('Boire, je dois boire . . . Boire et tuer en moi tout espoir de rachat et rester un schéma de Bicot'). The primary meaning of the word *bouc* is billy goat, but it is perhaps heard most frequently in the phrase *bouc émissaire*, scapegoat.

23 Spivak, *A Critique of Postcolonial Reason*, 255.

24 Chraïbi, *The Butts*, 61/93 ('Je ne me crois représentant de qui ou de quoi que ce soit, hormis de moi').

25 Ibid., 101, 112/155, 171 ('Waldick était pour eux un Chrétien'; 'les Boucs en ont marre – il se croit encore leur prophète!').

26 See Chraïbi, *Vu, lu, entendu*, 59.

27 Cf. the argument made by Floya Anthias and Nira Yuval-Davis, and cited by Robert Young, that the doctrine of multiculturalism encourages different groups to reify their individual and different identities at their most different, thus 'encouraging' extremist groups, who become 'representative' because they have the most clearly discernibly different identity (see Young, *Colonial Desire*, 5).

28 Deleuze and Guattari, *Kafka: Toward a Minor Literature*, 16/30.

29   Ibid., 19/35.
30   Ibid., 16, 61, 86, 24, 17/29, 111, 153, 45, 30.
31   Ibid., 17/30, 31.
32   Williams, *Keywords*, 185. Among the literature on this topic, see also George Steiner's 'To civilize our gentlemen', to which I alluded in chapter 3, and the discussion of Matthew Arnold in Young, *Colonial Desire*, 55–89, and Lloyd, 'Arnold, Ferguson, Schiller'.
33   Lanson, from *La Méthode de l'histoire littéraire* (1910); cited by Antoine Compagnon, *La Troisième République des lettres*, 169.
34   Memmi, *Anthologie des écrivains maghrébins d'expression française*, 10, 15, 17.
35   Bonn, 'La traversée, arcane du roman maghrébin?', 57.
36   See Foucault, 'What is an author?'. Foucault argues that the concept of the author guides interpretation of the text, and that different sorts of text are characterized by different 'author-functions' and different uses of personal pronouns. The sort of biographical information that might seem to many readers to serve a useful function in interpreting a poem, for example, fitting in with and constituting a certain *concept* of the author, would not appear pertinent in discussing a scientific proof.
37   Khatibi, *Le Roman maghrébin*, 38. Memmi in his preface of 1964, it may be noted, talked of 'North African literature' variously in terms of French literature, of 'emergent national literatures [*littératures nationales naissantes*]', and, tentatively, of 'universal' literature (15–16).
38   Rushdie, 'Introduction', xii–xiii; Maja-Pearce, *The Heinemann Book of African Poetry in English*, xiv; Ngũgĩ wa Thiong'o, *Penpoints, Gunpoints and Dreams*, 89.
39   Memmi, *Anthologie des écrivains maghrébins d'expression française*, 18.
40   Grégoire, cited by Calvet, *Linguistique et colonialisme*, 168. See also Miller, *Theories of Africans*, and Gordon, *The French Language and National Identity*, where he writes: 'To many a Frenchman his language is not a "mother tongue" rooted in nature, a medium of personal self-expression, but rather a function of civilization, a weapon against nature, and to talk correctly is a part of social behaviour.... The French *mission civilisatrice* is related to a subconscious faith that France is bearer of the universal idea that human nature is everywhere and at all times basically the same, that its laws have been most fully realized by France and that, therefore, one does not speak of "French civilization", but of civilization simply' (4, 6).
41   In the case of Algeria the link between Arabic and Islam is crucial, and, as Slimane Chikh notes (see 'L'Algérie face à la francophonie'), took on a particular consistency during the anti-colonial war because the Association of Algerian *Ulamas* (scholars of Islam) took the lead in spreading literacy as well as a deepened knowledge of Islamic culture and history among the Algerian population. The reach and authority of Arabic as a *national* and nationalist language were increased during the war through

the FLN's literacy programme, which, not least because it extended into jails, reached militants from different ethnic groups.

42 Reclus, *France, Algérie et colonies*, 447.

43 For a brief history of *francophonie* and a consideration of its implications at present, see Hargreaves, 'Francophonie and globalization'.

44 Benchama discusses the low level of interest in literature among North Africans in his 1994 book *L'œuvre de Driss Chraïbi*. He conducted a survey among a sample of teachers and students, and found that there was an average of only three answers per respondent in answer to the question 'Which Moroccan (North African) writers do you know?', and only 2.6 when it came to those the respondent had actually read – a large proportion of which, Benchama suggests, were texts which had appeared on a school or university syllabus. It will be particularly striking to those anglophone academic critics for whom Djebar has become an eminent figure that, among the 1185 answers to the first question, she was named just once. The frustration of reaching only a restricted readership in North Africa is not unique to 'francophone' writers, of course; it seems unlikely that the audience for Haddad's writing in Arabic, for instance, was much larger or less elite than that of his writing in French.

45 Haddad, 'Les Zéros tournent en rond', 34–5 ('même s'exprimant en français, les écrivains algériens d'origine arabo-berbère *traduisent* une pensée *spécifiquement algérienne,* une pensée qui aurait trouvé la plénitude de son expression *si elle avait été véhiculée par un langage et une écriture arabes*... Il n'y a qu'une *correspondance approximative* entre notre *pensée d'Arabes* et notre *vocabulaire de Français*').

46 Ibid., 32.

47 Henry argues categorically that '"modern" Arabic has established itself in the Maghreb over French, but also according to a very French model of a "national" language, seen as the kernel of a "national" culture, even if the latter relates partly to the mystical Arab Nation' (*Nouveaux enjeux culturels au Maghreb*, 18).

48 Fanon, *Black Skin*, 17–18; *Peau noire*, 13; Deleuze and Guattari, *Kafka: Toward a Minor Literature*, 24/44.

49 Chraïbi, *The Simple Past*, 202 ('Ce matin, en me rendant ici, j'ai rencontré un Américain de la Military Police. Il arrêta sa Jeep. "Toi Français?" me demanda-t-il. "Non," répondis-je: "Arabe habillé en Français." "Then... où sont Arabes habillés en Arabes, parlant arabe et... " J'étendis la main en direction du vieux cimetière musulman. "Par là"').

50 Ibid., 205–6 ('Un bon roman genre vieille école: le Maroc, pays d'avenir, le soleil, le couscous, les métèques, le Bicot sur le bourricot et la Bicote derrière, la danse du ventre, les souks... les cocotiers, les bananiers, les flèches empoisonnées, les Indiens, Pluto, Tarzan, le Capitaine Cook...').

51 Khatibi, *Le Roman maghrébin*, 28 ('Le roman ethnographique et folklorique').

52   Chraïbi, *The Simple Past*, 207 ('Je n'ignore point, messieurs les exam-
     inateurs, qu'une copie d'élève doit être anonyme, exempte de signature,
     nom, prénom ou marque propre à en faire reconnaître l'auteur. Je
     n'ignore point non plus cependant qu'une toile révèle aisément le pein-
     tre. C'est dire qu'il y a quelque temps déjà que vous avez percé ma
     personnalité: je suis arabe').
53   Quoted above from Memmi, *Anthologie des écrivains maghrébins d'ex-
     pression française*, 10, 15, 17.

Chapter 5
Writing and Voice:
Women, Nationalism and the Literary Self

1   Djebar, *Ces voix*, 224 ('"ce qu'ils n'aimaient pas en lui, c'était l'Algér-
     ien"'; 'je souris à cet Algérien-là, moi qu'on accueille de si loin et dans
     une université prestigieuse parce qu'écrivain, parce que femme et parce
     qu'algérienne: je note à mon tour, en contrepoint à Camus, "ce qu'ils
     reconnaissent en moi, c'est l'Algérienne." "Ce qu'ils reconnaissent?"
     Rectifions: "Ce qu'ils espèrent de moi, c'est l'Algérie-femme"'). Camus's
     The First Man contains a series of his manuscript notes.
2   Djebar, *Ces voix*, 18 ('sans doute trop jeune, pendant la guerre d'Algérie
     – l'autre, celle de mes vingt ans – et qui plus est, pas des essais nationa-
     listes, pas de profession de foi lyrique ou polémique (c'était ce genre de
     témoignage que l'on attendait de moi!), écrire donc des romans, qui
     semblaient gratuits'). Zhdanov (p. 87) was a Soviet theorist of art,
     whose purposes he thought should lie in supporting the socialist and
     proletarian ideology of the state. Djebar's first works were *La Soif*
     (1957), *Les Impatients* (1958), *Les Enfants du nouveau monde* (1962),
     and *Les Alouettes naïves* (1967). Of the texts in *Femmes d'Alger dans
     leur appartement* (1980), the 'Overture' ('Ouverture') and 'Postface'
     were written for that collection in 1979, but the others were written at
     different dates between 1959 and 1978. The English translation
     appeared in 1992.
3   Gafaïti, 'L'autobiographie plurielle', 150; Donadey, *Recasting Postcolo-
     nialism*, xxvi.
4   Djebar, *Women of Algiers*, 2/8 ('Depuis dix ans au moins – par suite sans
     doute de mon propre silence, par à-coups, de femme arabe – , je ressens
     combien parler sur ce terrain devient (sauf pour les porte-parole et les
     "spécialistes") d'une façon ou d'une autre une transgression. || Ne pas
     prétendre "parler pour", ou pire "parler sur", à peine parler *près de*, et si
     possible *tout contre*: première des solidarités à assumer pour les quel-
     ques femmes arabes qui obtiennent ou acquièrent la liberté de mouve-
     ment, du corps et de l'esprit').
5   Djebar, *Ces voix*, 85 ('une certaine critique qui, le domaine féminin sitôt
     approché, se contente de commentaires ou sociologiques ou biographi-

ques, recréant ainsi à sa manière un harem pseudo-littéraire'); 263 (vous ne direz pas 'nous', vous ne vous cacherez pas, vous femme singulière, derrière la "Femme"; vous ne serez jamais, ni au début ni à la fin, "porte-parole").

6   Aspects of Djebar's political involvement have been traced in her auto-biographical fiction and in interviews; cf. Zimra, Afterword, 189–90.

7   Partly because of the rhetorical uses made of the historical facts, the extent and nature of women's participation in the war is hard to estab-lish. Khalida Messaoudi, in *Une Algérienne debout: entretiens avec Elisabeth Schemla* (Paris: Flammarion, 1995), commented: 'Never, never would we have imagined that those by whose side we fought would conduct our country like that... Our "sequestration" did not begin in 1962 but before independence. Little by little during the war the FLN eliminated us from the maquis, sending us to the borders or abroad. Our role was defined at that moment. We did not have a place in the world "outside"' (84; quoted by Orlando, *Nomadic Voices*, 202–3). For a different view, see Lazreg, *The Eloquence of Silence*, chapter 8; and see Amrane-Minne, *La Guerre d'Algérie (1954–1962): femmes au combat* and *Des femmes dans la guerre d'Algérie*.

8   See Beauvoir and Halimi, *Djamila Boupacha*.

9   Djebar, *Women of Algiers*, 5/13 ('Tête de jeune femme aux yeux bandés, cou renversé, cheveux tirés').

10 Ibid., 50/68 ('Je ne vois pour les femmes arabes qu'un seul moyen de tout débloquer: parler, parler sans cesse d'hier et d'aujourd'hui, parler entre nous, dans tous les gynécées, les traditionnels et ceux des HLM').

11 Ibid., 36/51 ('Explique-lui que chez nous les "Fatma" s'appellent toutes Fatma!'). 'Fatma', the name of Muhammad's daughter by his first wife and the first name of many North African women (including Djebar, whose real name is Fatima Zohra Imalayen), is used in French as pejorative slang for Algerian women. In view of Djebar's project, in *Loin de Médine*, of fleshing out imaginarily the story of female figures from the Qu'ran, I wonder, too, whether one might detect some sort of ironic dissonance between this incident and the 'main de Fatma', a ubiquitous sign of good luck (which makes symbolic use of a historical figure about whom relatively little historical information is available).

12 Djebar, *Women of Algiers*, 122/152–3 ('les interminables formules de politesse'; '– Non! renâclait-elle – Papoter, manger des gâteaux, s'em-piffrer en attendant le lendemain, est-ce pour cela qu'il y a eu deuil et sang? Non, je ne l'admets pas... Moi, – et sa voix s'enveloppait de larmes – je croyais, vois-tu, que tout cela changerait, qu'autre chose viendrait').

13 See Giddens, 'Living in a post-traditional society'.

14 Djebar, *Women of Algiers*, 20/31. For a feminist critique of hawfis, see Titah, *La Galérie des absentes*, 53.

15 Djebar, *Women of Algiers*, 125/158 ('La pierre m'ouvrit le front juste au-dessus de l'œil (le Prophète, que la grâce soit sur lui, m'a protégée!) et mon mari se remit à prier imperturbablement').

16   Ibid., 10/18 ('Elle avait repris le rythme des accouchements "au lende-main de l'indépendance" (beaucoup de récits plus nobles commencent encore par cette expression oratoire . . .)').

17   Ibid., 14/24 ('De ses cinq ans de maquis, que m'a-t-il raconté? . . . La manière dont il avait ouvert le bal officiel du Kremlin, peu avant les années 60 (ils étaient les cinq premiers "fellaghas-étudiants" à être passés en U.R.S.S. par les maquis et les "pays frères") . . . Et de la vie de maquis, un seul détail "misérable": terrés dans des grottes, ils tuaient leur poux l'hiver! Un camarade de cette époque glorieuse avait même ajouté devant moi, un jour où il était pas mal éméché: "On en tuait un tel nombre et nous étions devenus si experts que les poux faisaient, en s'écrasant sous nos ongles, un vrai bruit de mitraillette"'). 'Fellah' is a word used for Arab peasants/smallholders.

18   Ibid., 111/141 ('Ces derniers jours, Hassan mesure le temps. D'autres déjà le résument: "sept ans", comme on dit dans des histoires classiques et conformes: "La guerre de sept ans", "la guerre de cent ans". Formule ici définitive: "La guerre de libération". Libération du décor et des autres, mais . . . ').

19   Ibid., 116/146 ('Un enterrement sans histoire certes, mais voilà que la mélancolie d'une cousine pauvre, la rêverie d'un métayer dans un cor-tège subsistent, tandis que sur le petit-fils seul les regards témoins se concentrent. En son cœur à lui, règne une étendue aride. Pire que l'oubli. || Or les morts parlent. La voix de la vieille murmure près de Aïcha . . . Qu'en aperçoit l'homme vers lequel les derniers espoirs de Hadda se sont tendus? Rien').

20   Ibid., 117/147 ('Longuement, il évoqua les morts, tous les morts enfouis dans les broussailles, morts au combat, morts des massacres, "tous les morts qui vivraient" disait-il. Il obtint succès si prolongé que les hulule-ments des femmes montèrent en vrilles langoureuses de l'esplanade au-dessus du port où se tenait le meeting, jusqu'au cimetière où Aïcha seule était venue se recueillir. C'était le septième jour de la mort de Yemma. A ses côtés, son garçonnet – cinq ans déjà – contemplait par-dessus le mur le panorama de la ville, qu'irisaient les taches mobiles et colorées du meeting'). 'Yemma', a respectful term for older women, means 'mother', and refers here to Hassan's grandmother, a mainstay of her own small community; Hassan's speech is delivered just after independence and only seven days after Yemma's funeral, a day that traditionally would have been a full day of ritual mourning and prayers over the grave. See Zimra, Afterword, 207–8.

21   See Anderson, *Imagined Communities*; Rose, *States of Fantasy*; and Žižek, *The Plague of Fantasies*.

22   Djebar, *Ces voix*, 32–3 ('Mon pays, sous véritable dictature culturelle, a été harcelé par un monolinguisme pseudo-identitaire'). See also 54, 56, 213.

23   Djebar, *Women of Algiers*, 13/22 ('se recycler dans la langue nationale').

24   Ibid., 68/90 ('moi, je n'éprouvais pas le besoin de secouer . . . mon esprit').

25 Ibid., 1/7 ('Je pourrais dire: "nouvelles traduites de...", mais de quelle langue? De l'arabe? D'un arabe populaire, ou d'un arabe féminin; autant dire d'un arabe souterrain').

26 Cixous, who is also from Algeria, published her influential *La Jeune née* (co-written with Catherine Clément) in 1975, and in the same year published *Souffles*, the first of many of her works to appear with 'des femmes', the original publisher of *Femmes d'Alger*. Irigaray's *Speculum: de l'autre femme* and *Ce sexe qui n'en est pas un* were published in 1974 and 1977 respectively. Both Cixous and Irigaray are referred to in *Ces voix*, but the question of their influence is not broached.

27 Ngũgĩ wa Thiong'o, *Penpoints*, 103. For a detailed account of Djebar's use of oral tradition in *Fantasia*, see Donadey, *Recasting Postcolonialism*, 50ff; and for a fascinating discussion of European assumptions about literacy, writing and oral culture in a different context, see V. Smith, *Literary Culture and the Pacific*.

28 Djebar, *Ces voix*, 43 ('J'ai utilisé jusque-là la langue française comme *voile*. Voile sur ma personne individuelle, voile sur mon corps de femme; je pourrais presque dire voile sur ma propre voix').

29 Ibid., 43 ('Voile non de la dissimulation ni du masque, mais de la suggestion et de l'ambiguité'); 97–8 ('Je livre d'abord un souvenir d'enfance; tous ceux qui ont vécu enfants au Maghreb, garçons ou filles, pourraient revivre la même scène du quotidien: quand je sortais, toute petite, avec ma mère, ou une tante, ou une autre parente, il y avait toujours un moment, dans le vestibule, où la dame voilée, avant d'affronter la rue, s'apprêtait lentement à déplier son voile. || Lorsqu'on déplie et qu'on déploie ce voile – dans mon souvenir, c'est toujours un voile de soie blanche et moirée –, ces quelques minutes pour s'apprêter, se protéger, pour manipuler le tissu, sont essentielles: car il y a une manière particulière de se voiler pour chaque femme!...Une façon de serrer le voile sur les hanches, de le plier au niveau des épaules, d'en ramener les pans sous le menton: de ces gestes rapides et sûrs, chaque enfant est conscient.... || Chaque enfant pensait, comme moi, que sa mère avait la façon la plus noble, la plus élégante de porter ce voile! Et, dans la rue, les hommes devaient reconnaître ma mère – sans doute parce que, dans la petite cité, ils me reconnaissaient... || Moi, fillette, j'étais tout à fait sûre que si l'on devait reconnaître ma mère, même voilée, c'était évidemment parce qu'elle avait les plus beaux yeux, et les plus belles chevilles (parce qu'effectivement on ne voyait d'elle que les yeux, au-dessus de la voilette posée sur le nez, et qu'on devinait à peine ses chevilles). Ou, parfois, d'une façon plus subtile, pensais-je alors, si on la reconnaissait, c'était, d'une certaine façon, les pans du voile qui la traduisaient (sa manière inimitable de s'envelopper dans cette soie). || Il y a mille façons de se voiler').

30 Djebar, *Women of Algiers*, 153/191 ('Les femmes voilées sont d'abord des femmes libres de circuler'). Djebar's use of 'd'abord' here may have a temporal dimension, pertaining to the historical role of the veil in

distinguishing free women from slaves (on which point, see Mernissi, *Le Harem politique*, chapter 9); the present tense suggests that its meaning is primarily conceptual, however, and that Djebar wants to present the veil as the condition on which those women who wear it enter the public space.

31 Lazreg, *The Eloquence of Silence*, 201.

32 See Alloula, *The Colonial Harem*, 29/24, 118/75; and see 122/78.

33 Haddour, *Colonial Myths: History and Narrative*, 128.

34 For a discussion of this issue in relation to Rushdie, see Brennan, *Salman Rushdie and the Third World*.

35 Djebar, *Women of Algiers*, 138/173 ('Ce regard-là, longtemps l'on a cru qu'il était volé parce qu'il était celui de l'étranger, hors du harem et de la cité. || Depuis quelques décennies – au fur et à mesure que triomphe çà et là chaque nationalisme –, on peut se rendre compte qu'à l'intérieur de cet Orient livré à lui-même, l'image de la femme n'est pas perçue autrement: par le père, par l'époux et, d'une façon plus trouble, par le frère et le fils').

36 As suggested earlier, the notions of 'Arab' and 'Muslim' frequently blur together in 'Western' representations of North Africa and the Middle East, as they do in a certain pan-Arab nationalism. Most Muslims, it should be remembered, are not Arabs (they are outnumbered by non-Arab Muslims around the world, including those in Indonesia, Pakistan, India, Iran, etc.), and not all Arabs are Muslims. Cf. Kandiyoti, 'Identity and its discontents: women and the nation'.

37 For a notable critique of practices of 'veiling' from an Islamic perspective, see Mernissi, *Le Harem politique*; and for further discussion of European perceptions of the veil, see Fanon, 'Algeria unveiled' (in *Studies in a Dying Colonialism*, 35–67/16–47); Haddour, *Colonial Myths*, chapter 7; and Gaspard and Khosrokhavar, *Le Foulard et la République*.

38 Djebar, *Ces voix*, 184 ('j'ai ressenti enfin combien la langue française que j'écris s'appuie sur la mort des miens, plonge ses racines dans les cadavres des vaincus de la conquête').

39 In interviews and conference papers Djebar's range of cultural reference is wide, stretching well outside France and North Africa. She makes it clear at one point that situating herself in an international (and non-French) literary context is a conscious decision: see Hornung and Ruhe, *Postcolonialisme et autobiographie*, 182.

40 Djebar, *Women of Algiers*, 137/172 ('absentes à elles-mêmes, à leur corps, à leur sensualité, à leur bonheur'). The phrase pertains to the new version of the painting created by Delacroix in 1849, *Femmes d'Alger dans leur intérieur*, wherein, in Djebar's interpretation, the figures seem all the more distant, the light more unreal, and the sense of the women's isolation more acute.

41 Cf. the actions of the women bomb-carriers whom Djebar discusses and who featured famously in Pontecorvo's *The Battle of Algiers*; as is suggested in both that film and the article by Fanon, 'Algeria unveiled',

that influenced it, the point is not only that those women's actions ran counter to French preconceptions about Algerian women's passivity and cloistered domesticity, but that it was precisely their knowing manipulation of the cultural conventions to which they were assumed to be passively subjected, and indeed of those French preconceptions, that made such actions feasible.

42   Djebar, *Women of Algiers*, 136/170 ('lumière de serre ou d'aquarium').

43   Djebar, *Ces voix*, 182 ('J'ai dû travailler avec cette contrainte, et je peux dire que j'ai cherché d'une certaine façon à la respecter, à faire que ce vide devienne fiction'). One might compare the remark I used as an epigraph in the Introduction.

44   Djebar, *Women of Algiers*, 153/191 ('Le talent novateur de Delacroix peintre s'oppose au traditionalisme de l'homme Delacroix').

45   Djebar captured something of this ambiguity in an elegant remark made at a conference: 'When one is writing the violence of history, one writes it as a *mise en scène* and that is a contradiction. I thought of Delacroix. When Delacroix paints the Chios massacres, he is not caught up in the pain of the massacres, he's caught up in his problem with the colour red, or with the woman's shoulder, he is caught up in these details, yet the motivation is to denounce that violence. But as soon as you start writing it, or inscribing it in colour or in words, the violence is in slow motion, it's anaesthetized by the style or the form that you impart to it' ['La violence de l'histoire quand on l'écrit, on l'écrit comme une mise en scène et c'est contradictoire. J'avais pensé à Delacroix. Lorsque Delacroix peint les massacres de Sion [*sic*], il n'est pas dans la douleur des massacres, il est dans ce problème du rouge, il est dans le problème de l'épaule de la dame, il est dans ces détails, pourtant la motivation est de dénoncer cette violence. Mais à partir du moment où vous l'écrivez, où vous l'inscrivez en couleurs ou en mots, c'est une violence au ralenti, c'est une violence anesthésiée par le style ou la forme que vous allez donner']. In Hornung and Ruhe, *Postcolonialisme et autobiographie*, 183.

46   See Hornung and Ruhe, *Postcolonialisme et autobiographie*, 244; Djebar, *Ces voix*, 107 ('je ne me contentais pas, après le succès d'estime de *Femmes d'Alger*, de creuser le sillon: "femmes du Maghreb, de l'Islam, malheureuses et victimes"!'). One might compare her ironic comment, 'in the West, people like to feel sorry for Arab women, or Muslim Women, or…' ('en Occident, on aime pleurer sur les femmes arabes, ou musulmanes, ou…' (ibid., 68)). The cover of *L'Amour, la fantasia* again bears a painting by Delacroix (*Exercice des Marocains*), and the title alludes to this, and also to Beethoven, via the Arabic *fantaziya*, 'ostentation', a term applied to the display of horsemanship depicted by Delacroix.

47   Djebar, *Fantasia*, 75/89 ('Pélissier n'eut qu'un tort: comme il écrivait fort bien et qu'il le savait, il fit dans son rapport une description éloquente et réaliste, beaucoup trop réaliste, des souffrances des Arabes…').

48   Ibid., 75, 78/89, 92 ('Les mots voyagent . . . une pulsion me secoue, telle une sourde otalgie: remercier Pélissier pour son rapport qui déclencha à Paris une tempête politique, mais aussi qui me renvoie nos morts vers lesquels j'élève aujourd'hui ma trame de mots français').

49   I return to this issue in the Conclusion. Cf. Djebar's remarks on Mouloud Feraoun's autobiographical *Le Fils du pauvre*, published as a novel just after the Second World War: 'He sheltered behind that fictional will; it's as if he veiled himself, perhaps because he was looking to reach a French audience above all' ('Il s'abritait derrière cette volonté fictionnelle; il se voilait presque, peut-être parce qu'il tentait d'avancer surtout au-devant d'un public français' (*Ces voix*, 118).

50   From Kacimi, *Une enfance ailleurs: 17 écrivains racontent*, ed. Huston and Sebbar (Paris: Belfond, 1993), 109; cited by Déjeux, 'Au Maghreb, la langue française "langue natale du je"', 185. A *zaouïa* is a religious community or its mosque, usually attached to the tomb of a holy man.

51   Déjeux, 'Au Maghreb, la langue française "langue natale du je"', 192. Djebar herself speaks of the taboos weighing on women who write 'in the first person and about singularity' ('à la première personne et de la singularité'; *Ces voix*, 70); and see her remarks in Hornung and Ruhe, *Postcolonialisme et autobiographie*, 182–3.

52   Mernissi, *Women's Rebellion*, 110.

53   Gusdorf, 'Conditions and limits of autobiography', 28.

54   Memmi, *Anthologie des écrivains maghrébins d'expression française*, 19.

55   See Hitchcott, *Women Writers in Francophone Africa*, chapter 4 and *passim*, for a challenge to the association between autobiography and individualism in relation to women writers from sub-Saharan Africa.

56   Cf. Hafid Gafaïti's remark, 'Djebar's production is illuminated by the principle that the history of the subject is a text inscribed in the general field of History' (cited in Hornung and Ruhe, *Postcolonialisme et autobiographie*, 101). Djebar herself, it should be noted, alludes to one of the best-known literary-critical models of autobiography, Lejeune's 'autobiographical pact', when she writes about Fadhma Aït Mansour Amrouche, implying that it is not fully adequate to that example. The latter was the first Algerian woman to write an autobiography in French, and the mother of the writers Taos and Jean Amrouche. She originally thought that her manuscript might serve as raw material for a novel by Jean, but he died young and in the end she dedicated the book to Taos, who, Djebar speculates, must have encouraged her mother to complete her own project (see *Ces voix*, 123).

57   Britton, 'The (de)construction of subjectivity', 44.

58   Ibid., 45–51. Ngũgĩ wa Thiong'o's notion of voice, it may be noted, is close to the one cited here: 'art', he writes, 'tries to give voice back to the silenced' (*Penpoints*, 25).

59   Smith and Watson, *Women, Autobiography, Theory*, 5.

60 Derrida, *Monolingualism*, 28/53. For a deft account of related concepts of the 'work of subjectivity', see R. Gordon, *Pasolini: Forms of Subjectivity*, Introduction.

61 The subtitle of *Ces voix qui m'assiègent*, '*en marge de ma francophonie*', is suggestive here, and symptomatically difficult to translate: 'en marge de' suggests being on (or outside) the periphery of French-speaking, and the (or 'my') French-speaking world.

62 Sheringham, *French Autobiography*, viii. The definition of literary form (and why 'form' may be a misleading term) will be clarified in the Conclusion.

63 Beckett, *The Unnamable*, 281/40 ('Cette voix qui parle... Elle sort de moi, elle me remplit, elle clame contre mes murs, elle n'est pas la mienne, je ne peux pas l'arrêter, je ne peux pas l'empêcher, de me déchirer,... de m'assiéger. Elle n'est pas la mienne, je n'en ai pas, je n'ai pas de voix et je dois parler, c'est tout ce que je sais, c'est autour de cela qu'il faut tourner, c'est à propos de cela qu'il faut parler, avec cette voix qui n'est pas la mienne, mais qui ne peut être que la mienne puisqu'il n'y a que moi'). Cited in *Ces voix*, 'Ecriture de l'autobiographie', 95.

64 Derrida, *Monolingualism*, 2/14 ('cette langue, la seule que je sois ainsi voué à parler tant que parler me sera possible,... jamais ce ne sera la mienne').

65 Djebar, *Ces voix*, 194 ('Littérature, lieu du non-lieu qui serait l'écriture du désastre qui s'ensable. Infinie déréliction du langage, dans l'impuissance bouche bandée, yeux dessillés, et dont, après Kafka, Beckett et Blanchot furent les augures!'). *L'Ecriture du désastre* is one of Blanchot's books.

66 Blanchot, 'The narrative voice', 385/565.

67 This translation is taken from Josipovici, *Text and Voice*, 67. Blanchot, *Le Livre à venir*, 259.

Chapter 6
Conclusion: Literature and the Work of Criticism

1 Slemon, 'Modernism's last post', 5.
2 Bhabha, 'Representation and the colonial text', 97, 100.
3 Derrida, *Acts of Literature*, 48.
4 Pavel, Review, 84.
5 Ibid. Cf. Pavel, *Fictional Worlds*, 16–17 and *passim*; and cf. his remark that 'realism is not merely a set of stylistic and narrative conventions, but a fundamental attitude toward the relationship between the actual world and the truth of literary texts' (p. 46).
6 Derrida, *Passions*, 94.
7 Rabinowitz, 'Reader response, reader responsibility', 139–40. The quotation is from Holland, *The Dynamics of Literary Response*, 5.

8   Iser, *The Fictive and the Imaginary*, 3; cited by Rabinowitz, 'Reader response, reader responsibility', 139.

9   On the latter point see Pavel, *Fictional Worlds*, 71, 80.

10   Derrida, *Acts of Literature*, 41, 44.

11   On Derrida's debt to Heidegger and Blanchot in this area, see Timothy Clark's excellent *Derrida, Heidegger, Blanchot: Sources of Derrida's Notion and Practice of Literature*.

12   Derrida, *Dissemination*, 245/299–300.

13   Derrida, *Passions*, 64, 66–8, 89–90.

14   See Webster, *A Brief History of Blasphemy*, 54. Rushdie's remark was made in *The Observer* (22 January 1989), and is reproduced in Appignanesi and Maitland, *The Rushdie File*, 74–5: 'Dr Aadam Aziz, the patriarch in my novel Midnight's Children, loses his faith and is left with "a hole inside him, a vacancy in a vital inner chamber". I, too, possess the same God-shaped hole. Unable to accept the unarguable absolutes of religion, I have tried to fill up the hole with literature. The art of the novel is a thing I cherish as dearly as the bookburners of Bradford value their brand of militant Islam . . . So the battle over *The Satanic Verses* is a clash of faiths, in a way. Or, more precisely, it's a clash of languages.' He goes on to talk in terms of a 'battle' between secularism and religion, light and dark, that has 'spread to Britain'. He had expressed some of the same ideas in the *Independent Magazine* (10 September 1988); see Ruthven, *A Satanic Affair*, 23.

15   Fish, *Professional Correctness*, 28–9. The Beverley quotation is from *Against Literature*, 25.

16   Derrida's own phrasing, it should be noted, does not indicate to what extent the association of certain forms of literary and political freedom should be considered merely coincidental.

17   Derrida, *Parages*, 149–50 ('La voix narratrice . . . répond à une "police", à une force de l'ordre ou de loi'); *Acts of Literature*, 38. The latter passage continues: 'This duty of irresponsibility, of refusing to reply for one's thought or writing to constituted powers, is perhaps the highest form of responsibility. To whom, to what? That's the whole question of the future or the event promised by or to such an experience, what I was just calling the democracy to come. Not the democracy of tomorrow, not a future democracy which will be present tomorrow but one whose concept is linked to the to-come [*à-venir*, cf. *avenir*, future], to the experience of a promise engaged, that is always an endless promise.'

18   On the notion of 'saying everything' in Sade and Freud, see Harrison, 'Tout dire', in *Circles of Censorship*, 205–21. The notion of literature as a space outside censorship is also invoked at points in Abdallah et al., *Pour Rushdie: cent intellectuels arabes et musulmans pour la liberté d'expression*, a collection to which Djebar contributed; see, for instance, Mohammed Berrada's essay, 'La forme littéraire', 109–11.

19   Bourdieu too, it may be noted, discusses literary 'autonomy' in such terms, writing: 'One of the properties of a "well-formed" discourse is

that it imposes the norms of its own perception; it says, "Treat me with due form", that is, in accordance with the forms I give myself, and above all don't reduce me to what I deny by taking on these forms. In other words, I am arguing here for the right to perform "reduction": euphemized discourse exercises a symbolic violence which has the specific effect of forbidding the only violence that it deserves, which consists in reducing it to what it says but in a form such that it claims not to be saying it' ('Censorship', 91). What is misleading in this, and in other discussions of artistic autonomy in Bourdieu, is how in his rhetoric that 'discourse', or the 'pure' work of art, despite possessing only an artificial autonomy, achieves agency: it seemingly speaks for itself and 'imposes' its own norms of perception (cf. *The Rules of Art*, 288/397). But, as we have seen, no work of art can do so; and relatedly, no reader or spectator ever experiences it or interprets it 'purely' in these terms.

20 For a closely related argument, which gives an account of how this literary/critical evolution has worked in the North African context, see Hallward, *Absolutely Postcolonial*, chapter 4. Hallward is discussing in particular the work of Mohammed Dib, and seeking to query its place within the sort of (Blanchotian) version of literary history offered by Charles Bonn in influential works including *Le Roman algérien de langue française*.

21 Eagleton, *Criticism and Ideology*, 135.

22 Watts, '"A bloody racist": about Achebe's view of Conrad', 415, 417.

23 Hampson, '*Heart of Darkness* and "The speech that cannot be silenced"', 210, 211.

24 Derrida, in Didier Cahen, 'Entretien avec Jacques Derrida', *Digraphe* (1987), 11–27: 18; cited by Clark, *Derrida, Heidegger, Blanchot*, 19 ('il y a peut-être des pensées plus pensantes que cette pensée qu'on appelle philosophie').

25 First quotation from Derrida, *Passions*, as above; second from Derrida, *Acts of Literature*, 37.

Chapter 7
Afterword: Theory and Relativism (Fanon's Position)

1 Cf. Djebar, *Ces voix*, 68.

2 This overlap is sometimes disguised or lost in English translation; this is true, I think, for many of the terms that have come into use through French theory ('interpeller', for example, is a relatively common and flexible word in French in a way that 'interpellate' is not in English), and it is notoriously true of Freudian theory, which in English is studded with scientistic neologisms replacing more ordinary German expressions. See Bettelheim, *Freud and Man's Soul*.

3 Freud, *Standard Edition* XIV, 190–1. The terms *Cs.*, *Pcs.* and *Ucs.* belong to Freud's first topography of the psyche, designating respectively the conscious, preconscious and unconscious systems.

4 Freud, *Standard Edition* XX, *The Question of Lay Analysis*, 212.

5 See Young, *White Mythologies*, 123, where he is discussing Barthes's 'The great family of man' in *Mythologies*. See also Ross, *Fast Cars, Clean Bodies*, and Young, *Postcolonialism*.

6 Ashcroft et al., *Key Concepts in Post-Colonial Studies*, 235.

7 Hallward, *Absolutely Postcolonial*, 177. The Appiah quotation is from *In my Father's House*, 92.

8 Hollis and Lukes, *Rationality and Relativism*, 1–20. For a history of ethnocentricity, relativism and universalism in French writing and thought, see Todorov, *Nous et les autres*.

9 Ashcroft et al., *Key Concepts in Post-Colonial Studies*, 236–7.

10 Fanon, *Black Skin, White Masks*, 16, 231/11, 187 ('Etant Antillais d'origine, nos observations et nos conclusions ne valent que pour les Antilles'; 'La densité de l'Histoire ne détermine aucun de mes actes. ‖ Je suis mon propre fondement').

11 Fanon, 'Maghreb [sic] blood shall not flow in vain', *Toward the African Revolution*, 91–6/95–9 ('Le sang maghrébin ne coulera pas en vain').

12 At one point, it is true, Fanon writes: 'Even today, in 1952, we hear Martiniquans insist that they (the natives of Guadeloupe) are more savage than we are' ('il nous arrive, en 1952, d'entendre un Martiniquais nous affirmer qu'ils (les Guadeloupéens) sont plus sauvages que nous'); but even this 'nous' is much more equivocal than it may seem out of context, because of Fanon's extensive use of free indirect discourse. Fanon, 'West Indians and Africans', *Toward the African Revolution*, 17–27: 21/22–31: 25–6.

13 Fanon, Preface, *Studies in a Dying Colonialism*, 23–33: 32/5–15: 15 ('la mort du colonialisme est à la fois mort du colonisé et mort du colonisateur. ‖ Les rapports nouveaux, ce n'est pas le remplacement d'une barbarie par une autre barbarie, d'un écrasement de l'homme par un autre écrasement de l'homme. Ce que nous, Algériens, voulons, c'est découvrir l'homme derrière le colonisateur... ‖ Nous voulons une Algérie ouverte à tous, propice à tous les génies').

14 Fanon, 'Letter to a Frenchman', *Toward the African Revolution*, 47–51: 48/46–49: 47 ('Inquiet de l'Homme mais singulièrement pas de l'Arabe').

15 Fanon, *The Wretched of the Earth*, 251/371, 372.

16 Fanon, Introduction, *Studies in a Dying Colonialism*, 24/6.

17 Fanon, *The Wretched of the Earth*, 39/81 ('Le problème de la vérité doit également retenir notre attention. Au sein du peuple, de tout temps, la vérité n'est due qu'aux nationaux. Aucune vérité absolue, aucun discours sur la transparence de l'âme ne peut effriter cette position.... Le vrai, c'est ce qui protège les indigènes et perd les étrangers. Dans le contexte colonial il n'y a pas de conduite de vérité. Et le bien est tout simplement ce qui *leur* fait du mal').

18 Ibid., 61/109 ('Pour le colonisé, l'objectivité est toujours dirigée contre lui').

19 Fanon, 'This is the voice of Algeria', *Studies in a Dying Colonialism*, 69–97: 76/51–82: 58 ('A la vérité de l'oppresseur, autrefois rejetée comme mensonge absolu, est opposée enfin une autre vérité agie. Le mensonge de l'occupant gagne alors en vérité, car il est aujourd'hui un mensonge en danger, acculé à la défensive. Ce sont les défenses de l'occupant, ses réactions, ses résistances qui soulignent l'efficacité de l'action nationale et la font participer à un monde de vérité. La réaction de l'Algérien n'est plus de refus crispé et désespéré. *Parce qu'il s'avoue troublé, le mensonge de l'occupant devient un aspect positif de la nouvelle vérité de la Nation*'). Fanon's use of the (historic) present tense in French gives his statements a generality that is lost in translation.

20 Fanon and Azoulay, 'La Socialthérapie dans un service d'hommes musulmans', 355 ('le psychiatre, irréflexivement, adopte la politique de l'assimilation... L'effort doit être fait par "l'indigène", et celui-ci a tout intérêt à ressembler au type d'homme qu'on lui propose. L'assimilation ici ne suppose pas une réciprocité de perspectives. Il y a toute une culture qui doit disparaître au profit d'une autre.... En fait, une attitude révolutionnaire était indispensable car il fallait passer d'une position où la suprématie de la culture occidentale était évidente, à un relativisme culturel').

21 Fanon, 'Letter to the resident minister', *Toward the African Revolution*, 52–4: 53/50–3: 51 ('La Folie est l'un des moyens qu'a l'homme de perdre sa liberté. Et je puis dire, que placé à cette intersection, j'ai mesuré avec effroi l'ampleur de l'aliénation des habitants de ce pays. ‖ Si la psychiatrie est la technique médicale qui se propose de permettre à l'homme de ne plus être étranger à son environnement, je me dois d'affirmer que l'Arabe, aliéné permanent dans son pays, vit dans un état de dépersonnalisation absolue.... ‖ La structure sociale existant en Algérie s'opposait à toute tentative de remettre l'individu à sa place'). The use of the French term 'aliénation' provides Fanon with a bridge between political and psychiatric vocabulary, one he uses extensively in *Peau noire masques blancs*. An extended analysis of the term is provided by Onwuanibe in *A Critique of Revolutionary Humanism: Frantz Fanon*.

22 Cf. Sartre, *Anti-Semite and Jew*, 148/180: 'Since he [the Jew], like all men, exists as a free agent in a situation, it is his situation that must be fundamentally altered. In short, if the perspective of choice is successfully changed, the choice itself will change.'

23 Fanon's approach in the article 'Attitude du musulman maghrébin devant la folie' is comparable. He and his co-author set about correcting the cultural misinformation and prejudice that make Western doctors misunderstand North Africans' approach to mental illness, and even suggest that certain practices based on superstition may have therapeutic worth; but, at the same time, they signal unequivocally their

belief that the superiority of Western medical knowledge is unchallenge-able. Similarly, Fanon's article 'L'Hospitalisation de jour en psychiatrie: valeur et limites' contains a certain subtextual element of political critique, but his explicit reason for presenting the material is that, from a methodological point of view, it is instructive to experiment with daycare in an underdeveloped country. For a critique of the former article, which argues that Fanon is confused about whether he is criti-cizing medical philosophy or practice, see McCulloch, *Black Soul White Artifact*, chapter 4.

24   Cf. Fanon and Sanchez, 'Attitude du musulman maghrébin devant la folie', 26: 'En définitive, nous assistons dans le Maghreb à une articula-tion harmonieuse de croyances...'.

25   Fanon, 'Medicine and colonialism', *Studies in a Dying Colonialism*, 121–45: 121–2/107–35: 108 ('Les statistiques sur les réalisations sani-taires ne sont pas interprétées par l'autochtone comme amélioration dans la lutte contre la maladie, en général, mais comme une nouvelle preuve de la prise en mains du pays par l'occupant... Il y a une véritable restriction mentale chez l'indigène, une difficulté de situation à être objectif, à séparer le bon grain de l'ivraie').

26   Djebar, *Women of Algiers*, 161/128 ('A cette époque... l'on disait "médecin et hôpital?... médecin de la France, et hôpital de la France"...').

27   Fanon, 'Medicine and colonialism', 140/130 ('La science dépolitisée, la science mise au service de l'homme est souvent un non-sens aux col-onies').

28   Ibid., 128/115 ('La vérité objectivement exprimée est constamment viciée par le mensonge de la situation coloniale').

29   A question that arises inevitably but which I cannot address here con-cerns the definition of science, and whether that definition includes the social sciences. Fanon himself is fairly scathing about sociologists and ethnographers in his article 'Algeria unveiled' ['L'Algérie se dévoile'], *Studies in a Dying Colonialism*, 35–67/16–47; again it is unclear, though, to what extent his criticisms are levelled at mispractice, and to what extent at the disciplines themselves.

30   Fanon, *The Wretched of the Earth*, 28, 31, 28/66, 71, 67 ('Le colon et le colonisé sont de vieilles connaissances. Et, de fait, le colon a raison quand il dit: "les" connaître. C'est le colon qui a *fait* et qui *continue à faire* le colonisé. Le colon tire sa vérité, c'est-à-dire ses biens, du système colonial'; 'La mise en question du monde colonial par le colon-isé n'est pas une confrontation rationelle des points de vue. Elle n'est pas un discours sur l'universel, mais l'affirmation échevelée d'une originalité posée comme absolue'; 'La décolonisation est véritablement création d'hommes nouveaux').

31   Cf. Fanon, *The Wretched of the Earth*, 170–1/257–8. The term *négri-tude* refers to the attempt to rediscover, promote and valorize African culture, and was coined by the activist and poet Senghor, later president

of Senegal, who first used it in 1934 in a revue he set up with Aimé Césaire.

32   To substitute gender-neutral terms would, I think, be to misrepresent Fanon's writing, whose gender politics are a complex matter.

33   Fanon, *The Wretched of the Earth*, 177/266 ('style heurté . . . de part en part habité par une vie éruptive'; 'des intellectuels colonisés qui décident d'exprimer cette phase de la conscience en train de se libérer'). As was pointed out to me by Jean Khalfa, Fanon's style also owes something to French translations of Hegel in his era.

References and Bibliography

Abbou, André, 'Les Paradoxes du discours dans *L'Étranger*: de la parole directe à l'écriture inverse', 'Albert Camus: langue et langage', ed. Brian T. Fitch, *Revue des lettres modernes*, 5 (1969), 35–76.

Abdallah, Anouar, et al., *Pour Rushdie: cent intellectuels arabes et musulmans pour la liberté d'expression* (Paris: La Découverte, 1993).

Achebe, Chinua, 'An image of Africa: racism in Conrad's *Heart of Darkness*', *Hopes and Impediments: Selected Essays, 1965–1987* (Oxford: Heinemann, 1988), 1–13.

Achebe, Chinua, and C. L. Innes (eds), *African Short Stories: Twenty Short Stories from Across the Continent* (London and elsewhere: Heinemann, 1985).

——— *The Heinemann Book of Contemporary African Short Stories* (Oxford: Heinemann, 1992).

Achour, Christiane, *Anthologie de la littérature algérienne de langue française* (Paris: ENAP – Bordas, 1990).

Adam, Ian, and Helen Tiffin, *Past the Last Post: Theorizing Post-Colonialism and Post-Modernism* (Hemel Hempstead: Harvester Wheatsheaf, 1991).

Adlai-Murdoch, H., 'Rewriting writing: identity, exile and renewal in Assia Djebar's *L'Amour, la fantasia*', *Yale French Studies*, 83 (1993), *Post/Colonial Conditions: Exiles, Migrations and Nomadisms*, vol. 2, 71–92.

Ageron, Charles Robert, *Histoire de l'Algérie contemporaine, 1830–1964* (Paris: PUF, 3rd edn, 1969).

Ahmad, Aijaz, *In Theory: Classes, Nations, Literatures* (London: Verso, 1992).

Akhtar, Shabbir, *Be Careful with Muhammad! The Salman Rushdie Affair* (London: Bellew, 1989).

Aldrich, Robert, *Greater France: A History of French Overseas Expansion* (Basingstoke: Macmillan, 1996).

Allégret, Marc, *Carnets du Congo: voyage avec Gide* (Paris: CNRS, 1987).

Allen, Richard, *Projecting Illusion: Film Spectatorship and the Impression of Reality* (Cambridge: CUP, 1995).

Allen, Richard, and Murray Smith, *Film Theory and Philosophy* (Oxford: OUP, 1997).

Alloula, Malek, *Le Harem colonial (images d'un sous-érotisme)* (Geneva and Paris: Slatkine, 1981).

—— *The Colonial Harem*, trans. Myrna Godzich and Wlad Godzich, introduced by Barbara Harlow (Manchester: MUP, 1987).

Amrane-Minne, Danièle Djamila, *La Guerre d'Algérie (1954–1962): femmes au combat* (Ryadh el Feth [Algieria]: Editions Rahma, 1993).

—— *Des femmes dans la guerre d'Algérie: entretiens* (Paris: Karthala, 1994).

Andersen, M. C., D. C. Byrne and M. F. Titlestad, 'Introduction' to teaching edition of *Heart of Darkness* (Pretoria: Unisa Press, 1999).

Anderson, Benedict, *Imagined Communities* (London: Verso, rev. edn, 1991).

André, Jacques, et al., *Frantz Fanon: mémorial international* (Paris and Dakar: Présence Africaine, 1984).

An-Na'im, Abdullahi, 'What do we mean by universal?', *Index on Censorship* (Sept/Oct 1994), 120–8.

Anon., *The Congo Reforms (by a Belgian Minister)*, trans. J. de Courcy Macdonnell (London: Alston Rivers, 1909).

Anon., 'La Révolte d'un jeune homme ou le Maroc mis à nu', *Bulletin de Paris*, 65 (7 January 1955), 9–10.

Ansell Pearson, Keith, Benita Parry and Judith Squires (eds), *Cultural Readings of Imperialism: Edward Saïd and the Gravity of History* (London: Lawrence & Wishart, 1997).

Anstey, Roger, *King Leopold's Legacy: The Congo under Belgian Rule, 1908–1960* (Oxford: OUP 1966).

Appiah, Kwame Anthony, *In my Father's House: Africa in the Philosophy of Culture* ([1992] London: Methuen, 1993).

Appignanesi, Lisa, and Sara Maitland (eds), *The Rushdie File* (London: Fourth Estate, 1989).

Apter, Emily, *Continental Drift: From National Characters to Virtual Subjects* (Chicago and London: University of Chicago Press, 1999).

Ascherson, Neil, *The King Incorporated: Leopold II in the Age of Trusts* (London: George Allen & Unwin, 1963).

Ashcroft, Bill, Gareth Griffiths and Helen Tiffin (eds), *The Empire Strikes Back: Theory and Practice in Post-Colonial Literatures* (London: Routledge, 1989).

—— *Key Concepts in Post-Colonial Studies* (London: Routledge, 1998).

Aubarède, Gabriel d', 'Instantané' [of Chraïbi], *Nouvelles littéraires* (24 January 1957), 4.

Austin, Mary, 'Joseph Conrad tells what women don't know about men', *Pictorial Review* (1923); corrected MS, Huntington Library, Pasadena, CA, AU266.

Azim, Firdous, *The Colonial Rise of the Novel* (London: Routledge, 1993).

Bagot, Françoise, *L'Etranger* (Paris: PUF, 1993).

Barker, Francis, P. Hulme and M. Iversen (eds), *Colonial Discourse/Postcolonial Theory* (Manchester: MUP, 1994).

Barker, Martin, 'The vicissitudes of identification', *Comics: Ideology, Power and the Critics* (Manchester: MUP, 1989), 92–116.

Barnes, Julian, *Flaubert's Parrot* (London: Jonathan Cape, 1984).

Barthes, Roland, *Le Degré zéro de l'écriture* [1953], *suivi de Nouveaux essais critiques* (Paris: Seuil, 1972).

—— *Writing Degree Zero and Elements of Semiology*, trans. Annette Lavers and Colin Smith (London: Jonathan Cape, 1984).

—— 'L'effet de réel' [1968], in *Le Bruissement de la langue: essais critiques IV* (Paris: Seuil, 1984), 179–87.

—— 'The reality effect', in *The Rustle of Language*, trans. Richard Howard (Oxford: Blackwell, 1986), 141–8.

—— *Mythologies* (Paris: Seuil, 1957).

—— *Mythologies*, trans. Annette Lavers (London: Vintage, 1972).

—— *Sade, Fourier, Loyola* (Paris: Seuil, 1971).

—— *S/Z* (Paris: Seuil, 1970).

Basfao, Kacem, 'Pour une relance de l'affaire du *Passé simple*', *Itinéraires et contacts de cultures*, 2/2 (1990), 57–66.

—— (ed.), *Epreuves d'écritures maghrébines* (Aix-en-Provence: Édisud, 1994).

Bate, Jonathan, 'Othello and the other: turning Turk: the subtleties of Shakespeare's treatment of Islam', *Times Literary Supplement* (19 October 2001), 14–15.

Baubérot, Jean, *Vers un nouveau pacte laïque?* (Paris: Seuil, 1990).

Beauvoir, Simone de, and Gisèle Halimi, *Djamila Boupacha* (Paris: Gallimard, 1962).

Beckett, Samuel, *The Unnamable*, in *The Beckett Trilogy* (London: Picador, 1979).

—— *L'Innommable* (Paris: Minuit, 1953).

Benchama, Lahcen, *L'œuvre de Driss Chraïbi: réception critique des littératures maghrébines au Maroc* (Paris: Harmattan, 1994).

Bencheïkh, M., et al., *Approches scientifiques du texte maghrébin* (Casablanca: Toubkal, 1987).

Benslama, Fethi, *Une fiction troublante: de l'origine en partage* (Tour d'Aigues: Editions de l'Aube, 1994).

Bensmaïa, Réda, 'Foreword: the Kafka effect', trans. Terry Cochran, in G. Deleuze and F. Guattari, *Kafka: Toward a Minor Literature* (Minneapolis: University of Minnesota Press, 1986), ix–xxi.

Berriedale Keith, Arthur, *The Belgian Congo and the Berlin Act* (Oxford: Clarendon Press, 1919).

Bersani, Leo, *The Culture of Redemption* (Cambridge, MA: Harvard University Press, 1990).

Best, Felton O., *Black Resistance Movements in the United States and Africa, 1800–1993: Oppression and Retaliation* (Lewiston, NY, Queenston, Ontario, and Lampeter, Wales: Edwin Mellen, 1995).

Bettelheim, Bruno, *Freud and Man's Soul* (London: Chatto & Windus, 1983).

Beverley, John, *Against Literature* (Minneapolis: University of Minnesota Press, 1993).

Bhabha, Homi, *The Location of Culture* (London: Routledge, 1994).

—— (ed.), *Nation and Narration* (London: Routledge, 1990).

—— 'Representation and the colonial text: a critical exploration of some forms of mimeticism', in F. Gloversmith (ed.), *The Theory of Reading* (Brighton: Harvester, 1984), 93–122.

Blanchot, Maurice, *L'Ecriture du désastre* (Paris: Gallimard, 1980).

—— *Le Livre à venir* (Paris: Gallimard, 1959).

—— *The Siren's Song*, ed. G. Josipovici (Brighton: Harvester, 1982).

—— 'La voix narrative (le "il", le neutre)', *L'Entretien infini* (Paris: Gallimard, 1969), 556–67.

—— 'The narrative voice, (the "he", the neutral)', *The Infinite Conversation*, trans. Susan Hanson (Minneapolis and London: University of Minnesota Press, 1993), 379–87.

Boehmer, Elleke, *Colonial and Postcolonial Literature* (Oxford: OUP, 1995).

Bongie, Chris, *Exotic Memories: Literature, Colonialism and the fin de siècle* (Stanford: Stanford University Press, 1991).

Bonn, Charles, *Le Roman algérien de langue française* (Paris: Harmattan, 1985).

—— 'La traversée, arcane du roman maghrébin?', in *Visions du Maghreb* (Aix-en-Provence: Edisud, 1987), 57–61.

—— (ed.), *Anthologie de la littérature algérienne 1950–1987* (Paris: Librairie Générale Française, 1990).

Bonn, Charles, Naget Khadda and Abdallah Mdarhri-Alaoui (eds), *La Littérature maghrébine de langue française.* (Paris: EDICEF-AUPELF, 1996).

Borch-Jacobsen, Mikkel, *The Freudian Subject* (Basingstoke: Macmillan, 1982).

Bordwell, David, *Making Meaning: Inference and Rhetoric in the Interpretation of Cinema* (Cambridge, MA: Harvard University Press, 1989).

Boudjedra, Rachid, *FIS de la haine* ([1992] Paris: Folio, 2nd edn, 1994).

Bouguerra, Tayeb, *Le Dit et le non-dit: à propos de l'Algérie et de l'Algérien chez Albert Camus* (Algiers: Office des Publications Universitaires, 1989).

Bounfour, Abdellah, 'L'autobiographie maghrébine et sa lecture', *Littératures autobiographiques de la francophonie*, ed. M. Mathieu (Paris: Harmattan, 1996), 195–201.

Bourdieu, Pierre, 'Censorship', *Sociology in Question* (London: Sage, 1993), 90–3.

—— *Ce que parler veut dire: l'économie des échanges linguistiques* (Paris: Fayard, 1982).

—— *Les Règles de l'art: genèse et structure du champ littéraire* (Paris: Seuil, 1992).

—— *The Rules of Art: Genesis and Structure of the Literary Field*, trans. Susan Emanuel (Cambridge: Polity, 1996).

—— *Sociologie de l'Algérie* ([1958] Paris: PUF, 7th edn, 1985).

Bouygues, Claude (ed.), *Texte africain et voies/voix critiques* (Paris: Harmattan, 1992).

Bowie, Malcolm, *Freud, Proust and Lacan: Theory as Fiction* (Cambridge: CUP, 1987).

Brantlinger, Patrick, *Rule of Darkness: British Literature and Imperialism, 1830–1914* (Ithaca and London: Cornell University Press, 1988).

Brennan, Timothy, 'The national longing for form', *Nation and Narration*, ed. H. Bhabha (London: Routledge, 1990), 44–70.

—— *Salman Rushdie and the Third World: Myths of the Nation* (Basingstoke: Macmillan, 1989).

Bristow, Joseph, *Empire Boys: Adventures in a Man's World* (London: HarperCollins, 1991).

Britton, Celia, 'The (de)construction of subjectivity in Daniel Maximin's *L'Ile et une nuit*', in *Francophone Texts and Postcolonial Theory*, ed. C. Britton and M. Syrotinski, *Paragraph*, 24/3 (2001), 44–58.

—— 'Fictions of identity and identities of fiction in Glissant's *Tout-monde*', *ASCALF Yearbook*, 4 (2000), ed. Sam Haigh, 47–59.

—— *Edouard Glissant and Postcolonial Theory, Strategies of Language and Resistance* (Charlottesville: University Press of Virginia, 1999).

Bruner, Charlotte, *Heinemann Book of African Women's Writing* (London: Heinemann, 1993).

Buford, Norman (ed.), *Ethnography in French Literature* (French Literature Series XXIII) (Amsterdam and Atlanta: Rodopi, 1996).

Bulhan, Hussein Abdilahi, *Frantz Fanon and the Psychology of Oppression* (New York and London: Plenum, 1985).

Burke, Seán, *Authorship: From Plato to Postmodern. A Reader* (Edinburgh: Edinburgh University Press, 1995).

Butler, Judith, *Bodies that Matter: On the Discursive Limits of 'Sex'* (London: Routledge, 1993).

Calvet, Louis-Jean, *Linguistique et colonialisme: petit traité de glottophagie* ([1974] Paris: Payot, new edn, 1988).

Camus, Albert, *Actuelles: écrits politiques* (Paris: Gallimard, 1950).

—— *Actuelles III: chronique algérienne 1939–1958* (Paris: Gallimard, 1958).

—— *Discours de Suède* ([1958] Paris: Seuil, 1997).

—— *Ecrits politiques* (Paris: Gallimard 1950).

—— *L'Etranger* (Paris: Gallimard, 1942).

—— *The Outsider*, trans. Joseph Laredo (Harmondsworth: Penguin, 2000).

—— *L'Exil et le royaume* (Paris: Gallimard, 1957).

—— *L'Homme révolté* (Paris: Gallimard, 1951).

—— *Le Premier homme* (Paris: Gallimard, 1994).

—— *The First Man*, trans. David Hapgood (London: Hamish Hamilton, 1995).

—— *Resistance, Rebellion and Death*, trans. Justin O'Brien (London: Hamish Hamilton, 1961).

—— *Le Mythe de Sisyphe* (Paris: Gallimard, 1942).

—— *Noces*, suivi de *L'Eté* (Paris: Gallimard 1959).

—— *Selected Essays and Notebooks*, ed. and trans. Philip Thody [from *Carnets*] (Harmondsworth: Penguin, 1984).

Capelle, Anne, interview with Visconti, *La Quinzaine littéraire*, 34 (1 September 1967), 26–7.

Carabine, Keith (ed.), *Joseph Conrad: Critical Assessments*, 4 vols (Mountfield, East Sussex: Helm Information, 1992).

Carroll, Noël, *Theorizing the Moving Image* (Cambridge: CUP, 1996).

—— *A Philosophy of Mass Art* (Oxford: OUP, 1998).

Cavalli-Sforza, Luca, P. Menozzi and A. Piazza, *The History and Geography of Human Genes* (Princeton: Princeton University Press, 1994; abridged pbk edn, 1996).

Cerf, Madeleine, et al., *Communications*, 9 (1967), *La Censure et le censurable*.

Cellard, Jacques, 'Le Vicaire et la rabouilleuse: autocensure et sexualité dans *La Comédie humaine*', *Censures: de la Bible aux 'Larmes d'Eros'* (Paris: Bibliothèque Publique d'Information, 1987), 140–5.

Certeau, Michel de, *L'Ecriture de l'histoire* ([1975] Paris: Gallimard, 2nd edn, 1978).

Chamberlain, Joseph, *Foreign and Colonial Speeches* (London: Routledge, 1897).

Chikh, Slimane, 'L'Algérie face à la francophonie', in S. Chikh et al., *Maghreb et francophonie* (Paris: Economica, 1988), 1–27.

Chikh, Slimane, et al., 'Fanon au futur', in *Révolution africaine (organe central du Parti du FLN)*, 1241 (11 December 1987), 27–46.

Childs, Peter, *Post-Colonial Theory and English Literature: a Reader* (Edinburgh: Edinburgh University Press, 1999).

Chraïbi, Driss, *L'Ane* (Paris: Denoël, 1956).

—— *Les Boucs* ([1955] Paris: Denoël, 1982).

—— *The Butts*, trans. Hugh A. Harter (Washington, DC: Three Continents Press, 1983).

—— *La Civilisation, ma Mère!* (Paris: Denoël, 1972).

—— *Une enquête au pays* (London: Bristol Classical Press, 1999).

—— 'François Mauriac, les Marocains et moi', *La Parisienne: revue littéraire mensuelle* (May 1956), 38–41.

—— *L'Inspecteur Ali* (Paris: Denoël, 1991).

—— *Inspector Ali*, trans. Lara McGlashan (Colorado Springs: Three Continents Press, 1994).

—— Letter in *Bulletin de Paris* (4 March 1955), 3.

—— 'Littérature nord-africaine d'expression française', *Confluent*, 5 (Feb 1960), 24–9.

—— *Le Passé simple* ([1954] Paris: Denoël, Collection Folio, 1993).

—— *The Simple Past*, trans. Hugh A. Harter (Washington, DC: Three Continents Press, 1990).

—— 'Préface' to Abdellatif Laâbi, *L'œil et la nuit* (Casablanca: Atlantes, 1969), i–ii.

—— *Succession ouverte* (Paris: Denoël, 1962).

—— *Vu, lu, entendu: mémoires* (Paris: Denoël, 1998).

Cixous, Hélène, *Souffles* (Paris: Des Femmes, 1975).

—— 'Guardian of language', Interview in *Pandora's Box* (Easter 1996), 4–5, 11.

Cixous, Hélène, and Catherine Clément, *La Jeune Née* (Paris: Union Générale d'Éditions, 1975).

Cixous, Hélène, and J. Derrida, *Voiles* (Paris: Galilée, 1998).

Clark, Timothy, *Derrida, Heidegger, Blanchot: Sources of Derrida's Notion and Practice of Literature* (Cambridge: CUP, 1992).

Clerc, Jeanne-Marie, *Assia Djebar: écrire, transgresser, résister* (Paris: Harmattan, 1997).

Clifford, James, *The Predicament of Culture: Twentieth Century Ethnography, Literature and Art* (Cambridge, MA: Harvard University Press, 1988).

Colbron, Grace Isabel, 'Joseph Conrad's Women', *Joseph Conrad*, ed. K. Carabine, vol. 1, 511–14.

Compagnon, Antoine, *La Troisième République des lettres* (Paris: Seuil, 1983).

Connerton, Paul, 'Freud and the crowd', *Visions and Blueprints: Avant-Garde Culture and Radical Politics in Early Twentieth-Century Europe*, ed. P. Collier and E. Timms (Manchester: MUP, 1988), 194–207.

Conrad, Joseph, *Heart of Darkness*, ed. Robert Hampson (Harmondsworth: Penguin, 1995).

—— 'Geography and some explorers' [1924], in *Almayer's Folly and Last Essays* (London: Nelson, 1957), 219–47.

—— 'An outpost of progress' [1897], in *Heart of Darkness and other Tales*, ed. Cedric Watts (Oxford: OUP, 1990), 1–34.

Conrad, Joseph, and Ford M. Hueffer, *The Inheritors: An Extravagant Story* (London: Heinemann, 1901).

Cookey, S. J. S., *Britain and the Congo Question 1885–1913* (London: Longmans, 1968).

Coombes, Annie E., *Reinventing Africa: Museums, Material Culture and Popular Imagination in Late Victorian and Edwardian England* (New Haven and London: Yale University Press, 1994).

Cribb, T. J. (ed.), *Imagined Commonwealths* (Basingstoke: Macmillan, 1999).

Davis, Colin, *Ethical Issues in Twentieth-Century French Fiction: Killing the Other* (Basingstoke: Macmillan, 2000).

Déjeux, Jean, 'Au Maghreb, la langue française "langue natale du je"', *Littératures autobiographiques de la francophonie*, ed. M. Mathieu (Paris: Harmattan, 1996), 181–93.

—— *Femmes d'Algérie: légendes, traditions, histoire, littérature* (Paris: La Boîte à Documents, 1987).

——*La Littérature féminine de langue française au Maghreb* (Paris: Karthala, 1994).

——*Maghreb littératures de langue française* (Paris: Arcantère, 1993).

Delacampagne, Christian, *Une histoire du racisme* (Paris: Librairie Générale Française, 2000).

Deleuze, Gilles, and Félix Guattari, *Kafka: pour une littérature mineure* (Paris: Minuit, 1975).

——*Kafka: Toward a Minor Literature*, trans. Dana Polan (Minneapolis: University of Minnesota Press, 1986).

Derrida, Jacques, *Acts of Literature*, ed. Derek Attridge (New York and London: Routledge, 1992).

——'Derrida l'insoumis', interview with Catherine David, *Nouvel Observateur* (9 September 1983), 84–90.

——*La Dissémination* (Paris: Seuil, 1972).

——*Dissemination*, trans. B. Johnson (London: Athlone, 1981).

——*L'Ecriture et la différence* (Paris: Seuil, 1967).

——*Le Monolinguisme de l'autre ou la prothèse d'origine* (Paris: Galilée, 1996).

——*Monolingualism of the Other, or The Prosthesis of Origin*, trans. Patrick Mensah (Stanford: Stanford University Press, 1998).

——*Parages* (Paris: Galilée 1986).

——*Passions* (Paris: Galilée, 1993).

Deurbergue, Jean, 'Notice et notes', in J. Conrad, *Œuvres* (Paris: Gallimard (Pléïade), 1985), Vol. II, 1257–80.

Dine, Philip, *Images of the Algerian War* (Oxford: OUP, 1994).

Djebar, Assia, *L'Amour, la fantasia* ([1985] Paris: Albin Michel, 1995).

——*Ces voix qui m'assiègent . . . en marge de ma francophonie* (Paris: Albin Michel, 1999).

——*Chronique d'un été algérien* [introduction to a volume of photographs] (Paris: Editions Plume, 1993).

——*Fantasia, An Algerian Cavalcade*, trans. Dorothy Blair (London: Quartet, 1989).

——*Femmes d'Alger dans leur appartement* (Paris: Des Femmes, 1980).

——*Women of Algiers in their Apartment*, trans. Marjolijn de Jager (Charlottesville VA, and London: Caraf Books, 1992).

——*Loin de Médine* (Paris: Albin Michel, 1991).

——*Ombre sultane* (Paris: J. C. Lattès, 1987).

——*Oran, langue morte* (Arles: Actes Sud, 1997).

Djemaï, Abdelkader, *Camus à Oran* (Paris: Michalon, 1995).

Donadey, Anne, *Recasting Postcolonialism: Women Writing between Worlds* (Portsmouth, NH: Heinemann, 2001).

Droz, Bernard, and Evelyne Lever, *Histoire de la guerre d'Algérie, 1954–1962* (Paris: Seuil, 2nd edn, 1991).

Dugas, Guy, *La Littérature judéo- maghrébine d'expression française* (Paris: Harmattan, 1990).

Dunwoodie, Peter, *Writing French Algeria* (Oxford: OUP, 1998).

Dunwoodie, Peter, and Hughes, Edward J., *Constructing Memories: Camus, Algeria and Le Premier homme* (Stirling: Stirling French Publications, 1998).

Dyer, Alfred Stace, *Christian Liberia, the Hope of the Dark Continent, with Special Reference to the Work and Mission of Edward S. Morris of Philadelphia* (London: Dyer Brothers, 1879).

Eagleton, Terry, *Criticism and Ideology: a Study in Marxist Literary Theory* ([1976] London: Verso, 1978).

Erickson, John, 'Albert Camus and North Africa: a discourse of exteriority', *Critical Essays on Albert Camus*, ed. Bettina Knapp (Boston, MA: Hall, 1988), 73–88.

—— *Islam and Postcolonial Narrative* (Cambridge: CUP, 1998).

Fabian, Johannes, *Language and Colonial Power: The Appropriation of Swahili in the Former Belgian Congo 1880–1938* (Cambridge: CUP, 1986).

Fanon, Frantz, *Les Damnés de la terre* ([1961] Paris: Gallimard, 1991).

—— *The Wretched of the Earth*, trans. Constance Farrington (Harmondsworth: Penguin, 1967).

—— 'L'Hospitalisation de jour en psychiatrie: valeur et limites', *La Tunisie médicale*, no. 10 (1959), Part I, 689–712, Part II (co-authored with C. Geronimi), 713–32.

—— *Peau noire masques blancs* (Paris: Seuil, 1952).

—— *Black Skin, White Masks*, trans. Charles Lam Markmann (London: Pluto, 1986; New York: Grove Press, 1967).

—— *Pour la Révolution africaine: écrits politiques* ([1964] Paris: Maspero, 1969).

—— *Toward the African Revolution*, trans. Haakon Chevalier (London: Writers and Readers, 1980).

—— *Sociologie d'une révolution* ([1959] Paris: Maspero, 1972).

—— *Studies in a Dying Colonialism*, trans. Haakon Chevalier (London: Earthscan, 1989).

Fanon, Frantz, and J. Azoulay, 'La Socialthérapie dans un service d'hommes musulmans', *L'Information psychiatrique*, 4th series, no. 9 (1954).

Fanon, Frantz, with J. Dequeker, R. Lacaton, M. Micucci and F. Ramee, 'Aspects actuels de l'Assistance Mentale en Algérie', *L'Information psychiatrique*, 4/1 (1955), 11–18.

Fanon, Frantz, and F. Sanchez, 'Attitude du musulman maghrébin devant la folie', *Revue pratique de psychologie de la vie sociale et d'hygiène mentale*, no. 1 (1956).

Feraoun, Mouloud, *Le Fils du pauvre* ([1950] Paris: Seuil, 1982).

Fincham, Gail, and Hooper, Myrtle, *Under Postcolonial Eyes: Joseph Conrad after Empire* (Rondebosch: University of Cape Town Press, 1996).

Firchow, Peter Edgerly, *Envisioning Africa: Racism and Imperialism in Conrad's 'Heart of Darkness'* (Lexington: University Press of Kentucky, 2000).

Fish, Stanley, *Professional Correctness: Literary Studies and Political Change* (Oxford: OUP, 1995).

Fitch, Brian T., *The Narcissitic Text: A Reading of Camus's Fiction* (Toronto: University of Toronto Press, 1982).

—— 'Narrateur et narration dans *L'Étranger*', *Archives des lettres modernes*, 6 (1960), no. 34.

Flaubert, Gustave, *Madame Bovary* ([1856] Paris: Flammarion, 1986).

Fontenot, Chester J., *Frantz Fanon: Language as the God Gone Astray in the Flesh* (Lincoln: University of Nebraska Studies, 1979).

Foucault, Michel, 'Qu'est-ce qu'un auteur', *Bulletin de la Société française de philosophie*, 3 (July–Sept 1969), 75–104.

—— 'What is an author?', in S. Burke, *Authorship* (Edinburgh: Edinburgh University Press, 1995), 233–46.

—— *Les Mots et les choses: une archéologie des sciences humaines* (Paris: Bibliothèque des Sciences Humaines, 1966).

—— *L'Ordre du discours* (Paris: Gallimard, 1976).

—— *The Order of Things: An Archeology of the Human Sciences* (London: Tavistock, 1970).

—— *The Archaeology of Knowledge*, trans. A. M. Sheridan Smith (London: Tavistock, 1972).

—— *Histoire de la sexualité* (Paris: Gallimard, 1976).

—— *The History of Sexuality, I*, trans. Robert Hurley (London: Allen Lane, 1979).

Freud, Sigmund, *The Standard Edition of the Complete Psychological Works of Sigmund Freud*, ed. James Strachey (London: Hogarth Press, 1953–66).

Fuss, Diana, *Identification Papers* (New York: Routledge, 1995).

Gafaïti, Hafid, 'L'autobiographie plurielle: Assia Djebar, les femmes et l'histoire', *Postcolonialisme et autobiographie*, ed. A. Hornung and E. Ruhe (Amsterdam and Atlanta: Rodopi, 1998), 149–59.

—— *Les femmes dans le roman algérien: histoire, discours et texte* (Paris: Harmattan, 1996).

Gandhi, Leela, *Postcolonial Theory: A Critical Introduction* (Edinburgh: Edinburgh University Press, 1998).

Gaspard, Françoise, and Farhad Khosrokhavar, *Le Foulard et la République* (Paris: La Découverte, 1995).

Gellner, Ernest, *Relativism and the Social Sciences* (Cambridge: CUP, 1985).

Genette, Gérard, 'Vraisemblance et motivation', *Figures, II* (Paris: Gallimard, 1969), 71–99.

Gervereau, Laurent, Jean-Pierre Rioux and Benjamin Stora, *La France en guerre d'Algérie* (Paris: BIDC, 1992).

Giddens, Anthony, 'Living in a post-traditional society', *In Defence of Sociology: Essays, Interpretations and Rejoinders* (Cambridge: Polity, 1996), 8–64.

Gide, André, *Joseph Conrad* (Liège: Lampe d'Aladdin, 1927).

—— *Voyage au Congo* ([1927] Paris: Gallimard, 1948).

Girardet, Raoul, *L'Idée coloniale en France de 1871 à 1962* (Paris: La Table Ronde, 1972).

GoGwilt, Christopher, *The Invention of the West: Joseph Conrad and the Double-Mapping of Europe and Empire* (Stanford: Stanford University Press, 1995).

Gontard, Marc, *La Violence du texte: études sur la littérature marocaine de langue française* (Paris: Harmattan, 1981).

—— *Le Moi étrange: littérature marocaine de langue française* (Paris: Harmattan, 1993).

Gordon, David C., *The French Language and National Identity 1930–1975* (New York and Paris: Mouton, 1978).

Gordon, Lewis R., *Fanon and the Crisis of European Man: An Essay on Philosophy and the Human Sciences* (London: Routledge, 1995).

Gordon, Lewis R., T. Denean Sharpley-Whiting and Renée T. White, *Fanon: A Critical Reader* (Oxford: Blackwell, 1996).

Gordon, Robert S. C., *Pasolini: Forms of Subjectivity* (Oxford: OUP, 1996).

Grant, Rena, 'Characterhysterics: Identification in Freud and Lacan', *Oxford Literary Review*, 15 1–2, *Experiencing the Impossible*, ed. Timothy Clark and Nicholas Royle, (1993), 133–61.

Green, Mary Jean, et al. (eds), *Postcolonial Subjects: Francophone Women Writers* (Minneapolis: University of Minnesota Press, 1996).

Gregory, Derek, *Geographical Imaginations* (Oxford: Blackwell, 1994).

Grenaud, Pierre, *La Littérature au soleil du Maghreb: de l'antiquité à nos jours* (Paris: Harmattan, 1993).

Grodal, Torben, *Moving Pictures: A New Theory of Film Genres, Feelings, and Cognition* (Oxford: Clarendon Press, 1997).

Guégan, Stéphane, *Delacroix et les Orientales* (Paris: Flammarion, 1994).

Gusdorf, Georges, 'Conditions and limits of autobiography' [1956], in *Autobiography: Essays Theoretical and Critical*, ed. J. Olney (Princeton: Princeton University Press, 1980), 28–48.

—— *Les Ecritures du moi* (Paris: Odile Jacob, 1991).

Haarscher, Guy (ed.), *Laïcité et droits de l'homme: deux siècles de conquêtes* (Brussels, Editions de l'Université de Bruxelles, 1989).

Haddad, Malek, 'Les Zéros tournent en rond', *Ecoute et je t'appelle* (Paris: Maspero, 1961), 9–46.

Haddour, Azzedine, *Colonial Myths: History and Narrative* (Manchester: MUP, 2000).

Halliday, Fred, 'The fundamental lesson of the fatwa', *New Statesman and Society* (12 February 1993), 16–18.

Hallward, Peter, *Absolutely Postcolonial: Writing between the Singular and the Specific* (Manchester: MUP, 2001).

Hampson, Robert, 'Conrad and the idea of empire', in *Under Postcolonial Eyes*, ed. G. Fincham and M. Hooper (Rondebosch: University of Cape Town Press, 1996), 65–77.

—— '*Heart of Darkness* and "The speech that cannot be silenced"', in *Post-Colonial Theory and English Literature*, ed. P. Childs (Edinburgh: Edinburgh University Press, 1999), 201–15.

—— 'Introduction' to *Heart of Darkness* (Harmondsworth: Penguin, 1995).

——*Joseph Conrad: Betrayal and Identity* (Basingstoke: Macmillan, 1992).

Hansen, Emmanuel, *Frantz Fanon: Social and Political Thought* (Athens, OH: Ohio State University Press, 1977).

Harbi, Mohammed, *1954, la guerre commence en Algérie* (Brussels: Editions Complexe, 1998).

Hargreaves, Alec G., 'Francophonie and globalization: France at the cross-roads', in K. Salhi (ed.), *Francophone Voices* (Exeter: Elm Bank, 1999), 49–57.

Harrison, Nicholas, *Circles of Censorship: Censorship and its Metaphors in French Literature, History and Theory* (Oxford: OUP, 1995).

——'Freedom of expression: the case of blasphemy', in *France During the Socialist Years*, ed. G. Raymond (Aldershot and Brookfield, VT: Dartmouth, 1994), 154–71.

——'Readers as *résistants*: *Fahrenheit 451*, censorship and identification', *Studies in French Cinema*, 1/1 (2001), 54–61.

——'Reading Sade through censorship', *Paragraph*, 23/1 (2000) 26–37.

Hawkins, Hunt, 'The issue of racism in *Heart of Darkness*', *Conradiana*, 14 (1982), 163–71.

——'Conrad's critique of imperialism in *Heart of Darkness*', *Publications of the Modern Language Association of America*, 94/2 (1979) 286–99.

Hawthorn, Jeremy, *Joseph Conrad: Narrative Technique and Ideological Commitment* (London: Edward Arnold, 1990).

——*A Concise Glossary of Contemporary Literary Theory* (London: Arnold, 3rd edn, 1998).

Heath, Stephen, 'Realism, modernism and "language-consciousness"' in *Realism in European Literature: Essays in Honour of J. P. Stern*, ed. N. Boyle and M. Swales (Cambridge: CUP, 1986), 103–22.

Henry, Jean Robert, et al., *Nouveaux enjeux culturels au Maghreb* (Paris: CNRS, 1986).

Hitchcott, Nicki, *Women Writers in Francophone Africa* (Oxford and New York: Berg, 2000).

Hochschild, Adam, *King Leopold's Ghost: A Story of Greed, Terror and Heroism in Colonial Africa* (London: Macmillan, 1999).

Holland, Michael (ed.), *The Blanchot Reader* (Oxford: Blackwell, 1995).

Holland, Norman N., *The Dynamics of Literary Response* (New York: Norton, 1975).

Hollier, Denis (ed.), *A New History of French Literature* (Cambridge, MA: Harvard University Press, 1989).

——'Fahrenheit 451 below', *Raritan*, 16/1 (1996), 93–102.

Hollis, Martin, and Steven Lukes, *Rationality and Relativism* (Oxford: Blackwell, 1982).

hooks, bell, *Reel to real: race, sex and class at the movies* (London: Routledge, 1996).

Hornung, Alfred, and Ernstpeter Ruhe (eds), *Postcolonialisme et autobiographie: Albert Memmi, Assia Djebar, Daniel Maximim* (Amsterdam and Atlanta: Rodopi, 1998).

Hourani, Albert, *Islam in European Thought* (Cambridge: CUP, 1991).

Huggan, Graham, 'Decolonizing the map: post-colonialism, post-structuralism and the cartographic connection', *Past the Last Post*, ed. I. Adam and H. Tiffin (Hemel Hempstead: Harvester Wheatsheaf, 1991), 125–38.

——*The Postcolonial Exotic: Marketing the Margins* (London: Routledge, 2001).

Hughes, Edward J., *Camus: Le Premier homme, La Peste* (Glasgow: University of Glasgow Press, 1995).

Huston, Nancy, and Leïla Sebbar (eds), *Une enfance ailleurs: 17 écrivains racontent* (Paris: Belfond, 1993).

Irigaray, Luce, *Ce sexe qui n'en est pas un* (Paris: Minuit, 1977).

——*Speculum: de l'autre femme* (Paris: Minuit, 1974).

Iser, Wolfgang, *The Fictive and the Imaginary: Charting Literary Anthropology* (Baltimore: Johns Hopkins University Press, 1993).

Itinéraires et contacts de cultures, II: L'Enseignement des littératures francophones (Paris: Harmattan, 1982).

Jameson, Fredric, *Nationalism, Colonialism and Literature: Modernism and Imperialism* (Derry: Field Day, 1988).

JanMohamed, Abdul R., *Manichean Aesthetics: The Politics of Literature in Colonial Africa* (Amherst: University of Massachusetts Press, 1983).

JanMohamed, Abdul R., and David Lloyd (eds), *The Nature and Context of Minority Discourse* (Oxford: OUP, 1990).

Jarvis, Simon, review of Richard Lansdown, *The Autonomy of Literature*, *Times Literary Supplement* (13 July 2001), 25.

Jean-Aubry, G., *Joseph Conrad in the Congo* (London: Bookman's Journal, 1926).

Jones, Susan, *Conrad and Women* (Oxford: OUP, 1999).

Josipovici, Gabriel, *Text and Voice: Essays 1981–1991* (Manchester: Carcanet, 1992).

Joyce, James, *Ulysses*, ed. Hans Walter Gabler (London: Bodley Head, 1986).

Kadra-Hadjadji, Houaria, *Contestation et révolte dans l'œuvre de Driss Chraïbi* (Paris: Publisud, 1986).

Kael, Pauline, 'The current cinema: politics and thrills', *New Yorker* (19 November 1973), 236–44.

Kandiyoti, Deniz, 'Identity and its discontents: women and the nation', *Colonial Discourse and Post-Colonial Theory*, ed. P. Williams and L. Chrisman (New York: Harvester Wheatsheaf, 1993), 376–91.

Kattan, Naïm, *Le Désir et le pouvoir: essai* (Montreal: Hurtubise, 1983).

——*Le Repos et l'oubli: essais* (Montreal: Hurtubise, 1986).

Kaye, Jacqueline, and Abdelhamid Zoubir, *The Ambiguous Compromise: Language, Literature and National Identity in Algeria and Morocco* (London: Routledge, 1990).

Kenny, Neil, 'Books in space and time: bibliomania and early modern histories of learning and "literature" in France', *Modern Languages Quarterly*, 61/2 (2000), 253–86.

Khatibi, Abdelkebir, *Figures de l'étranger dans la littérature française* (Paris: Denoël, 1987).
—— *Maghreb pluriel* (Paris: Denoël, 1983).
—— *Le Roman maghrébin* ([1968] Rabat, Morocco: SMER, 2nd edn, 1979).
King, Adele (ed.), *Camus's 'L'Étranger': Fifty Years On* (Basingstoke: Macmillan, 1992).
Knight, Diana, *Barthes and Utopia: Space, Travel, Writing* (Oxford: OUP, 1997).
Knowles, Owen, and Gene M. Moore, *Oxford Reader's Companion to Conrad* (Oxford: OUP, 2000).
Krausz, Michael, *Relativism: Interpretation and Confrontation* (Notre Dame, IN: University of Notre Dame Press, 1989).
Kristeva, Julia, *Etrangers à nous-mêmes* (Paris: Gallimard, 1988).
Lamchichi, Abderrahim, *Islam et contestation au Maghreb* (Paris: Harmattan, 1989).
Lanser, Susan Sniader, *Fictions of Authority: Women Writers and Narrative Voice* (Ithaca and London: Cornell University Press, 1992).
Lanson, Gustave, *Histoire de la littérature française* (Paris: Hachette, 9th edn, 1906).
Laplanche, Jean, and J.-B. Pontalis, *Vocabulaire de la psychanalyse* (Paris: PUF, 1967).
—— *The Language of Psychoanalysis*, trans. Donald Nicholson-Smith (London: Karnac, 1988).
Lazarus, Neil, *Nationalism and Cultural Practice in the Postcolonial World* (Cambridge: CUP, 1999).
Lazreg, Marnia, *The Eloquence of Silence: Algerian Women in Question* (London: Routledge, 1994).
Ledger, Sally, 'In darkest England: the terror of degeneration in *fin-de-siècle* Britain', extract in P. Childs, *Post-Colonial Theory and English Literature* (Edinburgh: Edinburgh University Press, 1999), 216–26.
Lee, Simon, *The Cost of Free Speech* (London: Faber, 1990).
Leiris, Michel, *L'Afrique fantôme* ([1934] Paris: Gallimard, 1981).
Lejeune, Philippe, *Le Pacte autobiographique* (Paris: Seuil, 1975).
Lemarchand, René, *Political Awakening in the Belgian Congo* (Berkeley and Los Angeles: University of California Press, 1964).
Letcher, Owen (ed.), *Congo Belge: A Work to Commemorate the Fiftieth Anniversary of the Founding of the Congo Free State and to Describe the Civilization of the Heart of Africa under Belgian Rule 1885–1935* (London: Waterlow, 1935).
Levering Lewis, David, *The Race to Fashoda: European Colonialism and African Resistance in the Scramble for Africa* (London: Bloomsbury, 1988).
Lévi-Valensi, Jacqueline (ed.), *Les Critiques de notre temps et Camus* (Paris: Garnier Frères, 1970).
Lichtman, Richard, *The Production of Desire: The Integration of Psychoanalysis into Marxist Theory* (London: Collier Macmillan, 1982).

Lindqvist, Sven, *'Exterminate all the Brutes'* (London: Granta, 1997).

Lindsay, Vachel, *The Congo and other Poems* (New York: Dover, 1992).

Lionnet, Françoise, *Postcolonial Representations: Women, Literature, Identity* (Ithaca: Cornell University Press, 1995).

Lloyd, David, 'Arnold, Ferguson, Schiller: aesthetic culture and the politics of aesthetics', *Cultural Critique*, 2 (1985–6), 137–69.

—— 'Ethnic minorities, minority discourse and the state', *Colonial Discourse/Postcolonial Theory*, ed. F. Barker et al. (Manchester: MUP, 1994), 221–38.

London, Bette, 'Reading race and gender in Conrad's dark continent', *Criticism*, 31/3 (1989), 235–52.

Loomba, Ania, *Colonialism/Postcolonialism* (London: Routledge, 1998).

Lowe, Lisa, *Critical Terrains: French and British Orientalisms* (Ithaca: Cornell University Press, 1991).

McClintock, Anne, 'The angel of progress: pitfalls of the term "postcolonialism"' *Colonial Discourse/Postcolonial Theory*, ed. F. Barker et al. (Manchester: MUP, 1994), 252–66.

McCulloch, Jock, *Black Soul White Artifact: Fanon's Clinical Psychology and Social Theory* (Cambridge: CUP, 1983).

McDonald, Peter M., *British Literary Culture and Publishing Practice 1880–1914* (Cambridge: CUP, 1997).

McGrath, William J., *Freud's Discovery of Psychoanalysis: The Politics of Hysteria* (New York: Cornell University Press, 1986).

McLynn, Frank, *Hearts of Darkness: The European Exploration of Africa* (New York: Carroll & Graf, 1992).

Maja-Pearce, Adewale (ed.), *The Heinemann Book of African Poetry in English* (Oxford and elsewhere: Heinemann, 1990).

Marchal, Jules, *L'Etat libre du Congo: paradis perdu: l'histoire du Congo 1876–1900*, 2 vols (Borgloon: Paula Bellings, 1996).

—— *E. D. Morel contre Léopold II: L'histoire du Congo 1900–1910*, 2 vols (Paris: Harmattan, 1996).

Marston, E., *How Stanley Wrote 'Darkest Africa'* (London: Sampson Low, 1890).

Martelli, George, *Leopold to Lumumba: A History of the Belgian Congo, 1877–1960* (London: Chapman & Hall, 1962).

Marx-Scouras, Danielle, 'Muffled screams/stifled voices', *Yale French Studies*, 82 (1993), ed. F. Lionnet and Ronnie Scharfman, *Post/Colonial Conditions: Exiles, Migrations and Nomadisms*, vol. 1, 172–82.

Mathieu, Martine (ed.), *Littératures autobiographiques de la francophonie* (Paris: Harmattan, 1996).

Mayne, Judith, *Cinema and Spectatorship* (London: Routledge, 1993).

Mazower, Mark, *Dark Continent: Europe's Twentieth Century* (London: Allen Lane, 1998).

Mbom, Clément, *Frantz Fanon: aujourd'hui et demain: réflexions sur le tiers monde* (Paris: Nathan, 1985).

Memmi, Albert, *Anthologie des écrivains français du Maghreb* (Paris: Présence Africaine, 1969).

—— *Anthologie des écrivains maghrébins d'expression française* (Paris: Présence Africaine, 1964).

—— *Ecrivains francophones du Maghreb* (Paris: Seghers, 1985).

—— *Portrait du colonisé* ([1957] Paris: Gallimard, 1985).

—— *The Colonizer and the Colonized*, trans. Howard Greenfield and Lawrence Hoey (London: Earthscan, 1990).

Mernissi, Fatima, *Beyond the Veil: Male–Female Dynamics in Modern Muslim Society* (London: Al Saqi, rev. edn, 1985).

—— *Le Harem politique: le Prophète et les femmes* ([1987] Brussels: Editions Complexe, 1992).

—— *Women's Rebellion and Islamic Memory* (London: Zed Books, 1996).

Metref, Arezki, 'Deux affaires de censure', *Autrement: série mémoires*, 33 (1994): *Aurès / Algérie 1954: Les Fruits verts d'une révolution*, 138–61.

Miège, Jean-Louis, *Le Maroc* (Paris: PUF, 1994).

Miller, Christopher L., *Blank Darkness: Africanist Discourse in French* (Chicago: University of Chicago Press, 1985).

—— *Nationalists and Nomads: Essays on Francophone African Literature and Culture* (Chicago and London: University of Chicago Press, 1998).

—— *Theories of Africans: Francophone Literature and Anthropology in Africa* (Chicago: University of Chicago Press, 1990).

Mimouni, Rachid, et al., *Visions du Maghreb* (Aix-en-Provence: Edisud, 1987).

Mongia, Padmini, 'Empire, narrative, and the feminine in *Lord Jim* and *Heart of Darkness*', *Under Postcolonial Eyes*, ed. G. Fincham and M. Hooper (Rondebosch: University of Cape Town Press, 1996), 120–32.

Moore, Gene M., *Conrad on Film* (Cambridge: CUP, 1997).

Moore-Gilbert, Bart, *Postcolonial Theory: Contexts, Practices, Politics* (London: Verso, 1997).

Morel, Edmund Dene, *The Congo Slave State* (Liverpool: John Richardson & Sons, 1903).

—— *King Leopold's Rule in Africa* (London: Heinemann, 1904).

—— *Red Rubber: The Story of the Rubber Slave Trade Flourishing on the Congo in the Year of Grace 1906* (London: T. Fisher Unwin, 1906).

Morris, William, *News from Nowhere* [1890], ed. Krishan Kumar (Cambridge: CUP, 1995).

Mortimer, Mildred, *Journeys through the African Novel* (Portsmouth, NH: Heinemann; London: James Currey, 1990).

Moynagh, Maureen, 'The ethical turn in postcolonial theory and narrative: Michelle Cliff's "No telephone to heaven"', *Ariel: a Review of International English Literature*, 30/4 (1999), 109–33.

Nadelhaft, Ruth, *Joseph Conrad: A Feminist Reading* (Hemel Hempstead: Harvester Wheatsheaf, 1991).

Naipaul, V. S., *A Congo Diary* (Los Angeles: Sylvester & Orphanos, 1980).

Naval Staff Intelligence Dept, *A Manual of Belgian Congo* (London: June 1919).

Ndaywel è Nziem, Isidore, *Histoire générale du Congo: de l'héritage ancien à la République Démocratique* (Paris and Brussels: De Boeck & Larcier, 1998).

Nelson, Cary, and Lawrence Grossberg (eds), *Marxism and the Interpretation of Culture* (Basingstoke: Macmillan, 1988).

Ngũgĩ wa Thiong'o, *Decolonising the Mind: the Politics of Language in African Literature* (London: James Currey; Nairobi/Portsmouth, NH: Heinemann; Harare: Zimbabwe Publishing House, 1986).

O'Brien, Conor Cruise, *Camus* (London: Fontana, 1970).

Ochert, Ayala, 'In Everyman's footsteps', *Times Higher Educational Supplement* (14 July 2000), 17.

Onwuanibe, R. C., *A Critique of Revolutionary Humanism: Frantz Fanon* (St Louis, MO: Warren H. Green, 1983).

Orlando, Valérie, *Nomadic Voices of Exile: Feminine Identity in Francophone Literature of the Maghreb* (Athens: Ohio University Press, 1999).

Ortony, Anthony (ed.), *Metaphor and Thought* (Cambridge: CUP, 1979).

Paccaud-Huguet, Josiane (ed.), *Joseph Conrad, I: La Fiction et l'Autre* (Paris: Lettres Modernes Minard, 1998).

Pariente, Jean-Claude, 'L'Étranger et son double', in 'Autour de *L'Étranger*' ed. Brian T. Fitch, *Revue des lettres modernes*, 1 (1968), 53–80.

Parry, Benita, *Conrad and Imperialism: Ideological Boundaries and Visionary Frontiers* (London: Macmillan, 1983).

——'Problems in current theories of colonial discourse', *Oxford Literary Review*, 9 (1987), 27–58.

——'Resistance theory/theorizing resistance, or two cheers for nativism', *Colonial Discourse/Postcolonial Theory*, ed. F. Barker et al. (Manchester: MUP, 1994), 172–96.

——'Narrating imperialism: *Nostromo's* dystopia', (*Cultural Reading of Imperialism*), ed. K. Ansell Pearson et al. (London: Lawrence & Wishart, 1997), 227–46.

Pauvert, Jean-Jacques, *Nouveaux (et moins nouveaux) visages de la censure, suivi de l'Affaire Sade* (Paris: Les Belles Lettres, 1994).

Pavel, Thomas G., *Fictional Worlds* (Cambridge, MA, and London: Harvard University Press, 1986).

——Review of Dorrit Cohn, *The Distinction of Fiction* (Baltimore: Johns Hopkins University Press, 1998), *Comparative Literature*, 53/1 (2001), 83–5.

Perinbam, B. Marie, *Holy Violence: The Revolutionary Thought of Frantz Fanon* (Washington, DC: Three Continents Press, 1982).

Pontecorvo, Gillo, *The Battle of Algiers* ([1966], Tartan Video, 1993) [videotape]

Porter, Bernard, *Critics of Empire: British Radical Attitudes to Colonialism in Africa, 1895–1914* (London: Macmillan, 1968).

—— *The Lion's Share: A Short History of British Imperialism, 1850–1995* (London and New York: Longman, 3rd edn, 1996).

Pratt, Katherine, ' "Comblant les béances de la mémoire collective": history, genre and orality in the novels of Assia Djebar', *ASCALF Yearbook*, 4 (2000), ed. Sam Haigh, 21–9.

Pratt, Mary Louise, *Imperial Eyes: Travel Writing and Transculturation* (London and New York: Routledge, 1992).

Prendergast, Christopher, *The Order of Mimesis* (Cambridge: CUP, 1986).

—— *The Triangle of Representation* (New York: Columbia University Press, 2000).

Quayson, Ato, *Postcolonialism: Theory, Practice or Process?* (Cambridge: Polity, 2000).

Quinzaine littéraire, 436 (16–31 March 1985), *Ecrire les langues françaises.*

Rabinowitz, Peter J., 'Reader response, reader responsibility: Heart of Darkness and the politics of displacement', *Heart of Darkness*, ed. Ross C. Murfin (Boston and New York: Bedford Books, 1996), 131–47.

Ramamurthi, Lalitha, and C. T. Indra (eds), *Joseph Conrad: An Anthology of Recent Criticism* (Delhi: Pencraft International, 1998).

Rancière, Jacques, *La Parole muette: essai sur les contradictions de la littérature* (Paris: Hachette, 1998).

Reclus, Onésime, *France, Algérie et colonies* ([1880] Paris: Hachette, 1887) [2 vol. edn with additional illustrations].

Reilly, Jim, *Shadowtime: History and Representation in Hardy, Conrad and George Eliot* (London: Routledge, 1993).

Ricoeur, Paul, *Soi-même comme un autre* (Paris: Seuil, 1990).

Roblès, Emmanuel, *Camus, frère de soleil* (Paris: Seuil, 1995).

Rorty, Richard, 'Freud, morality, and hermeneutics', *New Literary History*, 12 (autumn 1980), 177–85.

Rose, Jacqueline, *States of Fantasy* (Oxford: OUP, 1996).

Ross, Kristin, *Fast Cars, Clean Bodies: Decolonization and the Reordering of French Culture* (Cambridge, MA: MIT, 1995).

Rothman, William, 'Against "The system of suture" ' [1975], *Film Theory and Criticism: Introductory Readings* ed. Gerald Mast, Marshall Cohen and Leo Baudry (Oxford: OUP, 4th edn, 1992).

Ruedy, John, *Modern Algeria: The Origins and Development of a Nation* (Bloomington: Indiana University Press, 1992).

Rushdie, Salman, 'Introduction', *The Vintage Book of Indian Writing 1947–1997*, ed. S. Rushdie and Elizabeth West (London: Vintage, 1997), ix–xxiii.

—— *The Satanic Verses* (New York: Viking, 1988).

—— *The Moor's Last Sigh* (London: Jonathan Cape, 1995).

Ruthven, Malise, *A Satanic Affair: Salman Rushdie and the Rage of Islam* (London: Chatto & Windus, 1990).

Said, Edward W., *Culture and Imperialism* ([1993] London: Vintage, 1994).

—— *Joseph Conrad and the Fiction of Autobiography* (Cambridge, MA: Harvard University Press, 1966).

—— *Orientalism* (London: Routledge, 1978).

—— *Representations of the Intellectual* (London: Vintage, 1994).

—— *The World, the Text, and the Critic* ([1983] London: Faber, 1984).

Sarder, Ziauddin, and Merryl Wyn Davies, *Distorted Imagination: Lessons from the Rushdie Affair* (London: Grey Seal, 1990).

Sarocchi, Jean, *Le Dernier Camus ou Le Premier homme* (Paris: Nizet, 1995).

Sartre, Jean-Paul, 'Aminadab ou du fantastique considéré comme un langage', *Situations*, I (Paris, 1947), 122–42.

—— '"Aminadab" or the fantastic considered as a language', *Literary and Philosophical Essays*, trans. Annette Michelson ([1955] London: Hutchinson, 1968), 56–72.

—— 'Explication de L'Étranger', *Situations*, I (Paris, 1947), 99–121.

—— 'Camus's The Outsider', *Literary and Philosophical Essays*, 24–41.

—— *Qu'est-ce que la littérature?* (Paris: Gallimard, 1948).

—— *Réflexions sur la question juive* (Paris: Gallimard, 1954).

—— *Anti-Semite and Jew* (New York: Shocken Books, 1948).

—— *Situations*, II (Paris: Gallimard 1947).

—— *Situations*, V (Paris: Gallimard, 1964).

—— *Colonialism and Neocolonialism*, introduced by Robert Young and Azzedine Haddour, trans. (from *Situations, V*) A. Haddour, S. Brewer and T. McWilliams (London: Routledge, 2001).

Schorske, Carl E., *Fin-de-siècle Vienna, Politics & Culture* (London: Weidenfeld and Nicolson, 1980).

Schweinfurth, Georg, *Im Herzen von Afrika*, 2 vols (Leipzig: Brockhaus; London: Sampson Low, Marston, Low, & Searle, 1874).

—— *The Heart of Africa*, trans. Ellen E. Frewer (London: Sampson Low, Marston, Low, & Searle, 1873).

Sebbar, Leïla (ed.), *Une enfance algérienne* (Paris: Gallimard, 1997).

Seed, David, 'Introduction' to J. Conrad and F. M. Hueffer, *The Inheritors: An Extravagant Story* ([1901] Liverpool: Liverpool University Press, 1999), ix–xxviii.

Seidenfaden, Eva, *Ein kritischer Mittler zwischen zwei Kulturen: der marokkanische Schriftsteller Driss Chraïbi und sein Erzählwerk* (Bonn: Romantischer Verlag, 1991).

Sekyi-Otu, Ato, *Fanon's Dialectic of Experience* (Cambridge, MA: Harvard University Press, 1996).

Servier, Jean, *Les Berbères* (Paris: PUF, 2nd edn, 1994).

Shankar, S., 'The origins and ends of postcolonial studies', *Ariel: a Review of International English Literature*, 30/4 (1999), 143–55.

Sheringham, Michael, *French Autobiography: Devices and Desires, Rousseau to Perec* (Oxford: Clarendon Press, 1993).

Sherry, Norman, *Conrad's Western World* (Cambridge: CUP, 1971).

—— (ed.) *Conrad: The Critical Heritage* (London: Routledge & Kegan Paul, 1973).

Simiot, Bernard, 'Espoirs et tourments de la jeunesse marocaine', *Hommes et mondes*, 104 (1955), 463–80.

Slemon, Stephen, 'Modernism's last post', *Past the Last Post*, ed. I. Adam and H. Tiffin (Hemel Hempstead: Harvester Wheatsheaf, 1991), 1–11.

Smets, Paul F. (ed.), *Albert Camus* (Brussels: Université de Bruxelles, 1985).

Smith, Johanna M., '"Too beautiful altogether": ideologies of gender and empire in *Heart of Darkness*', *Heart of Darkness*, ed. Ross C. Murfin (Boston and New York: Bedford Books, 1996), 169–84.

Smith, Murray, *Engaging Characters: Fiction, Emotion and the Cinema* (Oxford: OUP, 1995).

Smith, Sidonie, and Julia Watson (eds), *Women, Autobiography, Theory* (Madison: University of Wisconsin Press, 1998).

Smith, Vanessa, *Literary Culture and the Pacific: Nineteenth-Century Textual Encounters* (Cambridge: CUP, 1998).

Souffles, 1 (1966); *Souffles*, 5 (1967).

Spivak, Gayatri Chakravorty, *A Critique of Postcolonial Reason: Toward a History of the Vanishing Present* (Cambridge, MA, and London: Harvard University Press, 1999).

—— 'Can the subaltern speak?', *Marxism and the Interpretation of Culture*, ed. C. Nelson and L. Grossberg, (Basingstoke: Macmillan, 1988), 271–313.

—— 'How to read a "culturally different" book', *Colonial Discourse/Postcolonial Theory*, ed. F. Barker et al. (Manchester: MUP, 1994), 126–150.

—— 'Reading *The Satanic Verses*', *Public Culture*, 2/1 (1989), 88–96.

—— *The Spivak Reader*, ed. D. Landry and G. MacLean (London: Routledge, 1996).

Sraïeb, Noureddine (ed.), *Pratiques et résistances culturelles au Maghreb* (Paris: CNRS, 1992).

Stacey, Jackie, *Star Gazing: Hollywood Cinema and Female Spectatorship* (London and New York: Routledge, 1994).

Staël, Madame de, *De la littérature considérée dans ses rapports avec les institutions sociales* ([1800] Paris: Garnier, 1998).

Stanley, Henry M., *The Congo and the Founding of its Free State* (London: Sampson Low, 1885).

—— *How I Found Livingstone* (London: Sampson Low, Marston, Low & Searle, 1872).

—— *In Darkest Africa, or The Quest, Rescue and Retreat of Emin, Governor of Equatoria* (London: Sampson Low, 1890).

—— Letter to James Osgood, 24 March 1874, Huntington Library, Pasadena, CA, MS HM2966.

—— *Through the Dark Continent* (London: Sampson Low, Marston, Searle & Rivington, 1878).

Stavrakakis, Yannis, *Lacan and the Political* (London: Routledge, 1999).

Steiner, George, 'To civilize our gentlemen', *Language and Silence: Essays 1958–1966* (London: Faber & Faber, 1967), 75–88.

Stora, Benjamin, *L'Algérie en 1995: la guerre, l'histoire, la politique* (Paris: Michalon, 1995).

—— *Histoire de l'Algérie coloniale (1830–1954)* (Paris: La Découverte, 1999).

—— *Histoire de la guerre d'Algérie (1954–1962)* (Paris: La Découverte, 1995).

—— *Histoire de l'Algérie depuis l'indépendance* (Paris: La Découverte, 1994).

—— *Algeria 1830–2000*: A Short History, trans. Jane Marie Todd (Ithaca: Cornell University Press, 2001).

Straus, Nina Pelikan, 'The exclusion of the Intended from secret sharing in Conrad's *Heart of Darkness*', *Novel*, 20/2 (1987), 123–7.

Strickland, Diana, *Journey Through the Belgian Congo* (London: Hurst & Blanchett, 1926).

Taussig, Michael, *Shamanism, Colonialism and the Wild Man: A Study in Terror and Healing* (Chicago: University of Chicago Press, 1987).

—— *Penpoints, Gunpoints and Dreams: Towards a Critical Theory of the Arts and the State in Africa* (Oxford: OUP, 1998).

Titah, Rachida, *La Galérie des absentes: la femme algérienne dans l'imaginaire masculin* (Tour d'Aigues: Editions de l'Aube, 1996).

Todorov, Tzvetan, *Nous et les autres: la réflexion française sur la diversité humaine* (Paris: Seuil, 1989).

—— *On Human Diversity: Nationalism, Racism and Exoticism in French Thought* (Cambridge, MA: Harvard University Press, 1993).

Toso Rodinis, Giuliana (ed.), *Le Banquet maghrébin* (Rome: Bulzoni, 1991).

Twain, Mark [Samuel Clemens], *King Leopold's Soliloquy: A Defense of his Congo Rule* [Boston: Warren, 1905]; facsimile in Twain, *'Following the Equator' and Anti-Imperial Essays* (New York and Oxford: Oxford University Press, 1996).

Vansina, Jan, *The Children of Woot: a History of the Kuba Peoples* (Madison: University of Wisconsin Press, 1978).

Vidan, Ivo, 'Conrad in his "Blackwood's" context', *The Ugo Mursia Memorial Lectures*, ed. M. Curreli (Milan: Mursia, 1988), 399–422.

Wack, Henry Wellington, *The Story of the Congo Free State* (New York and London: G. P. Putnam's Sons, 1905).

Walker, Keith L., *Countermodernism and Francophone Literary Culture: The Game of Slipknot* (Durham, NC, and London: Duke University Press, 1999).

Watt, Ian, *Conrad in the Nineteenth Century* (London: Chatto & Windus, 1980).

Watts, Cedric, '"A bloody racist": about Achebe's view of Conrad', *Joseph Conrad: Critical Assessments*, ed. K. Carabine, vol. 2, 405–18.

—— *Conrad's 'Heart of Darkness': A Critical and Contextual Discussion* (Milan: Mursia, 1977).

Weber, Samuel, *The Legend of Freud* ([1979] Minneapolis: University of Minnesota Press, 1982).

Webster, Richard, *A Brief History of Blasphemy: Liberalism, Censorship and the 'Satanic Verses'* (Southwold: Orwell Press, 1990).

West, Russell, *Conrad and Gide: Translation, Transference and Intertextuality* (Amsterdam and Atlanta: Rodopi, 1996).

White, Andrea, *Joseph Conrad and the Adventure Tradition: Constructing and Deconstructing the Imperial Subject* (Cambridge: CUP, 1993).

Williams, Patrick, and Laura Chrisman (eds), *Colonial Discourse and Post-Colonial Theory: A Reader* (New York: Harvester Wheatsheaf, 1993).

Williams, Raymond, *Keywords: A Vocabulary of Culture and Society* (London: Fontana, 1976).

—— *Culture and Society (1780–1950)*, London: Chatto & Windus, 1958).

Willmott, Robert E. A., *Pleasures, Objects and Advantages of Literature* ([1851] London: Melrose, 1906).

Wilson, Emma, *Sexuality and the Reading Encounter: Identity and Desire in Proust, Duras, Tournier, and Cixous* (Oxford: OUP, 1996).

Winch, Robert F., *Identification and its Familial Determinants. Exposition of Theory and Results of Pilot Studies* (Indianapolis: Bobbs-Merrill, 1962).

Woolf, Virginia, *The Essays of Virginia Woolf*, ed. Andrew McNeillie, Vol. 2 (London: Hogarth, 1987); Vol. 3 (London: Hogarth, 1988).

Yacono, Xavier, *Histoire de la colonisation française* (Paris: PUF, 1994).

Yétiv, Isaac, *Le Thème de l'aliénation dans le roman maghrébin d'expression française de 1952 à 1956* (Sherbrooke, Quebec: CELEF, 1972).

Young, Robert J. C., *Postcolonialism: An Historical Introduction* (Oxford: Blackwell, 2001).

—— *Colonial Desire: Hybridity in Theory, Culture and Race* (London: Routledge, 1995).

—— *White Mythologies: Writing History and the West* (London: Routledge, 1990).

Youngs, Tim, *Travellers in Africa* (Manchester: MUP, 1994).

Zahar, Renate, *Colonialism and Alienation: Political Thoughts of Frantz Fanon* ([1969] Benin: Ethiopia Publishing Corporation, 1974).

Zide, Arlene R. K. (ed.), *In their own Voice: the Penguin Anthology of Contemporary Indian Women Poets* (New Delhi: Penguin, 1993).

Zimra, Clarisse, Afterword (and interview), in A. Djebar, *Women of Algiers in their Apartment* (Charlottesville, VA, and London: Caraf Books, 1992), 159–211.

Žižek, Slavoj, *Looking Awry: an Introduction to Jacques Lacan through Popular Culture* (Cambridge, MA, and London: MIT Press, 1991).

—— *Enjoy your Symptom: Jacques Lacan in Hollywood and Out* (London: Routledge, 1992).

—— *The Plague of Fantasies* (London: Verso, 1997).

—— *The Sublime Object of Ideology* (London and New York: Verso, 1989).

—— (ed.) *Everything You Always Wanted to Know about Lacan (but Were Afraid to Ask Hitchcock)* (London: Verso, 1992).

Index

abstraction 6, 38–9, 46, 140
Achebe, Chinua, and representation
  of Africa 2, 4, 23, 26, 30–1,
  38–9, 43, 48–50, 58–9, 61, 64,
  84, 95, 143, 148–9, 164n.2,
  165n.5
Africa, representation of *see* Achebe,
  Congo
Ahmad, Aijaz 165n.12
Algeria 7, 8, 17, 66, 93, 96,
  101, 107, 114, 156–61,
  172n.10, 178n.41, 181n.7
  and Algerian identities
  66–72, 108, 112, 172n.12
  see also Camus, Djebar, Fanon
Allen, Richard 176n.52
Alloula, Malek 123–4, 127
Amrane-Minne, Danièle
  Djamila 181n.7
Amrouch, Fadhma Aït Mansour,
  Taos and Jean 186n.56
Anderson, Benedict 119
Anthias, Floya, and N. Yuval-
  Davis 177n.27
anthologies, selection criteria
  of 93–5, 104, 105
Appiah, Kwame Anthony 154
Apuleius 119, 131
'Arab' slave traders 18, 39, 54, 71;
  see also slave trade

Arabic as national
  language 108, 110, 119–21,
  178n.41, 179n.47; *see also*
  language politics
Ascherson, Neil 16–17
Ashcroft, Bill, G. Griffiths and H.
  Tiffin 73, 153, 155
Aubry, Jean 171n.71
Augustine 131
Austin, Mary 38
author-function, notion of 178n.36
autobiography 5, 128–34, 143,
  186n.51, n.55, n.56
autonomy, literary/artistic 5–6,
  85, 105, 138–9, 144, 146,
  188n.19

Bakhtin, Mikhail 37
Barker, Martin 175n.51
Barnes, Julian 174n.31
Barthes, Roland 62–4, 77, 79,
  83, 85, 134, 172n.2, n.4
Bate, Jonathan 173n.24
Beauvoir, Simone de 114–15
Beckett, Samuel 102, 104,
  133–4
Belgian Congo, Belgium, *see* Congo
Benchama, Lahcen 179n.44
Berbers and Berber culture 71, 75,
  119, 121, 127, 173n.18

Berlin West Africa
    Conference 13, 54
Berrada, Mohammed 188n.18
Bettelheim, Bruno 189n.2
Beverley, John 144
Bhabha, Homi 33, 138, 154,
    167n.17
Blackwood's Magazine 37, 46,
    57, 60
Blanchot, Maurice 134,
    142, 143, 145, 149, 151
Boehmer, Elleke 165n.7
Boer War 47, 54
Bonn, Charles 104, 189n.20
Borch-Jacobsen, Mikkel 175n.46
Bouhired, Djamila 114
Boupacha, Djamila 114
Bourdieu, Pierre 68, 84, 188n.19
Boyce Davies, Carole, and E. Savory
    Fido 132
Brantlinger, Patrick 56
Brazza, Pierre de 44
Brée, Germaine 176n.4
Brennan, Timothy 184n.34
Bristow, Joseph 35
British Empire 8, 13, 52, 54; *see also*
    East India Company
Britton, Celia 131-2

Calvet, Louis-Jean 106-7
Camus, Albert, and *The
    Outsider* 4, 62-91, 97, 104,
    124, 136-7, 139, 141, 173n.14,
    n.18, 174n.33, n.36
    The First Man 67, 70, 112,
    172n.12
canonical literature 4, 10, 105,
    140-1, 153; *see also* 'minor'
    literature, national literatures
Canrobert, Lieutenant-Colonel 129
capitalism, as driving force of
    imperialism 7-8, 13, 16-17
Carlyle, Thomas 44
Carroll, Noël 176n.52
Casement, Roger 55-6
Cavalli-Sforza, Luca 73-5

Cellard, Jacques 46
Césaire, Aimé 192n.31
CFS *see* Congo
Chamberlain, Joseph 47, 166n.20
Chikh, Slimane 178n.41
Chraïbi, Driss, and *The Simple
    Past* 4-5, 92, 95-111, 137-8,
    141, 144-5
    The Butts 100-1, 146, 177n.22
Cixous, Hélène 120, 183n.26
Clark, Timothy 188n.11
Clifford, Hugh 49
Clinton, Bill 75
colonialism, definition of 7-9,
    173n.18; *see also* imperialism
commonwealth literature *see*
    'postcolonial' literature
Conan Doyle, Arthur 55-6
Congo, and Congo Free State
    (CFS) 3, 11-21, 39-45, 47,
    51-6, 143-4, 169n.51
Congo Reform Association (CRA)
    see Morel
Connerton, Paul 89
Conrad, Joseph, and *Heart of
    Darkness* 1-4, 11, 14,
    19, 21, 22-61, 77, 83, 105,
    136-7, 139-41, 143-4,
    146-50, 165n.6, 169n.52
    'An outpost of progress' 40-1,
    53, 171n.66
    The Inheritors 47-8, 53, 143-4
    The Nigger of the Narcissus 60
Cookey, S. J. S. 56
Coombes, Annie 167n.18
Cosmopolis magazine 40-1, 57
Courtney, Leonard 42
Cunninghame Graham, R. B. 57,
    60, 171n.66
Curle, Richard 169n.52
Cuvier, Georges 73

Davis, Colin 174n.32
Déjeux, Jean 130
Delacroix, Eugène 123-8, 184n.40,
    185n.45, n.46

Deleuze, Gilles, and Félix
    Guattari 102–3, 105, 109
Derrida, Jacques 66–7, 132, 134,
    138–9, 142–9, 151, 188n.11,
    n.16, n.17
Deurbergue, Jean 58
Dib, Mohammed 105, 189n.20
Dilke, Charles 40, 41, 168n.32
discourse, notion of 19–21, 26
Djebar, Assia, 4–5, 112–35,
    143, 145, 153, 165n.5,
    179n.44, 180n.2, 181n.11,
    183n.30, 184n.39, n.40,
    185n.45, 186n.56, 188n.18
    Ces voix qui m'assiègent
    (*Voices*) 1, 114, 133, 151,
    187n.61
    *Fantasia: An Algerian
    Cavalcade* 128–33, 141
    *Women of Algiers in their
    Apartment* 112–29,
    137, 146, 151, 160–1,
    183n.26
Donadey, Anne 113, 137–8,
    183n.27
Dunwoodie, Peter 173n.14
Durand, Anne 174n.33

Eagleton, Terry 147, 189n.21
East India Company 51, 170n.56
English literature 105, 109–10, 153;
    see also national literatures,
    Steiner

Fanon, Frantz 20, 52, 68–70, 109,
    114, 153–63, 184n.37,
    190n.12, 191n.19, n.21,
    n.23, 192n.24, 193n.32, n.33
Feraoun, Mouloud 176n.4, 186n.49
fiction and fictionality 1, 48, 59–60,
    84–5, 90–1, 127–8, 130, 132–3,
    134, 138–9, 141, 143, 144, 147;
    see also literarity and notion of
    literature
Firchow, Peter 168n.39
Fish, Stanley 144

Fitch, Brian 81, 174n.35
Flaubert, Gustave, *Madame
    Bovary* 76, 90
FLN *see* Algeria
Ford, Ford Madox *see* Hueffer
Foucault, Michel 19, 104, 178n.36
France and French Empire 8, 13,
    16, 17, 44, 66–70, 152; *see also*
    Algeria, Camus, Chraïbi,
    Djebar, Fanon, French
    literature, Morocco
'francophone' literature and
    francophonie 104, 107, 109,
    179n.43; *see also* language
    politics, 'minor' literature
Franklin, John 45
freedom of expression,
    literary 142–6, 188n.18
French literature, association with
    Frenchness 106–9, 126; *see also*
    canonical literature,
    'francophone' literature,
    language politics, national
    literatures
Freud, Sigmund 88–9, 151–2,
    162–3, 175n.46, n.47,
    188n.18, 189n.2, 190n.3
'functional' model of literary
    criticism 27, 37, 63, 77

Gafaïti, Hafid 113, 186n.56
Gandhi, Leela 166n.27
Garnett, Edward 42, 165n.9
Gaspard, Françoise, and F.
    Khosrokhavar 184n.37
gender, as factor in colonial/
    postcolonial identities 8, 35–6,
    71, 112–32, 168n.23
Genette, Gérard 23–8, 30, 37, 46,
    63, 91, 143
genre, as factor in reception 37–8,
    53, 57, 58, 128–9, 155–6;
    see also autobiography
Giddens, Anthony 116
Glave, E. J., 41
Gordon, David 178n.40

Gordon, Robert 187n.60
Gramsci, Antonio 176n.8
Grant, Rena 89
Grégoire, Abbé 106
Gusdorf, Georges 130–1

Haddad, Malek 108
Haddour, Azzedine 124, 172n.2,
    173n.14, 184n.37
Hallward, Peter 154, 166n.27,
    189n.20
Hampson, Robert 28, 30, 33, 35,
    36–7, 44, 58, 148–9
Hargreaves, Alec 179n.43
Hawkins, Hunt 45, 47, 169n.42
Hawthorn, Jeremy 166n.24
Heath, Stephen 27
Henry, Jean Robert 179n.47
Hitchcott, Nicki 186n.55
Hochschild, Adam 15, 17,
    165n.1
Hodister, Arthur 40
Holland, Norman 140
Hollis, Martin, and S. Lukes 154–5
Holt, John 170n.58
hooks, bell 90
Hueffer, Ford M. 47
Huggan, Graham 165n.6
hybridity and hybridization 33, 70,
    74, 110, 121, 167n.17

identification and identity 31,
    65–6, 69, 84, 85–91, 132–3,
    139, 175n.42, n.46, n.51
illusion and illusionism 26, 86,
    89–90, 91, 138, 176n.52
imperialism, definition of 7–9
    motives for 11–12, 16–19, 20,
    34
indeterminacy see literarity and
    notion of literature
Indian literature 94–5, 105–6, 107,
    110
Innes, C. L. 95
Irigaray, Luce 120, 183n.26
Iser, Wolfgang 140

Islam 96, 108, 117, 125–6, 130,
    177n.21, 178n.41, 181n.11,
    184n.36; see also veil

Jackson, John Payne 167n.18
Joyce, James 102, 171n.62

Kacimi, Mohammed 130
Kadra-Hadjadji, Houaria, 177n.15
Kael, Pauline 175n.49
Kandiyoti, Deniz 184n.36
Khatibi, Abdelkebir 104–5, 108,
    111
Kipling, Rudyard 55, 60
Kitchener, Herbert 42
Knight, Diana 172n.4

Lacheraf, Mostefa 176n.4
language politics 5, 16, 87, 102–11,
    119–24, 133–4, 178n.40,
    n.41
Lanson, Gustave 103
Laplanche, Jean, and J.-B.
    Pontalis 88
Lazreg, Marnia 123, 181n.7
Ledger, Sally 44–5
Lejeune, Philippe 186n.56
Leopold II of Belgium see Congo
Letcher, Owen 169n.51
Lindqvist, Sven 40, 42, 48, 171n.75
literarity and notion of
    literature 2, 3, 4, 6, 30, 46,
    59–60, 63, 64, 84, 103, 113,
    117, 132–5, 138–50;
    see also fiction and fictionality
literary criticism, conventions and
    purposes of 1–2, 5–6, 10,
    58–60, 64, 87–8, 90, 97, 103,
    105, 140–1, 144–50
London, Bette 171n.70

McClintock, Anne 6
McCulloch, Jock 191n.23
McDonald, Peter 46
Maja-Pearce, Adewale 106
Marchal, Jules 170n.57

Marx, Karl 9, 170n.56
Memmi, Albert 93–4, 100, 104,
  106, 111, 131, 145, 178n.37
Mernissi, Fatima 130, 184n.37
Messaoudi, Khalida 181n.7
Miller, Christopher 33, 46
'minor' literature 5, 93–5, 102–4
'minority' group, notion of 99–100,
  177n.19
modernism/modernity 27–30, 116,
  143, 147
Moore-Gilbert, Bart 165n.8
Moors and Moorishness 63, 67,
  71–2, 74, 77, 173n.24
Morel, Edmund Dene 54–6, 143,
  170n.58
Morocco 93, 96, 97, 108, 110–11,
  173n.18; see also Chraïbi
Morris, William 13, 51, 170n.55
Murphy, J. B. 40

Nadelhaft, Ruth 46
national literatures, notion
  of 4, 87, 103–5, 178n.32, n.37
Ndaywel è Nziem, Isidore 12, 16,
  51, 56
négritude 161–2, 192n.31
neo-colonialism/neo-imperialism,
  definition of 8
Ngũgĩ wa Thiong'o 106, 121,
  186n.58

O'Brien, Conor Cruise 65, 78, 82,
  172n.6
Onwuanibe, R. C. 191n.21
oral culture 121, 141, 183n.27
Orientalism see Delacroix, Said
Ouled Riah, massacre of 129

Parminter, Alfred 40
Parry, Benita 35, 44, 165n.12,
  166n.20
Pasha, Emin 13, 168n.37
Pavel, Thomas 139, 187n.5
Pélissier, Colonel 129
Picasso, Pablo 127, 128

pieds noirs, 68, 173n.18, n.19,
  174n.33; see also Algeria,
  Camus
plausibility see vraisemblance
Pontecorvo, Gillo, and The Battle of
  Algiers 175n.49, 184n.41
Porter, Bernard 170n.55
positionality 10, 156, 162–3
'postcolonial', definitions 6–9
'postcolonial' literature 104, 113;
  see also 'minor' literature
post-traditional society see Giddens
Prendergast, Christopher 20, 26,
  176n.52

Rabinowitz, Peter 139–40
'race' and racism 2–3, 18, 22–3, 27,
  31, 38–9, 59, 72–7, 139, 152
reading and reception, traditions and
  conventions of 5, 46, 58–9,
  64–5, 76–7, 79, 84–5, 90–1,
  92, 97, 103, 112–13, 137–50;
  see also anthologies, genre,
  identification and identity,
  realism, representation and
  representativity
realism 23–30, 64–5, 76–7, 79, 85,
  129, 136, 138–9, 147, 187n.5
reception see reading and reception
Reclus, Onésime 107
Reilly, Jim 170n.62
relativism 19–20, 74, 153–63
representation and
  representativity 19–20,
  92–111, 113–14, 122, 131–2,
  138–9, 142–3, 176n.4, n.7
Rushdie, Salman 94, 105,
  110, 144, 145, 146, 184
  n.34, 188n.14, n.18

Said, Edward 7, 19–20, 59, 62–6,
  70–1, 77, 84, 172n.6
Salusbury, Philip 40
Sartre, Jean-Paul 62,
  65, 68, 86, 90, 191n.22
Schweinfurth, Georg 11, 19

science, relation to politics 74–5, 158–62, 174n.29, 192n.29
Sefrioui, Ahmed 98
Seidenfaden, Eva 177n.15
Senghor, Léopold Sédar 192n.31
Shankar, S. 16, 166n.15
Sheringham, Michael 133
Sherry, Norman 40, 171n.71
Sjöblom, Edward Wilhelm 40, 41
slave trade 11, 12, 13, 18, 42, 55–6, 170n.58
Slemon, Stephen 136–8
Smith, Murray 175n.42, 176n.52
Smith, Sidonie, and J. Watson 132
Smith, Vanessa 183n.27
Spencer, Herbert 73
Spivak, Gayatri Chakravorty 95, 101, 103, 170n.56, 176n.8
Stanley, Henry Morton 11–15, 18, 38, 39, 42, 43, 44, 152
Steiner, George 87–8, 90, 175n.50
stereotyping 100, 127; see also 'race' and racism, representation and representativity
Stokes, Charles 40, 45
subversiveness, ascribed to literature 50, 52–3, 57, 144–50
Symons, Arthur 60

Taussig, Michael 49–50, 149
theory, as category of writing 6, 151–63
Times, The 11, 40, 44
Tippu Tip 18, 39, 54
Titah, Rachida 181n.14

Todorov, Tzvetan 190n.8
torture 114–15, 157, 159, 161
Twain, Mark 55–6, 170n.62

universalism and universals 62, 65, 105, 140–1, 152–8, 190n.8

veil, representation of 121–4, 125–6, 183n.30, 184n.37, n.41
voice, notion of 4, 5, 111, 131–5, 186n.58
vraisemblance 23–8, 37, 83

Watt, Ian 50, 60, 168n.30
Watts, Cedric 23, 26, 44, 52, 148–9
Webster, Richard 144
White, Andrea 37, 52, 57
Williams, George Washington 39, 168n.29
Williams, Patrick, and L. Chrisman 7
Williams, Raymond 7–8, 99, 103
Willmott, Robert Aris 86, 90
'worldliness' of literature 139, 147; see also realism, representation and representativity

Yacono, Xavier 172n.10
Young, Robert 3, 99, 152, 153, 165n.9, n.13, 166n.26, 168 n.32, 174n.28, 177n.19
Youngs, Tim 168n.37

Zhdanovism 112, 145, 180n.2
Zimra, Clarisse 181n.6, 182n.20
Žižek, Slavoj 87, 90, 91, 175n.50